KNIGHTS OF FREEDOM

Here I am, six years old, lifted by my dad onto the back deck of an M48 Patton tank right next to its 90mm gun—my lifelong fascination in Dad's World War II experiences as a tanker was born. The photo was taken in 1954 while Dad was a major serving as the executive officer of the 749th Tank Battalion. (FCB)

KNIGHTS OF FREEDOM

WITH THE HELL ON WHEELS ARMORED DIVISION IN WORLD WAR II
A STORY IN PHOTOS

LIEUTENANT COLONEL FREDERICK C. BREMS,
USAR (RET.)
WITH FRED G. BREMS

STACKPOLE
BOOKS

Essex, Connecticut
Blue Ridge Summit, Pennsylvania

STACKPOLE BOOKS

An imprint of Globe Pequot, the trade division of
The Rowman & Littlefield Publishing Group, Inc.
4501 Forbes Blvd., Ste. 200
Lanham, MD 20706
www.rowman.com

Distributed by NATIONAL BOOK NETWORK

Photo Credits:
(FCB) Frederick C. Brems
(FGB) Fred G. Brems
(EF) Ed Fawks
(EH) Ed Huckaby
(DAC) Don Critchfield
(RS) Rodney "Ray" Stewart
Others as credited

COVER PHOTO: Lieutenant Brems next to his burned-out tank *Freedom*, which had been knocked
out near Kaldenhausen. (FCB)

British Library Cataloguing in Publication Information available

Library of Congress Cataloging-in-Publication Data
Names: Brems, Frederick C., 1919–2014, author. | Brems, Fred G., 1948–
Title: Knights of freedom : with the Hell on Wheels Armored Division in World War II, a story in
    photos / Lt. Col. Frederick C. Brems, USAR (Ret.) ; with Fred G. Brems.
Other titles: With the Hell on Wheels Armored Division in World War II, a story in photos
Description: Essex, Connecticut : Stackpole Books, 2023 | Summary: "Through over 600 photos, many
    never before published, supplemented by firsthand accounts from the author, this book follows the
    tanks of the 2nd Armored Division through some of the toughest fighting of World War II"
    —Provided by publisher.
Identifiers: LCCN 2023031254 (print) | LCCN 2023031255 (ebook) | ISBN 9780811773768
    (paperback) | ISBN 9780811773775 (epub)
Subjects: LCSH: Brems, Frederick C., 1919–2014. | United States. Army. Armored Regiment, 66th.
    Company F—Biography. | World War, 1939–1945—Regimental histories—United States. | World
    War, 1939–1945—Personal narratives, American. | World War, 1939–1945—Campaigns—Western
    Front. | World War, 1939–1945—Tank warfare.
Classification: LCC D769.3055 66th .B74 2023 (print) | LCC D769.3055 66th (ebook) | DDC
    940.54/1273—dc23/eng/20230815
LC record available at https://lccn.loc.gov/2023031254
LC ebook record available at https://lccn.loc.gov/2023031255

∞™ The paper used in this publication meets the minimum requirements of American National
Standard for Information Sciences—Permanence of Paper for Printed Library Materials,
ANSI/NISO Z39.48-1992.

14DEC1941 LETTER HOME FROM CAMP POLK

Sent after the United States declared war on Japan on 8 December 1941:

Things go along the same, but now perhaps with more purpose in each act. You can just feel that unity. It's great! We'll win! This world won't be the kind I will want to live in if we don't. Even if we do win, I'm sure that we are all in for many changes in life as we now know it. Those who lead us after this is over, truly, their job will be gigantic.

A note from my mother . . . sent to me in February 1945 while I was in combat overseas. I read it often as the war wound down. (FCB)

Contents

Preface ix

Introduction 1

Chapter 1. Training 7

Chapter 2. From the United States to the 2nd Armored Division 35

Chapter 3. On to Company I 45

Chapter 4. Company F to Merzenhausen 65

Chapter 5. The Battle of the Bulge 93

Chapter 6. Operation Grenade: Schiefbahn 131

Chapter 7. Operation Grenade: Kaldenhausen. 151

Chapter 8. Off to Paris! 161

Chapter 9. The Central European Campaign: Encircling the Ruhr River Basin. 173

Chapter 10. The Central European Campaign: The Run to Magdeburg and the Elbe. 185

Chapter 11. The Occupation of Germany Begins 205

Chapter 12. A Day Trip to Braunschweig 229

Chapter 13. The Move to Preusslitz 237

Chapter 14. The 2nd Armored Division Occupies Berlin 245

Chapter 15. Back to France for Class 257

Chapter 16. Back to Berlin. 265

Chapter 17. Leaving Berlin for Frankfurt 279

Chapter 18. Marseille and Going Home. 299

Epilogue: Everything After This Will Be Gravy 307

Appendix: My Visual Short Snorter 313

Preface

These 2¼-inch by 2¼-inch photos had been around the house in envelopes and boxes and a book Dad had put together toward the end of the war. There are nearly five hundred of them, all contact prints. As a kid, I was mightily impressed by the shots of tanks and trucks and airplanes, but they were all so small that I could not make out much detail. I knew Dad had taken them during the war, but 1950s technology didn't offer options for enhancement. Computers, scanning, Photoshop and digitizing were decades away, and we could not even imagine enhancement as a possibility. I probably could have used a magnifying glass, but I mistakenly thought there was not much more detail to see. Still, each was a treasure, since Dad had taken them during the war, so we took great care with them.

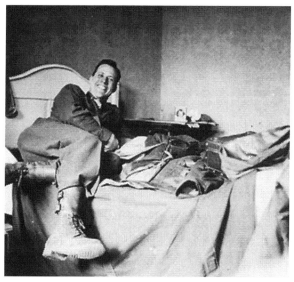

"I used the self-timer on this and took my own pic— made quite a dash. This is my present bunk." (FCB)

What we always had were his stories. Dad was never hesitant to tell training and battle action stories, and I remember them all well, over time writing many of them down. He had received years of training and put that training to good use in action, winning the Silver Star and a Bronze Star. He completely believed and knew they were fighting a just war that had to be fought and won, so there was never any reluctance on his part to discuss the details and the sacrifices. He also had stayed in the reserves after the war, ending up as a lieutenant colonel after nearly twenty-seven years' total service. Mom and I often accompanied him to the monthly weekend training of his various units and traveled to Camp (now Fort) McCoy in Wisconsin for his two-week summer camps. The war was part of his years of duty to his country, and sharing his stories with me perhaps had been a part of that duty as well.

I was always intrigued by this particular photo and caption; this is the actual size—2¼ by 2¼ inches—with its faded color. What was he smiling about? Dad did not remember anything in particular, so I let it go at that. Dad would always rather smile than frown. Maybe he was just happy to have a bed under him and a roof over his head.

But then in 2006 I started wondering whether there might be something invented that could help us look at these photos more closely. I have to thank my cousin Mark Charette, a professional photographer, for doing more than just answering my question about what to do; he took me to his darkroom resource, who said he could digitize the photos for me. Each would be in the 12Mb range, which we could then enlarge to search for more detail. It was not going to be cheap, but we discovered that the cost was worth every penny.

The details that were revealed in many of the photos were amazing. And there *was* a reason Dad was smiling in this photo. It is right there on the table behind him.

I knew it as soon as I saw it. It was this color-enhanced photo of my mother that he was smiling about. I knew this photo well, as a larger framed version hung on our family wall. I am only sorry my mother never got to see this detail in the photo. She would have seen once again how much she meant to Dad.

Not only is this photo in the picture, but his Rolleiflex camera is on the bed as well. Hidden treasures.

(FCB)

What we found in the photos awaits you in this book, accompanying the stories I grew up on. Dad did not have a telephoto lens, but he eventually had his Rolleiflex camera, which caught great resolution, much to our satisfaction.

Dad was often asked whether he ever felt like an underdog. He knew well that the Germans had some very effective tanks and guns that could knock out a Sherman tank easily, but he never felt the underdog. He knew he had been well trained and was as ready as he could be for combat without ever having been in combat before. He also knew that the GIs beside him were the best.

Reporter Wes Gallagher accompanied the 2nd Armored Division in November 1944 and wrote an article that appeared in the 4 December 1944 *Kansas City Star*. In it, he quoted Dad: "If you get the drop on them (German tanks) and fire first, it's okay, but you can't stand and slug with them. We are getting Tigers [German tanks] because our boys have more guts than the Germans and take better advantage of the terrain, and not because we've got better tanks. When one of our tanks gets hit, the crew stays in and fights it out if it can. When the German tank gets hit, they come boiling out and head for the woods." A member of Dad's platoon knocked out the first Royal Tiger tank destroyed by the Ninth Army (an event detailed in chapter 6).

Here is another photo taken on the streets of Berlin while the 2nd Armored Division occupied the city. The original is on top. The details we had not seen are in the enhancement on the bottom. (FCB)

Dad repeatedly said that throughout the war he firmly believed it was the right thing to fight the Nazis, and that if any war was the right war, this one was. This belief allowed him to open up after the war about the horrible things he had witnessed. He was also carried by the faith that he would survive; he had just gotten married, he was a strong Roman Catholic, and his mother and father gave him their full support. Plus he was an Eagle Scout, with all the optimism and survival and orienteering skills that implies.

The fact that the Brems family is of German origin certainly did not interfere with his commitment to fight for the United States in Europe. He repeatedly stated that he was fighting Nazis and Hitler, not the German people. The German he picked up at home and at DePaul Academy in Chicago helped him as well.

Perhaps Dad was in a unique position. His first real job was at the Boston Store in Chicago, where he worked in the photography section and discovered he had a real love for photography. From July 1941 (when he was drafted) until the end of the war, he had at least one camera with him at, as you will see, nearly all times, and he took nearly five hundred photographs, most of which we have, with only two rolls lost. (He sent them in for developing but never got them back. Dad could not remember what photos were lost.)

As an officer, Dad had a heightened perspective of the battlefield; not only was he often in on the planning, but he also had his head out of the turret much of the time. He was never wounded, so he spent all his time in Europe with his unit at the front or refitting (except for two weekend passes, one a three-day trip to Paris, detailed in chapter 8). In addition, he wrote many letters, and his parents and my mother, Helen, saved them all. Lastly, he had a good memory and never tired of telling me oft-repeated anecdotes of his experiences. He also started writing his stories down over time.

I hope that Dad's effectiveness as a soldier, who simply did what he was supposed to do and had been prepared to do, comes through in the following pages. Dad always believed that we won even against often superior equipment because U.S. soldiers were not underdogs, as the U.S. military had spirit and belief on its side.

If you like vehicles and airplanes, you will thoroughly enjoy the collection of photos showcased here. If you are a veteran or your father or grandfather fought in the war, a photo of someone who will look familiar might appear. Though many of the photos in chapter 1 were taken by his bunkmates and others, most of the photos from chapter 2 on were taken by my dad and are in that "never-before-seen" category. Thanks to Jon Critchfield, son of Lieutenant Don Critchfield—a fellow platoon commander in F Company with Dad—who has allowed me to insert his dad's photos, also "never before seen." This is a fitting tribute to the friendship the two of them formed during the war. In addition, the families of 2nd Platoon Bow Gunner Rodney Stewart, F Company Commander Ed Fawks and 66th Armored Regiment Chaplain Luke Bolin have contributed photos to this work.

I must thank the staff at the U.S. Army Heritage and Education Center in Carlisle, Pennsylvania, who supplied me with all their primary source material on the 66th Armored Regiment and the end-of-day reports of its battalions. The staff warmly shared in my surprise and joy at my first encounter of my dad in the material, running over to me as I nearly shouted, "That's my dad! That's my dad!"

Thanks to the more than fifty readers who encouraged me with their comments and their requests for more chapters to read. A special thanks to Eirwyn Rogers for his intense historical curiosity, rich suggestions and spot-on edits, and to Dylan Soal for his willingness to provide excellent drawings of events that could not have been caught on camera. Also thanks to Wayne and Mark, who accompanied me on the very emotional trip to Dochamps. Another big thank-you to Jerry Whitaker, a neighbor of ours and former U.S. Army intelligence officer who translated the German account of the action around Schiefbahn covered in chapter 6. Gerry O'Neill's patience with all my picky demands for the great maps that he produced is appreciated more than he knows. Fred Haub has been a font of many great suggestions and helped with the cover. A special thank-you to Dad's fellow tankers Mike Skovira and Ray Stewart, and to Stewart's daughter Karen and son Mike for all their stories, photos and friendship. Warm thanks also go to Ed Fawks's son Marvin "Bud" Fawks, Don Critchfield's son Jon, the family of Ed Huckaby and Reverend Luke Bolin's daughter Beth Cooper. There are so many others, many of whom are recognized in the course of this book. I apologize to those whom I have missed, as I know there are many.

And, finally, a very special thanks to Susan, my wife, who has supported these efforts and been accepting of the time I have had to spend on the book, and for her ideas and impeccable editing of the manuscript.

It is an honor to write this book. Dad is my hero, and this is an important way for me to pay homage to him and all the other heroes of the U.S. military who fought in World War II.

Fred G. Brems
25SEP2021

Visit https://www.knights-of-freedom.com to expand each chapter with numerous never-before-published photos, video interviews, original battle maps, color postcards and more.

Introduction

Although I served in six armored divisions during my twenty-seven-year military service, I have always considered Company F, 1st Battalion, 66th Armored Regiment, 2nd "Hell on Wheels" Armored Division, my home unit. I was proud to serve in action with the men of Company F from 14 October 1944 until 24 March 1945, when I moved to battalion headquarters. I led the 2nd Platoon and then the company after Captain Ed Fawks was wounded during the Battle of the Bulge, returning to the 2nd Platoon when Captain Johnson returned to command after he had spent some time in convalescence.

What we experienced in those nearly six months is for the books: the seventy-five-mile march in less than twenty-four hours on ice and through snow in blackout conditions to arrive in a position directly on the northern flank of the German Ardennes Offensive; the slicing southeast attack into Dochamps and on to Samrée and Wibrin; the counterattack by Panzer Lehr at Schiefbahn; and the charge to break through a battalion of 88s and tanks in an attempt to capture a bridge over the Rhine at Kaldenhausen. These are the subjects of just a few of the chapters Company F wrote.

I learned from the best, serving under Captain Henry Chatfield of Company I before moving to F; Captain Ed Fawks, with whom I remained friends after the war; and Captain Henry Johnson, who sadly lost his life at Magdeburg. All knew their trade well, and each led by example.

I had the opportunity to command or ride in at least nine different tanks, starting with the M2A2 two-turreted "Mae West," the M2A4 with Guiberson diesel engines, Stuart light tanks, variants of the Shermans, a Grant and a Chaffee, a Pershing and even a German Panther tank!

As for the men with whom I served, there were none better. I will not try to name all, as I would certainly miss some, and that would not be right. I will name Lieutenant Don Critchfield, though, fellow platoon leader in F Company. Don was one of the old hands, one of the "Benning to Berlin" guys, who were looked on with awe. Critch had seen it all: Africa, Sicily, Italy, France, Belgium and finally Germany, having four tanks knocked out from under him for his trouble. (Funny how the old cavalry phrase "from under him" was still applied to armor.) We hung out a lot together, traveling the countryside when time permitted, both of us taking our fair share of photographs.

I truly wish I had followed up with Critch after the war. I was at one 2nd Armored Division reunion and noticed he had signed up to join us. I was looking forward to seeing him! Apparently he actually got to the reunion, registered, and then for some reason turned around and went home. Critch passed away in 2004, but many of his photos (credited DAC) and stories are still alive in this book, with many thanks to his son Jon for sharing.

The M2A4 tank, prototype for the M3 Stuart Light Tank, on the left and the M3 Lee Medium Tank on the right. To add to the "M3" confusion, the British called their version of the Lee the Grant. The M4 Sherman replaced the Lee. This photo was taken sometime after August 1941, when full-scale manufacturing of the Lees began. (FCB)

Ed Fawks, me and Critch. (FCB)

I would be more than remiss if I did not point out a special relationship at several of our annual 2nd Armored Division reunions. I am sure that rarely at World War II divisional reunions these days are there men from the same battalion or even the same regiment, let alone the same platoon. Mike Skovira, Ray Stewart and I are from the same platoon, 2nd Platoon of Company F. I am not sure when our last reunion might be, but we will go as long as we can make it.

As for all the other men with whom I had the honor of serving, an appendix is devoted to the soldiers of whom I have photos, with their names where possible. Many identified photos appear throughout the book as well.

Critch. (FCB)

Loader Mike Skovira then and now. (FCB)

"Lieutenant Brems and I snapped in my room sitting on my wee little bed. My camera (I like to brag) has a device where you can take a picture of yourself. Very clever gadget. Rolleiflex." (DAC)

Assistant driver and bow gunner Ray Stewart then and now. (FCB)

A couple of photos of yours truly. (FCB)

Mike Skovira, Ray Stewart, General Donald Campbell (commanding general of Fort Knox, Kentucky) and me in 2008. (FCB)

Everything since the war has been gravy. I've been a lucky guy. Between Helen Charette, who passed away in 1985, and Margaret Walker, I have had over sixty years of married love and life. I have a son and daughter-in-law and granddaughter of whom I am very proud, and Margaret's family has been a second family to me. I have many friends old and new. Plus I am still upright. Very lucky indeed.

With ninety-three years now under my belt, the list of people to whom this book could be dedicated would require another book, but I think it has to be dedicated to the men in F Company, 66th Armored Regiment, 2nd Armored Division, as this book is mostly about them and our shared joys and horrors, gains and losses, and the ultimate victory. We worked together, fought hard, laughed and cried, and we did what we set out to do, accomplishing great deeds with honor and dignity.

Thanks, guys. If you are not here on earth now, I know you still hear me.

Lieutenant Colonel Frederick C. Brems, USAR (Ret.) 2014

Mike Skovira, me and Ray Stewart at Fort Knox in front of an Easy Eight; we all wish we'd had these earlier in the war. (FGB)

(FCB)

MAP SYMBOLS

On some of the maps that follow, standard military symbols for units will often be used. Types of units are indicated like this (note that there were no cavalry units present):

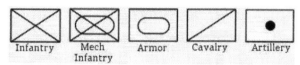

The size of units is indicated by placing marks over the middle top of the above rectangles, shown here from smallest unit to largest:

• = squad
•• = section
••• = platoon
I = company
II = battalion
III = regiment
X = brigade/combat command
XX = division
XXX = corps
XXXX = army
XXXXX = army group

On a map, the unit I was about to join would look like this—size on the top line (a company) with the company designation on the left (I Company) and the parent organization on the right (66th Armored Regiment, or 66th AR). You won't see my unit much on any but the most detailed tactical-level maps.

You will see the 2nd Armored Division symbol; it will look like this:

(From the U.S. Army Training Manual)

This 1938 photo sets a base for much of my experience in the military. The lineage of the 66th Armored Regiment in which I served while with the 2nd Armored Division is traced directly to the 66th Infantry (Light Tanks) Provisional Battalion, shown here on parade at the 75th Commemoration of the Battle of Gettysburg. The name of the unit indicates that even as late as 1938, tanks were not seen to be anything more than support for the infantry, a concept that changed soon after the start of World War II. I am also linked to the tanks in the photo as my first training in any actual tank was in the M2A2 type tank shown here on parade. (Courtesy of the *Gettysburg Times*)

1

Training

In five years of active duty, I spent only a bit over a year and a half overseas, as I kept getting stateside assignments, mainly to attend classes or schools. Much of this was a matter of the timing of the orders I received. For example, one morning I was assigned to the 8th Armored Division and ordered to a thirty-day gunnery course at Fort Knox, but that same afternoon I received orders for overseas shipment as a casual officer—a general replacement assigned to no specific unit. The orders to the gunnery course took precedence, as they were issued before the overseas shipment order. If I'd received the orders to go overseas first, there is a very good chance that I would have taken part in the invasion of North Africa.

I kept getting sent to various training schools, Advanced Tank Tactics for three months, for example. I was part of the cadre that was assigned to form the new 14th Armored Division at Camp Chaffee, then assigned as the executive officer of Company B, 47th Armored Regiment, and later became the commander of a light tank company for over a year. As it worked out, those courses and that experience were of real value when I finally got involved in combat operations.

At the camera section of the Boston Store in Chicago, 1939. (FCB)

I worked in the camera department at the Boston Store in Chicago and got great experience using cameras and working with film. This would turn out to be a lifelong hobby.

For lunch, I would often go to the nearby Nanking Restaurant. A new waitress there stopped me in my tracks, definitely a "love-at-first-sight" kind of thing. I made sure to sit in her section every lunch, and I finally asked her out on the first of many dates.

15APR1941

I received my notice of 1-A Classification from my local draft board. The day I received my classification, I knew what I had to do. With induction no doubt soon to follow, I decided to ask Helen M. Charette of Marinette, Wisconsin, to marry me. Much to my delight, Helen answered, "Yes."

(FCB)

The induction process began soon thereafter. I vividly recall one part of the physical. We were in a line of maybe twelve men waiting to have blood drawn, and it was obvious that the technician drawing blood was a novice at it. Everyone in line stared as he made repeated jabs in each draftee's arm in attempts to find veins. When I got to be fourth in line for this procedure, the fellow two in front of me flat out fainted and hit the floor with a thud. I am lucky that I have fairly evident veins; it only took the technician three times to hit one correctly.

09JUN1941

Drafted. The United States was not officially at war and would not be until 8 December 1941, the day after Pearl Harbor was attacked. At the time, I saw this as a just-in-case measure.

13JUN1941

I was inducted into the U.S. Army. It is interesting to me now that I was drafted six months prior to the attack on Pearl Harbor. I was processed through Camp Grant, Illinois, becoming one of the fillers (because we "filled out" units with our bodies) for the activation of the 3rd Armored Division at Camp Polk, Louisiana.

14JUN1941 POSTCARD HOME

Dear Mother and Dad,

It's O.K. So many things going on. We were just issued our summer uniforms, pack, canteen, meat pan, fork, etc. Good food. Everything is so new. They say we will be out of here in three days. I have a swell bunk. Slept like a log or soldier last night. Love, Frederick

We were run through heavy calisthenics every day! Here I am in my calisthenics shorts standing on our barrack's "patio." (FCB)

Palmer Maroni of Chicago in the barracks. (FCB)

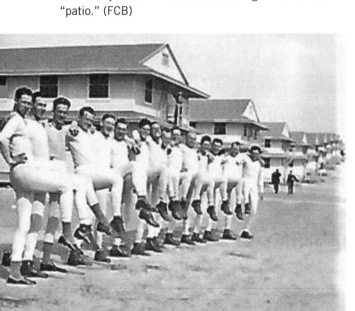

This was not one of our official exercises, but it made us laugh. (FCB)

I am standing third from the left. Steve Kelly, my best-man-to-be, is seated in the first seat on the left. (FCB)

Each of us was issued a complete set of these clothes, one of each, including wrap-around leggings (see the wrapping below the knees of the fellow looking down—that's me; the leggings were extremely itchy), very heavy woolen trousers, a backpack, helmet and more—all surplus from World War I. Steve Kelly is fourth from the end. (FCB)

An early version of the Dodge WC series half-ton truck designed for reconnaissance, called "jeeps" even before the Willys MB quarter-ton truck came along. Turns out that the word "jeep" likely originated in Elzie Segar's comic strip *Thimble Theater*, best known for Popeye the Sailor and Olive Oyl. In March 1936, a new character was introduced named Eugene the Jeep, a rodent-like character the size of a small dog whose only sound was *jeep!* Eugene the Jeep became very popular, and the exclamation "Jeep!" was applied to this vehicle and the quarter-ton truck because, like Eugene the Jeep, this vehicle could "go anywhere." (FCB)

30JUN1941 LETTER HOME

We were issued pair of galoshes (big uns!), mosquito net, and two pair of coveralls, nice ones of a green color. It's hot here today; calisthenics really pulled sweat out. Then this p.m. I played volleyball. Now I'm just sittin' in shorts and still sweatin'. Mother—will you send me my camera? I think it will be nice to have.

02JUL1941 LETTER HOME

It's 9:30 a.m. Today I am on K.P. duty; it isn't so bad. Washed out a couple of big iceboxes, cleared some tables, ground some meat. I'm not off duty until 10:00 p.m.

I can hear the various groups outside drilling. To help keep fellows in step and develop keeping together; the man in charge gives the command, "In cadence—COUNT!" All the fellows call out—"Step 1, 2, 3, 4, 1, 2, 3, 4!" Left foot should touch ground at 1 & 3, right foot 2 & 4. Then they continue marching, not counting until the next command, whatever it might be, is given. Hot and sweaty; that's me.

3:15 p.m. We peeled 100 pounds of potatoes. Were we lucky! It started to rain, torrents, and other fellows had to go sloshing around while we were in the mess hall. K.P. was a pleasure today. I wish you could see it rain here;

Me on cleanup duty after a heavy rain at Camp Polk. (FCB)

it just digs out the earth; rushing rivers all over the place. It's hard to buy stamps here. I've been borrowing them from the fellow next to me.

10JUL1941

I am out there in the crowd somewhere as Brigadier General Alvan C. Gillem Jr. addressed the entire 3rd Armored Division. (U.S. Army Photo in the Author's Collection)

Two M3A1 scout cars are part of the general's entourage. Note the bulldozers parked by the buildings. We did not have tanks yet, but we used these to learn how to drive tracked vehicles. (FCB)

28JUL1941 Letter Home

10:15 p.m. It's past lights out, and I'm sitting in the regimental office, where I started a new job today. I'm in the Intelligence Office of the 32nd Armored Regiment (Light Tanks). (Intelligence office? Hmmmm, unbelievable.) It will probably be just plain clerical work; later, as I learn more about it, it will no doubt be more interesting.

In actual combat, we would be at the field headquarters and take information from scouting parties, observation squads, planes, etc. and seek information about the enemy, such as their location, strength, equipment, and activities. We would take this information, consolidate it and see that it gets to the proper authorities. One thing which should be interesting is the map work, especially studying aerial photos. For example, an observation plane will take a picture of a certain area one day and the next day take another photo of the same area. The two photos would be compared to see if any differences show up, such as trails or vehicle tracks, which weren't there the day before. If a difference shows up, something is going on!

They held a court-martial tonight. Some fellow had an accident with a motorcycle; also there was something about someone who took money which didn't belong to him. After court was over, I walked into the regimental recreation center where the trial was held. I found a paper with random doodling on it, evidently the work of one of the officers serving on the court.

Sergeant F_____ was our supply sergeant at the time. He was nasty. I went in to requisition toilet paper, and he pointed to some brown craft paper, telling me to grab some of that. He got called away, so I jumped over the counter and grabbed a bunch of real toilet tissue off the shelf and took it back to the barracks.

Sergeant F_____ was one to resort to fisticuffs, and I remember him punching Private Strefling once while the sergeant was a bit intoxicated. I walked in and told him that he if was going to act like that, he should stop drinking. Mind you, I was a private at that point, and I do not know what you would call what I did—moxie or stupidity! I got out of there fast.

30AUG1941

Ordered to attend Division Intelligence School from 2–20 September 1941.

19SEP1941 Letter Home

Releases for men over twenty-eight years old are coming through. Things can't be so tough if they pass out discharges at this time. Sounds good to me; however, they are subject to recall in case of any emergency. Surprising how many are getting out. I'm only twenty-two, so I am here for a while.

I was called up to regimental headquarters (HQ), and as I entered, I was told to report to Technical Sergeant Cascio.

Sam Weinberg getting ready to go home; he was definitely over twenty-eight years old! I think he was actually in his thirties. (FCB)

Here I am in front of the same door as Sam at Camp Polk. At least I had lost the leggings! (FCB)

Seemed like we were always running somewhere. (FCB)

"Brems," he says to me, "G-2 [intelligence] informs me that you worked for a paper, and they would like you to interview two men in the regiment; one is an accomplished pianist and the other is a journalist. Find out how they feel they are getting along in the army."

My response was "I'm sorry, Sergeant, but I never worked for a newspaper."

He said, "You must have. G-2 says so!"

It dawned on me what had happened. I told Sergeant Cascio that I had worked for a *wholesale paper company* selling paper to printing companies, not at a newspaper.

"!#$*7^," he responded. "I guess I'll have to write it myself!"

I thought fast and told him I had worked for school papers and done a bit of reporting on different occasions and that I would be willing to take a shot at it.

"Hey," he said, "I'd appreciate that."

I talked to the two guys, wrote up a couple of short paragraphs and gave them to Cascio. A couple of days later, he saw me in the company area and told me that G-2 liked what I had written, and he thanked me. A week later, nine of us in the HQ Platoon were called up to regimental HQ to report to Sergeant Major Hunt. He lined us up and told us we were in line for a lot of good assignments. All the positions called for promotion from private to what were various levels of private first class.

Now Technical Sergeant Cascio sees me in the line and beckons for me to come over to him.

"Brems, how would you like to work for me in the S-2 Section?"

I know I said something like "Sarge, I don't even know what S-2 means!"

He looks at me kind of sour like and says, "Well you can type, can't YA?"

"Yes, Sergeant."

"Okay, I'll tell Hunt I want you to work for me."

It turned out S-2 was the intelligence section.

The position was the only opening of the nine spots that called for three stripes, a buck sergeant! So after only three and a half months in the army, I'm promoted to sergeant, but I was a so-called "jaw-bone" sergeant because you had to have been in the army four months before you could be paid at full rate for that grade. So for a half month I got $21.00, and then on the fourth month I moved up to $40.00. When Cascio left for Officer Candidate School (OCS), I got his job.

One of the smartest things I ever did was take typing in high school. Among the first things I typed was a list of experiences officers had had with tank accidents. Tanks could be very dangerous even in peacetime.

25SEP1941

Appointed sergeant, Headquarters Company, 32nd Armored Regiment (Light), at Camp Polk, by Lieutenant Colonel R. R. Allen. If you know anything about tanks, you will have a hard time seeing the purpose of an entire regiment of light tanks. Speed but no firepower. This was changed not too long after.

These were the days when, in training exercises, trucks became "tanks"; large signs were attached to the trucks that read, "TANK." In those early days, wood rods became tank guns.

I remember one of the fellows coming into the barracks and announcing, "Hey! There's a tank in the motor park!" We all rushed down there, and, I must say, I was not very impressed.

A mere draftee, what did I know about tanks other than the very sturdy toy tank I had received from Santa one Christmas? It was very solid. I could stand on it without damaging it at all. To me, my toy looked more like a tank than the one I first saw in the motor pool.

The M2A2 was powered by a Continental W670-9A air-cooled radial engine. Very soon we received the M2A4 with the Guiberson T-1020 Series 4 diesel engines. You started the M2A4 engines by firing a shotgun shell to get the pistons turning. It sometimes took an entire box of shells to get one going. After you got one or more of the tanks started, you could use

This is what the smile on a new buck sergeant looks like, the 3rd Armored Division patch prominent on my left sleeve. (FCB)

No one had checked to see whether the bridge could hold the weight of the tank. This was an early Sherman, which was a medium tank and not one of the early light tanks. The top hatch is open, so at least some of the crew was able to get out on their own despite their no doubt bruised condition. (EF)

I am washing the bogies of an M2A3, the tank that followed the M2A2, with its distinctive octagon turret and longer track base. (FCB)

Two of my messmates standing next to an M2A2. (FCB)

Here I am with a "peep," the more popular name we had for the "jeep." (FCB)

those tanks to pull start the others, certainly not an efficient process. Only 375 of the M2A4s were produced, all used for training by both us and the British, who got some through the Lend-Lease program. Production of the M2A4 ended in April 1942.

Radio communications among units and vehicles were very primitive, nearly nonexistent. For quite a while, motorcyclists had to act as couriers to carry all orders up and down a march column. An armored division on a road march could extend eighty or more miles, making for a long ride and a long delay in receiving messages and orders, with all the accompanying consequences of delay to command and control.

When a commander in the column needed to contact any of the units on a march, he would fill out a message form, attach the message to a wooden rod with a clip pin, give the rod to a motorcyclist and send the message on its way. The cyclist was able to deliver the message to the person on top of the highest vehicles by extending the rod to the recipient.

This was hazardous duty for the motorcyclists, with many accidents, injuries, and some deaths. As there was no option, cyclists were used come rain or shine, dark or light, and often over dusty or muddy secondary roads. Add to that the threat of civilian cars that would on occasion recklessly attempt to pass the column.

After the war, the *Saturday Evening Post* carried an article noting that, in spite of the danger, the division never lacked for volunteer motorcycle riders. I could see why.

Without any radio/intercom communication within a tank, alternative ways to send orders and give directions had to be developed among a tank's crew members.

The "tap" method was adapted in light tanks and worked like this: If the tank commander standing in the turret and looking out of the hatch wanted to turn right, he signaled the driver below him by stepping on the driver's right shoulder; a tap on the left shoulder meant turn left; a tap or kick on the gunner's head meant to fire the main gun. A kick to the lower back meant to back up. Various types of taps signaled any other directions that would be required to move the tank.

At some point, the tank company commander received FM voice radio for contact with battalion HQ and his platoon leaders, but this was initially limited, with individual tanks only being able to receive, not transmit.

Eventually, almost all tanks and vehicles had the capability of two-way receiving and transmitting and could even establish contact with air support and artillery forward observers. This change was accelerated by tankers who cannibalized knocked-out tanks for their radios and improvised with what they found. Eventually, the radio became a crucial component of a tank's equipment.

What the motorcycle looked like overseas; this in Schulenberg, 1944. The bike is loaded down with gear while the rider makes a repair. (FCB)

I learned to ride a motorcycle at Camp Polk, Louisiana, in 1941. I took every opportunity I could get to ride a bike. I slipped a few times but never fell. Notice the 3rd Armored Division triangle on the front fender. (FCB)

Tap practice, Fort Benning, Georgia, March 1942. Here the sergeant is giving the signal to go forward. Even though intercoms and radios were introduced in November 1941, touch signals were still useful to light tank crews in the noise of battle. (U.S. Army Signal Corps Photo)

Bill Munch was with me in basic training at Camp Polk. He became an officer, then a communications officer in the reserve and eventually a major general. We were old friends. Years later, we were marching our battalion on parade. I yelled out, "Left turn. . . . March!" and from the side of the reviewing stand comes, "Hey Freddie! How the hell are you!" It was Colonel Munch, temporary commanding officer of our regiment! The guys in the ranks got a big kick out of that.

It wasn't *all* training! (FCB)

Driving in the mud, a given at Camp Polk. (FCB)

A long time after the war, I ran into Bill in Chicago, and he had made brigadier general. As we talked, he said, "Remember that no good Sergeant F_____?"

"Sure, I remember him."

"Well, I took care of him."

I assume he had him busted.

Because I was assigned to the Headquarters Company, I decided to keep a daily log. My first entry is on 29 September 1941 and tells of our preparations for the many upcoming maneuvers, but the rest of that first day was inauspicious. The biggest thing was sewing sergeant chevrons onto the rest of my shirts and going to a movie. 30 September was payday and another slow day, with some letter writing and a shower thrown in. However, 1 October changed all that, as we undertook a mounted march, covering 102 miles through dust, mud and woods, followed by a much-appreciated shower, a letter home and a very solid sleep. The next day I celebrated my first week as a sergeant with my third tetanus shot.

The subsequent log entries chronicle tactical problems, mock battles, blackout movements, map and photo work, application of planimetrics, rain and sun ("war weather"), occasional twenty-four-hour or weekend passes, full-dress parades, entire days in half-tracks, riding motorcycles, firing weapons, attending Mass when I could, tear-gas training and lots of dust and sweat, but I was a "happy goon." I learned I could sleep anywhere, even in a moving half-track or all night on pine boughs. When in camp, I wrote letters to Helen, went to movies with Ed Furman and Steve Kelly (including *Dive Bomber* and *Charley's Aunt*) and enjoyed ice cream. Helen sent me cookies, assorted nuts and salami, all very welcome.

13OCT1941

I celebrated four months in the army and decided to write to my Boy Scout buddy Frank Capos, who was posted to the Philippines.

I'm leaning on an early version of the half-track. This design did not change much over time. (FCB)

Sergeant Pareid's tank platoon is ready to move out. These look to be M2A4s with the 37mm gun, the proto-type for the M3 series, which would be designated the Stuart light tank. Notice the use of signal flags. We had no tank-to-tank radio communication yet. (FCB)

It seemed we were always going on tactical marches in all kinds of weather (but mostly bad), over increasingly rough terrain and in various unit sizes from platoon up to battalion. The marches included all the vehicles we had, from tanks to half-tracks to "peeps."

Manning the Browning .50 caliber machine gun that faced front on the half-track. (FCB)

Maneuver observers. (FCB)

USO show at Theater #1, Camp Polk, Louisiana, featuring the Three Dennis Sisters with emcee Clarence Stroub. (FCB)

Half-track coming and Dodge recon vehicle going. (FCB)

23OCT1941 Letter Home

Been considering purchasing a better camera when I get home . . . but I want to pick it out, nothing expensive, don't know exactly what. Might not even do it. The rumor of our being transferred to Fort Meade, Maryland, has again been revived. Right now I am in the orderly room taking Ed Furman's "charge of quarters" while he goes to the movie. I am going later; Bob Hope in "Caught in the Draft."

(FCB)

08NOV1941 Letter Home

Another week fades away. We have recovered almost completely from our field trip. They are anything but picnics. Most of us sport red and swollen eyes from wind, dust, cold; we all have bright rosy cheeks.

Started squatting on my cot at 2:00 p.m. Left for chow at 4:30 p.m. (we eat a half hour earlier on Saturdays, Sundays and holidays), came back after chow; it is now 6:45 p.m., and I'm still squatting on my cot. Nice to just sit. Listening to Wayne King; sounds nice. Praying for furlough to be home for Christmas. Have a feeling it will come through.

13NOV1941 Letter Home

My cot has been moved. I now have a spot in the corner of the barracks; they want a non-commissioned (non-com) officer in each corner. Have cot right up to a window and can look out as I lay here. Also a window at head of the cot. Ideal spot—I like it. I'm next to the fire-escape ladder.

We were issued winter combat uniforms; they look much like an aviator's or parachutist's outfit. Very good and very warm. We also wear a wool-lined helmet with flaps for over the ears and a big flap which hangs over the back of the neck. Itches like crazy . . . but very warm. Still I believe I will sew a lining in it.

17NOV1941

I finished my physical for OCS with X-ray, blood tests, everything. Because of the physical, I missed the bivouac, which broke my heart.

29NOV1941

The 3rd Platoon was organized into squads; Furman, Dillard and I each got a squad.

There was no soap to clean the greasy silverware, so I talked to the company commanding officer. My first official gripe. Also saw Captain Ludes, the dentist, and got four fillings! He checked the fillings using the "stoop" method: You bend over, open your mouth and shake your head. If the fillings stay in your teeth, you're okay.

07DEC1941

I went to Mass and took communion in the morning and heard that Japan had bombed Pearl Harbor. I think we all knew we were going to be at war, considering all the preparation we had been going through. Many of us worried about getting our Christmas furloughs approved, as this might be our last chance to be home for a while.

08DEC1941

United States declares war on Japan. Furloughs???

14DEC1941 LETTER HOME

My furlough blank has been signed by the regimental commander, the Colonel; so far so good. Steve Kelly left last night for Detroit. That is a very good sign that I shall be able to go, but that can still change.

Saturday we received a shipment of new men. Selectees. I worked from 7:30 a.m. until 9:00 p.m. First Lieutenant Crawford (swell fellow) and I had the job of assigning the men to the various companies in the regiment. No kidding, I really enjoyed it; made the day go by much faster. It was interesting to meet all these new fellows. I know just how they feel, not knowing just what they are getting into, not knowing in their minds. I know since that's just how I felt. I had a good time just kidding them along. When I first joined, if somebody had some kind word for me or just shot a line of bull at me, it helped, I think. They all seem rarin' to go.

Things go along the same, but now perhaps with more purpose in each act. You can just feel that unity. It's great! We'll win! This world won't be the kind I will want to live in if we don't. Even if we do win, I'm sure that we are all in for many changes in life as we now know it. Those who lead us after this is over, truly, their job will be gigantic.

Steve Kelly helping his friend figure out how to work his new camera. The 3rd Division Armored patch is on his sleeve. (FCB)

A Christie T3E2 tank was on display at Camp Polk. The Christie suspension was not adopted by the U.S. Army, but the Russians liked the suspension and used it on many of their vehicles, including what was arguably the best tank in the war, the T-34. (FCB)

15DEC1941 Letter Home

We went out on the shooting range before dawn again. Fired a "Tommy" gun for the first time and made a score of 11 hits out of 15. Wasn't at all difficult to shoot. I can't help but admire how perfectly that gun functions.

The instructor came over and asked me where I had learned to shoot a Thompson like that.

I immediately responded, "I'm from Chicago! What do you expect?"

I have never seen an instructor laugh like he did.

19DEC1941

My furlough began! I took a train to Chicago and made it home: 2210 North Lamon Avenue (the house is still there). In the Brems family tradition, Mother, Dad, Helen and I celebrated Christmas on Christmas Eve with gifts, a tree and all the fixings.

Here I am shouldering a .45 caliber Thompson submachine gun. (FCB)

On 27 December, I spoke at the Order of the Arrow Banquet about how scouting skills helped in the U.S. Army. Very good crowd! Note the Sam Browne belt. (FCB)

(FCB)

In the snow in Chicago. (FCB)

With Mother in our backyard. (FCB)

With Helen in the same spot. (FCB)

On 28 December, Helen and I went to a Sonja Henie ice show and were inspired enough to go ice skating ourselves two days later. Dick Jergens, Frank Capos with his date and Helen and I went to the Aragon Ballroom to celebrate New Year's Eve.

03JAN1942

Left for Camp Polk and was kept busy enough that I did not miss home too much. I had to fill out my application for OCS and was assigned to help the athletic and recreation officer, assist the new morale officer, set up sand tables demonstrating areas where training exercises were to be held, and got to work at S-2 (Intelligence) again. I saw lots of movies (including *The Bugle Sounds*, much of which was shot at Camp Polk, and we saw many places we all knew) and held bull sessions with Steve Kelly.

(FCB)

21JAN1942 LETTER HOME

Steve and I are going to see "Tarzan" tonight. Hope he yells tonight. I collected my furlough ration money—allowance comes to $.44 a day.

05FEB1942

Went before the OCS board.

12FEB1942

OCS application accepted; selectees announced during a radio show.

21FEB1942

Promoted to technical sergeant by order of HQ, 32nd Armored Regiment, Camp Polk, Louisiana, by order of Colonel Jones and signed by Captain H. W. Gardner, 32nd Armored Regiment Adjutant.

    Before I left for OCS, Captain Streater, S-2, said, "Brems, if you had stayed, you would have made technical sergeant, so we might as well give it to you." Streater was a West Pointer and a good guy. I was off to OCS as a technical sergeant!

(FCB)

11MAR1942

1700: Left Camp Polk for OCS at Fort Knox, Kentucky.

12MAR1942–12JUN1942

I spent three months at Officer Candidate School Armored School at Fort Knox. I graduated one year to the day that I entered the army. The army was growing mighty fast after 7 December and here I had been a technical sergeant with only nine months' experience in the army! So what did I *really* know about the army? Being in such a short time did not exactly work to my advantage at OCS, but it all ended well.

    We had families and girlfriends visiting the barracks all the time, and I was concerned about the language the guys were using, mostly the "f—" word with the "mother" variant. At one morning inspection I told the gathered troops that we had to be more mindful of our language, considering mothers and girlfriends were so frequently within earshot.

    Worst mistake I ever made. Every other word out of anyone's mouth was now "f—" this and "'f—" that! Once on maneuvers, while in the cab of the truck, I counted the "f—" word and variants used thirty-seven times in four minutes. Interestingly, it was also used as a positive. One fellow said, "You know what my f— wife did? She went and put $4,000 in our savings account!"

    A salesman I worked with told the story of his first meal with his parents right after he had just gotten home from the war, "Pass the f— salt and pepper, please." You got to a point where you just shut off your ears and lived with it.

An army picnic: my right foot and full plate in foreground with Ed Furman and Steve Kelly, our best man to be! We've had many road marches and two weeks of tank driving as well. (FCB)

17JUL1942

We took Company C out on a road march and overnight bivouac. The weather was extremely hot and humid, so much so that several members of the company succumbed to heat stroke. If nothing else, they learned the importance of water.

(FCB)

For a reason that escapes me to this day, I had to be discharged from the army in order to convert to a second lieutenant in the army. The Enlisted Record on the back noted that I had been a noncommissioned officer, a technical sergeant, and that my specialty to that point had been chief clerk. The record also noted that I had no horsemanship skills. The answer on the blank space: "Not Mounted." Also on the back was a note that I would lose no service time because of the discharge. I was happy to see that.

13JUN1942–04SEP1942

Transferred to tank platoon leader, 80th Armored Regiment, 8th Armored Division, located at Camp Chaffee, Arkansas.

The 8th was a training division with the task of forming units and readying them for overseas shipment.

There was no relief from the heat except to drink water. (FCB)

The man on the ground with his head in his hands is just coming around from sunstroke. (FCB)

08AUG1942 LETTER HOME

Received my orders tonight relieving me from assignment to the 8th Armored Division [AD] and assigning me to station at Camp Bowie, Texas and the 14th AD upon activation. First I report to the Armored Force School for the purpose of pursuing (that's what it says here) a course of instruction. Probably be on tank maintenance (and imagine . . . I have to pursue the thing yet). Upon completion of the course, I shall proceed to my new permanent station reporting there at not later than 10OCT1942.

I actually went to Camp Chaffee, Arkansas, and not Camp Bowie.

05SEP1942–31DEC1942

Transferred to executive and company motor officer, Company B, 47th Armored Regiment, 14th Armored Division.

One day, as I walked down the middle of the bachelor officers' quarters, I met face-to-face with First Lieutenant Lewis, whom I considered a fine officer and who had been in charge of the platoon in which I had received my basic training at Camp Polk. He took a quick second look at me and my shiny new gold bars and said, "This man's army is sure goin' to hell!" He laughed and shook my hand, slapped my back and wished me well.

03OCT1942–10OCT1942

Leave granted to go to Fort Knox.

06OCT1942

Tent City Chapel, Fort Knox

Helen and I got married! The ceremony was performed by Father Tom A. Bartley (to the right in the photo). My best man was Steve Kelly, and the maid of honor was Lucy Fleming. We received twenty congratulatory telegrams. I know because I still have all of them.

(FCB)

I didn't take a photo of the Tent City Chapel at the time of the wedding, but we went back to Fort Knox in 1954, and the chapel was still standing. It has long since been demolished. In the photo on the right, our six-year-old son Fred (Rick), Helen and I stand in front of the chapel. We had silhouettes made of us when we got to Camp Chaffee in Arkansas. (FCB)

A typical tent barracks, perhaps at Chaffee. The shoulder patch on the jacket hanging in the middle rear is definitely a triangle, indicating an armored division. (FCB)

Helen and I opted to rent a house in nearby Fort Smith, Arkansas. (FCB)

My next assignment was to join the cadre forming the 14th Armored Division, stationed at Camp Chaffee in Arkansas. Chaffee was a new camp that had only been activated March 27, 1942. From that date until 1946, the 6th, 14th and 16th Armored Divisions trained there. The camp was

On parade in Camp Chaffee: this is the M2A4, introduced in early 1941, with the 37mm gun, co-ax, .30 machine gun plus two more machine guns in the side sponsons, one machine gun in the hull front and a fifth on an anti-aircraft mounting on the turret. The number of machine guns indicates the concept was to support infantry. (FCB)

named after Major General Adna R. Chaffee Jr., an artillery officer who, in Europe during World War I, determined that the cavalry was outmoded and, unlike other cavalry officers, advocated the use of tanks. Probably Chaffee is remembered best as the post where Elvis Presley received his first military haircut in 1958 in Building 803! He was in the 3rd Armored Division.

05DEC1942

I was promoted to first lieutenant. At the time, I was serving as motor officer for Company B of the 47th Armored Regiment, 14th Armored Division.

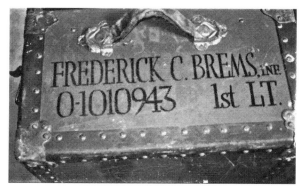

Dad lettered the footlocker showing my change in rank. It went overseas with me. We had to change the branch from INF. to ARMOR, though. (FCB)

01JAN1943

Appointed company commander, Camp Chaffee, Company B, 47th Armored Regiment, 14th Armored Division.

Untrained men in large vehicles they were not used to driving led to numerous accidents. While our company was on night maneuvers, Lieutenant Heist's light tank drove over the side of a bridge and fell into a river, rolling completely over. We went back and got the men out of the upside-down tank. Amazingly, they were all safe. Lieutenant Heist was surprisingly calm, even telling us baseball stories. On another maneuver, a tank commander rolled his tank while he was half out the turret, killing him instantly.

A Stuart tank charging. (U.S. Army Signal Corps Photo)

01FEB1943–12FEB1943

Camp Chaffee, Arkansas

I conducted tank crew training while waiting to be assigned overseas.

01JUL1943

Reappointed company commander, Company B, 47th Armored Regiment, 14th Armored Division.

21SEP1943–31DEC1943

Appointed company commander, Company B, 25th Tank Battalion, 14th Armored Division.

After we had some training under our belts, we gave several demonstrations for the division cadre and visitors. During one demonstration, we maneuvered the tanks from column to line, and I gave the signal to charge up a ridge to our front. The Stuart was fast, and we tore across the field and up the slope, declaring victory at the top.

Afterward, I was approached by several of the observers who must have been old

Those may be tanks lined up along the far edge of the field. (U.S. Army Photo)

cavalry officers. Each declared that the charge I had conducted was exactly the way armor was supposed to be used in battle.

Although the charge was exhilarating and the response from the observers good for the spirit, experience made it clear that if we were to actually do this in combat, we would all be knocked out. As it turns out, we *did* make an old-style cavalry charge once, and its result was predictable. Nine of our seventeen tanks were knocked out. See chapter 7 and our attack on Kaldenhausen.

The following are Signal Corps photos from the twelve-day "Tank Formation Class" I conducted at Camp Chaffee, Arkansas, with a mix of M2A4 and M5 light tanks. These are part of an instructional series taken by members of the 164th Signal Photo Company.

Proof of the value of the leather helmet came during the war from Lieutenant Goodnight, battlefield commissioned, who wore the football helmet under his steel helmet. A projectile pierced the front of his "pot" and ran around inside without any damage to him. I talked to him afterward and asked, "Hey Goodnight, you gonna turn that pot in for a new one?" His response: "Hell NO! This is my good luck piece!"

164-009-43-211

Camp Crowder, Missouri.   11 Feb 43

47th AR B Btry of 14 AD Camp Chaffee, Ark., 12 day class in light tank operation directed by Lt. Frederick C. Brems, tanks in wedge formation.

164-009-43-211   Photo By:
                        164th Signal Photo Co.

Sgt. William J. Randolph.

Camp Crowder was a U.S. Army Signal Corps Replacement Training facility and probably where the film was developed. Sergeant Randolph mislabeled the unit, calling it a "Btry" (battery). The unit was part of Company B. (U.S. Army Signal Corps Photo)

164-009-43-214

Camp Crowder, Missouri.   11 Feb 43

Section commanders tank crew.
Front L. to R. Lt. Albert R. Waldron – Bow Gunner
                        Pvt. Wagner – Driver
Rear L. to R. Lt. Frederick C Brems–Tank Commander
                        2nd Lt. Conrad Dienstbach,
                                    57 mm Gunner.
At Camp Chaffee, Ark.

164-009-43-214   Photo By:
                        164th Signal Photo Co.

Pvt. Robert W. Curry.

As the instructor, I got number-one tank. Here I am on the upper left. Errors were common, as we were all new at what we were doing. The M5 had a 37mm gun, not a 57mm gun. (U.S. Army Signal Corps Photo)

The differences between the M2A4 and the M-5 tanks can be seen here. The M2A4, on the left in the photo, is boxy with two hatches below the turret. On the M5 to the right, the front hatches have been replaced by a slanted glacis plate designed to deflect enemy shot upward. (U.S. Army Signal Corps Photo)

After a reorganization, we became the 25th Tank Battalion. Andrew W. "Wini" Winiarczyk (he and I graduated from the same OCS class) was my executive officer. Other officers were William A. Reed, Lloyd G. Price, John A. Houlihan, and Edgar Heist. First sergeant was Bernard Oldinsky.

Other members were C. P. Koster (NCO Maintenance), Charles Craig, Edgar Derbin, K. G. Farnan, A. Gladding, E. Lebanowski, S. McLaughlin, A. E. Clary, E. Shafer, G. T. Smith, B. A. White and D. C. Midyette. For the most part, these men made up the original cadre of the new 14th Armored Division.

Sometime after the war, I met a member of the 14th Armored Division Association at the Marine Exchange at Quantico, Virginia. He knew Wini and told me Wini was very active in the association.

I was able to locate Wini, and we talked for quite a while. He partially answered one pressing question I had: "Whatever became of 'Tough Guy' Captain L_____?"

Let me explain. I was one of three first lieutenants who were company commanders in the battalion. Lieutenant Colonel Hart, the battalion commanding officer when I first arrived, was, I suspect, over age in grade. He was shortly replaced by Lieutenant Colonel Maulsby.

One afternoon all three of us were called to battalion HQ where Lieutenant Colonel Hart announced, "I am not accustomed or used to working with such young company commanders, but I am submitting your promotions to captain. If you will take your example from Captain L_____, you will . . ." I do not remember his exact words, and I mean no disrespect to Lieutenant Colonel Hart, but I know my thoughts went something like this: "If I have to operate like that guy, I don't know if I want to be a captain!" Not really true (but a real

(U.S. Army Signal Corps Photo)

thought); Captain L_____ was the only company commander with the appropriate rank, and we did *not* like the way he operated.

One example: If a soldier screwed up, he would be required to dig a six-by-six hole and then fill it up. I also heard that he had "busted" a tank commander to sergeant for chewing gum while in his turret, although it is hard to believe that one.

But this one I know for sure. We were on a night problem. All companies were off the narrow road that led to our route of advance and in the woods. Captain L_____ moved his company onto the road, blocking my entrance to the road. I had to maneuver my company around to get on the road and therefore was late crossing the Initial Phase line (IP). However, it gave L_____ an open road. I was standing in the turret of my tank when I finally hit the IP.

The battalion executive officer called up to me as my tank rolled by, "You are X minutes late!"

I was ticked, and I shouted back to the major, "If my 'sister company' had not blocked my entrance onto the road, I would not have been late! SIR!"

I am on the left with Quinto Chelli and Andrew "Wini" Winiarczyk at our rental home in Fort Smith, Arkansas, while stationed at Camp Chaffee. (FCB)

I still get my hackles up thinking of it. We were called up to battalion headquarters and lectured on the fact that, I don't really know how it went, but we "have to be a team" would sum it up.

I heard rumors when I had my pass to Paris after Kaldenhausen that "Captain Tough" had been sent home in "irons."

So I asked Wini whether he had heard anything about that.

Now you have to know Wini. He stayed in the army and retired as a colonel, and he didn't usually talk like this; his response: "That son of a bitch!" venting the old resentments from our training days. Apparently L_____ had seen one of his officers blown to bits in combat, and he lost it. Certainly a horrible experience, but many of us saw this happen and were able to—had to—continue. He was not sent home in irons, but his toughness now appeared to be a veneer.

As you can guess, we did not get our promotions at that time.

25DEC1943

I have a copy of the Christmas Menu of Company B when it was still designated as part of the 47th Armored Regiment. The menu includes a roster of all 105 men who had recently been sent to the division to fill out the company. Of some interest might be what made up the Christmas Menu: roast turkey and sage dressing, cranberry sauce, mashed potatoes, giblet gravy, buttered peas, candied yams, creamed corn, buttered cauliflower, hot rolls and butter, white or rye bread, apple pie, ice cream, coffee, lemonade, mixed candy, mixed nuts, cigarettes and cigars!!! No complaints here.

The armored school sent a batch of captains to the division for hands-on experience in leading troops. The division had a surplus of captains, so we continued as first lieutenants.

Gas mask training—just in case. (FGB)

NOV1943–JAN1944

14th Armored Division takes part in the intense training at the Tennessee Maneuvers.

01JAN1944–04FEB1944

Assigned as Battalion S-2, 25th Tank Battalion, 14th Armored Division.

01FEB1944

Granted leave of absence.

05FEB1944–06MAY1944

After Tennessee Maneuvers I was sent to Fort Knox to attend the three-month Officers' Advanced Course (Tank) at the Armored School. I graduated from this school on 6 May 1944.

11MAY1944–08AUG1944

Casual officer now assigned the address FFRD No S, APO 545 CP 11, meaning I was off to Europe.

03JUN1944

Departed for Europe.

After three years in the army, I finally got orders to go overseas. I was as prepared as I could be.

(U.S. Army Signal Corps Photo)

2

From the United States to the 2nd Armored Division

While I was in Boston waiting to board the RMS *Mauretania*, the ship that would take us to the European Theater of Operations, I telephoned my dad primarily to tell him I was in Beantown but also to ask permission to buy a pipe. Here I am, twenty-four years of age (at least chronologically), calling my father to ask his permission to buy a pipe.

His response was "Go ahead and enjoy, Frederick."

I smoked the pipe for a while, but then it became cumbersome, so I put it aside, doing nothing to replace it. It was some time afterward that I smoked my first cigarette. Four Viceroys came as part of each box of K-rations. Good marketing by Viceroy to a captive audience.

03JUN1944

I departed for Europe on the RMS *Mauretania*, bound for Greenock, Scotland.

06JUN1944

We were on the North Atlantic when the captain of the ship announced that the Allies had landed on the Normandy beaches. It was D-Day. A big cheer went up. I thought we were cheering because the

invasion had started, we were on the Continent and ready to destroy Hitler and his cronies, but later a second thought occurred to me—that we on the ship might be cheering because we had been spared from having to make what was surely going to be a very costly, very deadly operation, as it proved to be.

09JUN1944

The *Mauretania* docked in Greenock, Scotland, and we traveled by train to England.

The RMS *Mauretania* in her gray paint scheme.

11JUN1944

We arrived in England, and I ended up at a replacement depot just outside of Frome. From there we went on to Tidworth Barracks, where we waited to be sent to Southampton to get on ships to cross the Channel. When I say we, I am talking about an entire shipload of perhaps as many as seven thousand men: enlisted men, noncommissioned and commissioned officers, with almost every military occupational specialty available in the army. It was a sobering realization that we were all replacements for soldiers who had gone before us and been wounded or killed.

My washday at Tidworth Barracks. We had sunny weather and my whites dried right away. (FCB)

The Tidworth Barracks had been built around a nineteenth-century mansion—Tedworth House—on that estate's extensive tracts. A number of barracks were completed in 1905, all named after battles of the Indian Mutiny and of the Afghan wars. Starting in 1944, the barracks became a temporary home to various units of the U.S. Army. The 7th Armored Division was there at the same time as my group of replacements.

To keep us officers busy, stacks—and I mean stacks—of mail were given to us to censor. We knew none of the men whose letters we were censoring, so we had to be serious about it, not like when we censored men in our own units back in the States. The men there had learned what information was allowed in their letters and what was not allowed and were very careful. Not so with this group.

At Frome, we got a lot of "I haven't heard *frome* you for a long time." Cut.

At Tidworth, one incident stands out in my mind. An officer on the first floor called out, "I have a guy here who writes he is in love and has been engaged to and loves, well, six women already."

Another officer chimes in, "So what? I have a guy that is married to three women."

I ran into the same thing. We got together to compare notes and found out it was the *same guy*. I cannot remember how many women he was engaged to, married to, or in love with, but it was quite a high number. We considered switching letters but thought that wasn't the proper thing to do. We just censored them

Stonehenge, located only thirteen miles away from Tidworth. (FCB)

Salisbury Cathedral was sixteen miles to our south. We went here the same day as Stonehenge. (FCB)

(actually there was nothing we had to cut out), but we all agreed that the best thing that could happen to this guy would be if he were killed in action.

I had no idea that we would be able to sightsee at all before being assigned to a unit. After seeing my photos from the trips we took while barracked in England, I decided that I would make sure to keep my eye out for a better camera. I have always wished that I could have gone back to these places to photograph them again and do them justice.

09AUG1944–24AUG1944

Appointed casual officer with the mailing address Repl (Replacement) Depot No 2 APO 117.

12AUG1944 LETTER HOME

Do you remember that little seven-year-old girl I wrote about? Her aunt is the one who gave me the Sacred Heart medal she had obtained at Lourdes many years ago. I never saw their home in Swindon, although I did see the town. Little girl's name was Janet Knighton.

22AUG1944

We sailed from Southampton for Normandy. Southampton was in bad shape. The Germans had bombed the city hard during the Blitz, afterward aiming at the Spitfire factory located there.

25AUG44–29AUG1944

Appointed casual officer (meaning unassigned) at the 19th Replacement Depot.

25AUG1944

We arrived in Normandy, and I frankly do not remember how we disembarked at Omaha Beach. I know we didn't have to go down nets, nor do I believe we unloaded on the piers, but somehow we got on smaller boats, or we could have taken a landing ship, tank, all the way across the Channel.

By the time we got to Omaha, the beach had been well policed, two months having passed since the landings. German bunkers were still recognizable, though all showing signs of hits by artillery or ships' heavy guns. Our engineers protected the beach by sinking merchant ships; in addition, a good number of ships had been sunk and placed to serve as landing docks. The concrete piers constructed in England and floated over to the beach were now in place as well. It was a busy port, bringing in mountains of supplies. I found out later that by D+60 (sixty days after D-Day) ten thousand tons of supplies were being unloaded everyday at Omaha. I remember walking up a long sloping road on the left side of the beach as you faced the land.

We loaded onto two-and-a-half-ton trucks for transport to the replacement depot, or "repple depple," as they were called.

The carnage from the invasion was all around us. The notorious hedgerows still trapped burned-out tanks and vehicles from both sides. Bodies of bloated cattle were scattered about. Our truck hit the main road east, N13, just before Bayeux.

N13 (now E46) was located just inland from the D-Day beaches. The route I took to the front passed through Bayeux and to Caen, where our truck convoy turned north to Rouen and eventually Liège. I ended up 450 miles from where I'd landed. Although I had no idea at the time, I was close to my future unit, the 2nd Armored Division, then in action to the north and east of Aachen, Germany. This was a very long ride in that two-and-a-half-ton truck.

Replacement depots were roughly equivalent to a brigade or group headquarters and usually attached to one of three armies (First, Third or Ninth). Each depot controlled, in theory, a number of replacement battalions, each battalion of men being assigned to a specific division. The depot headquarters was supposed to be an administrative

An early GMC CCKW two-and-a-half-ton, six-by-six closed-cab, short-wheelbase transport, Pontiac, Michigan, United States, 1940–1942. (U.S. Army Photo)

entity that controlled the movement of replacements as they arrived from the United States and forwarded them to the replacement battalion where they were readied for combat and eventually sent to the units that requested replacements for wounded and killed GIs.

The system worked fairly well in England, but once operations on the Continent began, it quickly fell apart. Casualties were much higher than expected and more heavily concentrated in infantry, while manpower limitations (and mistakes in manpower planning) limited the number of replacements available.

The expansion of the Normandy bridgehead began to really speed up in late July, the rapid advance lasting until mid-September. This caused the replacement system basically to collapse. It would take months to rebuild it, and a lot of us got caught in the massive confusion.

Transportation was a huge problem. Replacements were loaded on whatever vehicle was available, frequently open trailers or "cattle cars" towed by trucks; the replacement battalion headquarters were left in place to receive and pass forward more replacements, while the repple depples moved on, essentially becoming traveling mobs of officers and men that were herded randomly from place to place without any permanent accommodations. Our accommodations were our shelter halves pitched each night in soaked farm fields. Soldiers stayed with the depot until frontline units requested troops. We were sent off to those units "by the numbers."

That arrangement led to the well-known phenomenon of the "f—ing new guy," or FNG, the poor guy whose name nobody knew or wanted to know because, with no experience, he was likely to be a casualty in his first action.

Finally, by late September, the frontline did not change much, which allowed the replacement battalion to catch up to the repple depples and move into more permanent quarters behind the front, but by then the replacement shortage was so dire that most men went directly from U.S. ports to Le Havre, got onto a train and were trucked to a repple depple or replacement battalion, where, if they were lucky, they had time for a meal before they were sent on to a unit.

The time spent in the replacement depot system was, I believe—I am trying to think of the proper word—the most "disliked" period I spent in the army. My fellow officers and enlisted men were all of the same opinion. It was certainly not typical of what we expected from the service, and it was the most degrading period in all my twenty-seven years of Active Duty and Reserve time. Ask anyone who has gone through the experience, and I am almost certain that they will agree with that assessment. I include colonels and enlisted men of all grades who I am sure shared that feeling.

Although I was unaware of it at the time, as I moved through the repple depple system I was following the advance through Normandy of the 2nd Armored Division, "Hell on Wheels," to which I was to be ultimately—and, it turns out, fortunately—assigned.

25AUG1944–09SEP1944

Trucks slowly crossed France, not crossing into Holland until sixteen days after I disembarked on Omaha Beach on D+80.

30AUG1944–23SEP1944

Appointed casual officer in the 3rd Replacement Depot.

Keeping track of each of us and our military occupational specialties in order to match us with the incoming requests for replacements had to be a nightmare. I am sure many mistakes were made. I was lucky.

04SEP1944 Letter Home from Somewhere in France

After a few days of rain, sunshine today—feels very good. Just fine; lunch is C-rations again. Now I'm squatting in front of my shelter tent, digesting and relaxing.

Had a field mass yesterday, threatened by rain, which fortunately held off. Went to communion—haven't missed at all lately—can't remember when the last time was that I didn't receive. Made very easy for us, absolutely no fasting required. And if Father doesn't have time to hear all confessions, he gives a general absolution. Then he tries to hear all confessions in whatever time he has after mass. I've been going after mass.

Took a complete bath yesterday, hair and all, in three helmets of water.

We are set up in a grassy field near an apple orchard with plenty of company in the form of cows, horses, a few chickens, ducks and turkeys.

This afternoon at about 1530 another officer and I "took off" and scoured the countryside for anything to supplement our rations. We send scouting parties out every now and then (have one out right now). Today, I did the talking. Our mission was cabbage, tomatoes, onions, chicken. We did get a cabbage and tomatoes; it's lots of fun. Cabbage is des choux, tomatoes is des tomatoes. We have a stew on the fire now. It contains: one rabbit, two heads of cabbage, tomatoes, one onion, a few potatoes and a pot of fresh green beans.

It's hard keeping account of days; gotta watch the calendar. I check off each day.

YOW! I thought a riot had broken out, but it's all right. Someone was indiscreet enough to say, "What I wouldn't do for a chocolate malted milk!" He's lucky he isn't a bloody pulp right now.

My bill is signed by a lot of guys, including Bing Crosby. Look hard just below the 7996C—it's there in fine blue ink. I never did get asked to produce the bill, though. I am not sure what that meant. (FCB)

Most of us carried a "short snorter," which was a dollar bill that you would have men from your outfit or anyone else sign. I found out after the war that apparently the short snorter started in 1925 in Alaska, where bush pilots would have passengers of their planes sign a dollar bill (everyone had a dollar bill in his pocket). If they met up again, the signee could ask the collector of his signature to produce the bill; if the bill was not produced, the collector was bound to buy the signer a drink. The tradition was a confirmation that the pilot and his passenger were still alive, which was celebrated with a "short snort." The tradition passed on to pilots and on to the army.

Among the numerous signatures I collected, my fellow platoon leaders in Company F Lieutenants William Trinen and Don Critchfield signed the bill, as did Captain Henry Chatfield, under whom I proudly served while with Company I. Rather than collect signatures, some would keep track of the towns we went through on their snorter, although this was frowned upon by the intelligence guys.

07SEP1944 LETTER HOME

Sunny day after a really cold night. I'm feeling well. Yesterday for the first time I missed both mass and communion. Couldn't be helped. On the go again. My status remains the same; waiting assignment.

Set up in a woods now. Quite a number of birch trees. We are really seeing the world from the back of a G.I. truck.

An interesting thing happened to one of our officers. He was walking along a path when he met two small children; he gave them each a couple of pieces of hard candy. Just then the mother came up and saw what he'd given them. She immediately handed him two eggs and began to spout oodles of French mentioning the word "Boche" (French for "German") quite frequently. She had tears in her eyes when she finished and said, "Vive le Americain." Usually when people here mention the "Boche" they draw their finger across their throat as if it were a knife. See you soon—with you always.

08SEP1944

A huge number of GIs, more than a thousand is my guess, gathered in a large meadow somewhere in France to see Bing Crosby. We were in front of a stage that had been erected by the USO just for this show. I believe most (if not all) of us were from the repple depple, all still waiting to be transferred to units at the front.

Letter Home

Just moved out of my tent; now leaning against a tree.

I had the good fortune to see and hear Bing Crosby. I have always enjoyed his singing. When Bing came out on the stage he was in regular Army fatigues, but he opened up the jacket to the wildest tie you could imagine! At one point, he sang his 1943 song with lyrics expressing the heartfelt wish of every soldier fighting overseas, "I'll Be Home For Christmas." There was not a dry eye in the house.

After the show he came down into the field. That's when I got his autograph on my dollar bill and also on a ten franc note that I've already sent home.

Earlier in the day, I saw something that I shall never forget. We all had watched a huge flight of our planes going out, stretching from what seemed horizon to horizon. It was a very inspiring sight. A steady drone. Beautiful to see. An unrelenting force. You felt that nothing could stop them or turn them from their steady and what appeared to be slow course.

While in the field sitting on the ground waiting for Bing's show to start, the bombers started to return. All formation was lost, and the planes were scattered all over the sky. We noticed one lone B-24 coming along at a low altitude and on a course which would carry the plane right over our heads. The pilot appeared to be crabbing the plane into the wind. As he passed over our heads we saw why. One propeller was stopped, with the engine dead, and in the wing to the rear of the engine were two large irregular holes.

The starboard side of the aircraft had a huge hole in it as well. The plane was so low we could see members of the crew standing up in the opening; some waved to us, and it was as if someone had given the order for all of us to jump to our feet and cheer. We shouted, waved our arms, and applauded wildly, hoping to convey to those airmen that we wished them a safe flight over the Channel back to England. It was quite a sight and very emotional for all of us. I'll never forget that.

My status is still the same. All's well!

09SEP1944 Letter Home

Sunny day in France, and we took good advantage of it. This morning three other officers and I found a very fine spring, nice, clear, cold water. We dipped it out with our helmets and had a very fine bath . . . boy, that water was cold. But it sure was refreshing. I washed out a couple of things in addition to the collar of my shirt, which now feels more wearable—around the neck anyway.

13SEP1944 Letter Home

We are somewhere in Belgium now. A little tired today but otherwise okay. I no sooner finished a letter to Helen last night than I was alerted and told to get ready to move again, which I naturally did.

I was able to get a seat in the cab of a truck. Poor driver was really worn out, and I relieved him for a while. It was an interesting experience wheeling that big thing. Who would ever have thought I would someday drive a truck over Belgian roads!

My signature on the outside left hand corner of the envelope is my certificate that I understand all censorship regulations & that I have censored my own letter. We are liable to spot-checks.

We are restricted to our camp area, and all towns are off limits. These people are very friendly. They wave, cheer, give the "V" for victory symbol, sometimes toss flowers, which usually miss us, and toss kisses, which the men receive with much wolfish howling and glee. If the trucks stop, the people sometimes rush out with fruit. I had some plums the other day. Then we toss C rations, cigarettes & gum to them.

One night we were talking to a friendly group of about ten people, four grown-ups, the rest all ages of children. When I say talking, I mean we stumble along with our wee knowledge of French and German. All of a sudden there was a large boom and a couple of small ones.

We three were just as suddenly all alone. Boy did those people scatter. It shows what life has been like for them. We stood outside and soon they were back. They had thought of nothing but cover. We found out later that some German infantry had been hiding out in some chateau and were being blasted out.

Off to formation.

14SEP1944 LETTER HOME

A super day yesterday. I received 21 letters. I knew that sooner or later they would catch up. Surely was a grand feeling when they handed me the bundle.

Had a swell night's sleep. Rained last night, sounded good hitting the canvas. Had a couple of pears from this orchard we are in.

I am much closer to an assignment than before, but my main activity now is waiting & moving.

Took a helmet bath yesterday. Cold. How much I shall appreciate those many little things that make for good living yet which we take so for granted.

14SEP1944 SECOND LETTER HOME
OF THE DAY

My mail will get to me now that I am assigned. I'm quite proud to be a part of the 2nd Armored Division.

The Hershey bar enclosed in letter of Aug 20 was very good; rather cracked up but still edible. None of your letters has been censored. No packages yet, but they should be getting here, too.

17SEP1944 LETTER HOME

Well, well, I do get around, don't I. Today I am somewhere in Holland. It has been another beautiful, sunny day, for which I am very grateful, since it has thoroughly dried my O.D. (olive drab) trousers and shirt. Washed both with much misgiving yesterday, fearing that they might not dry for days. Worked out very well.

Just took time out to dig a drainage ditch along one side of my tent, since, even though the past two days have been super sunny, storm clouds now gather in the west.

Blackout time is approaching; it's 1830 now; blackout tonight is 1930. After blackout absolutely no lights are permitted, for very good reasons.

At 1000 hours today I walked over to the Chaplain's area for mass. A very impressive setting under a bright sunny sky and a thick grass carpet under apple trees. I was able to take communion.

Feel great. As happy as can be without my loved ones. Inside of me all is in good order. I feel swell. Do miss the mail much, but it will catch up.

Lt. Clark and I have started a new cooperative called Slit Trench Co-op. We work together and dig a good deep hole for our mutual benefit and use. The present hole is a beaut!

19SEP1944 LETTER HOME

A bit of sunshine today, so I made it a laundry day. Shorts, T-shirts, handkerchiefs, socks, not much, because every time I've been able to take a helmet bath I've washed the understuff I had been wearing.

I've been able to write almost every day; the longest gap was, I believe, three days when I was unable to write—moving and stuff.

20SEP1944 LETTER HOME

I went to chow, where they made the announcement that Fred Astaire was going to put on a show nearby! Off we went! A very good show; the emcee was very good, a Mr. W. Shaw, who was a very good accordionist and dancer.

Astaire was, naturally, very good. He sang: "I'm . . . puttin' on my top hat" among other songs.

All's well. I feel great. I miss you very, very much, but soon a better world.

One night we were standing around our area listening to a plane circling overhead. We thought it sounded like a Jerry, but really had no idea. Then suddenly we heard a whistle. I had never heard a bomb drop before, but no one had to tell me what it was. I made it to my hole (which I had just dug as a warm-up exercise), jumped in and landed on the back of a captain who had thought that the hole did not belong to anyone in particular. I don't know how he beat me to it, because I made it in a split second. The bomb landed some distance away.

The captain excused himself and said, "I'll find another hole." It was rather crowded in my hole, and there were some extra holes in the area, so he left.

Then the plane came back over again. I looked out and saw a fellow who was frantically looking for cover, so I yelled over for him to get in with me. In he squeezed. But the plane only had one bomb, I guess, and left. We all crawled out and had a great time discussing the situation.

I saw the captain later and told him I was sorry I had jumped on his back; I did not know he was there. He answered, "I never felt it, and besides it

Fred Astaire dances for American service members in the Palace Garden at Versailles, France, in September 1944. He knocked himself out for us singing and dancing on 20 September somewhere in Holland.
(USO Photo)

was very comforting to have someone on top of me. And also it was, after all, your hole." Actually, it was a very minor incident, but for a few seconds we surely scrambled. For us new guys, it was a world-shaking (our world) major occurrence.

21SEP1944 LETTER HOME

Still somewhere in Holland, the land of the windmills & wooden shoes. It certainly has been a beautiful day. We are again bivouacked in an apple orchard with a plum orchard next to us. We've sampled and approved of both. Also a very picturesque little stream running through our area. Clear & cold. You guessed it. Lt. Clark and I took the big bath today. Also I took a bold step and washed our shirts and trousers, which we've been wearing every day for a month. Now we pray they will dry before we make any changes.

Gave all equipment an exposure to the sun today to rid it of dampness.

People are very friendly. We're restricted to our tent area so no local sightseeing is possible. Not exactly desirous either.

26SEP1944

Today I was officially transferred from the replacement depot to Company I (medium tanks: Shermans) of the 1st Battalion, 66th Armored Regiment, 2nd Armored Division. Companies C (Light Tanks: Stuarts) and F (Medium Tanks) rounded out the battalion. I quickly learned that the 66th Armored Regiment was the oldest armored regiment in the entire U.S. Army and that the 2nd Armored Division had been commanded by George S. Patton Jr. from November 1940 to January 1942. During that time, Patton stated that his division would be "Hell on Wheels" when it met the enemy. The phrase stuck.

3

On to Company I

On 25 September 1944, I was assigned to a tank company in the 2nd Armored Division (2nd AD), although which company was not specified. Whichever company, I was going to be the last link in a chain of command that started miles to the rear with the Twelfth Army Group.

General Omar N. Bradley's Twelfth Army Group was the largest body of American soldiers ever to serve under one field commander, ultimately comprising forty-three divisions with 1.3 million men. (U.S. Army Photo)

The Ninth Army had just been reconstituted and moved to the front. To build it up, on 12 September 1944 Bradley transferred the XIX Corps from the First Army to the Ninth Army, also shortening the First Army's front. The Ninth Army was commanded by Lieutenant General William H. Simpson. (U.S. Army Photo)

The XIX Corps, with the 29th and 30th Infantry Divisions and 2nd AD, was under Major General Charles H. Corlett. (U.S. Army Photo)

Company I was in the 66th Armored Regiment's 1st Battalion, under Lieutenant Colonel Carl O. "Shorty" Parker. (FCB)

The 2nd AD was under the command of Major General Ernest N. Harmon, who had just taken over the division on 12 September 1944. (U.S. Army Photo)

I would initially join Company I, 66th Armored Regiment (66th AR), which was led by Captain Henry Chatfield. Unfortunately, I have no photo of Captain Chatfield.

I am not sure I was aware of most of this chain of command, but I did feel that I was part of something very big, and that, wherever I ended up, I would definitely be at the receiving end of everything that rolled downhill.

The 2nd AD was one of two armored divisions (the other being the 3rd AD) under the old, "heavy" table of organization and equipment with a triangular form of organization: three platoons to a company, three companies to a battalion, and three battalions to a regiment. Essentially, this left the 2nd AD with forty more tanks than newer armored divisions. The 66th AR originally had a battalion (three companies) of M5 Stuart light tanks and two battalions of M4 Sherman medium tanks.

It became clear fairly early on that an entire battalion of light tanks made no sense, as the Stuart, though well suited for infantry support and reconnaissance, was no match for the German armor of 1944. In June 1944, before I joined the 2nd AD, the 66th AR had been reorganized with the light tank battalion's three companies of light tanks distributed among the three battalions. This meant that each of the three tank battalions was made up of one company of light tanks and two of medium tanks, giving each battalion more operational flexibility.

This reorganization, however, messed up the alphabetic symmetry of the battalions. The 1st Bat-

An M4 Sherman with the 75mm howitzer. The Sherman had more armor than the Stuart, and a bigger gun, but the early Sherman had to be close or have a lucky shot to take out a German tank. (FCB)

An M5 Stuart light tank with the 37mm gun. It was fast, but it did not have the firepower to take on German armor. (U.S. Army Signal Corps Photo)

talion no longer had Companies A, B and C, but rather 1st Battalion, my battalion, retained Company C (M5 Light Tanks) and gained Companies F and I (M4 Shermans).

A tank battalion had, at full strength, fifty-one tanks in three companies of seventeen tanks each. C Company had three platoons of five Stuart tanks each, plus two company command tanks. Both F and I Companies had three platoons of five Shermans and two company command tanks.

The 2nd AD had its armor organized into two regiments, the 66th and 67th, and had artillery, infantry, engineers and signal units attached to the division. We did not have units designated specifically as "tank battalions" at that time in the 2nd AD. However, there were independent tank battalions that were corps and army troops, meaning they were used where and as needed and were not attached to an armored division. Unlike those battalions, the 66th AR had a "home" within the division structure, and therefore we were afforded some consideration and protection. We referred to those separate tank battalions as "poor bastard outfits." They could be assigned to an infantry division on the front line, watch that infantry division be pulled back for some rest and relaxation (R&R) and be forgotten on the line, only to be attached, without any R&R, to the next fresh infantry division entering the front line.

The Panzerkampfwagen Mark IV, a German medium tank, was developed in the late 1930s. It was the most numerous German fully tracked fighting vehicle of the war, remaining in continuous production until the war's end. In total, 8,552 Panzer IVs of all versions were made. (Wikimedia Commons)

Included from here until June 1945 are pertinent sections of the 1st Battalion's daily reports, written up by Colonel Parker and Training and Operations Officer (S-3) Jarvis.

I did not join I Company until 26 September 1944, but I start with battalion reports from 19 September 1944 to provide a context to the battalion's activities just prior to my joining the unit and as a run-up to what I was about to experience.

19SEP1944 BATTALION DAILY REPORT

Near Gillrath, Germany. Weather good. Visibility excellent. 1400 crossed the German border. Set up our security and established road blocks by 1630. 1730 we were counterattacked from the east by 8 Mark IV tanks and a reinforced infantry regiment.

We were to hold while Task Forces A and B were to attack the enemy forces on the right flank and road. Artillery destroyed two Mark IVs while we destroyed two 75mm self-propelled (SP) guns.

Our attack on their right flank drove the infantry into one of our road blocks consisting of one platoon of medium tanks. No estimation of enemy killed is available as yet as the bodies are in no man's land. Counterattack beaten back at 2000.

During the night one listening post challenged an individual coming into his area. Upon receiving no reply, and the individual continued to move, the intruder was shot dead. Inspection this morning showed that the individual was a German soldier who had put on civilian clothes over his uniform.

No vehicular losses, and all vehicles had been resupplied with ammo and fuel.

Approximately 90% of full track vehicles need new tracks.

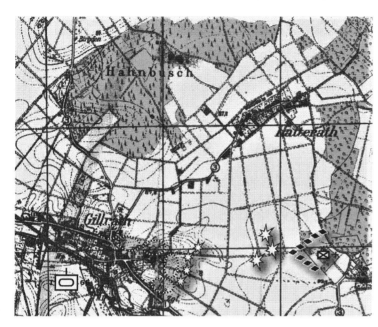

Woods at Hahnbusch

Hallerath

Gillrath

Attack by eight Mark IV tanks came from this direction.

(Map courtesy of U.S. Army Map Service; adapted by Gerry O'Neill)

20SEP1944 BATTALION DAILY REPORT

Approximately 1500, a patrol of one medium tank platoon and one light tank platoon went on a patrol into the wooded area located to our N and NE to seek information as to possible enemy troop movements. No contact was made. All tanks returned to their respective outpost areas. Interdictory artillery fire was placed on the wooded areas N, NE, and E of our position.

At first dark, trip wire warning devices were put out by engineers at 200–300 yards to our front. We received sporadic mortar and artillery fire.

22SEP1944 BATTALION DAILY REPORT

Trip wires improved around the outer perimeter and completed. An additional platoon of A Company, 702nd Tank Destroyer (TD) Battalion (BN) was received making a total of two platoons (ten TDs) of TDs.

23SEP1944 BATTALION DAILY REPORT

Gillrath, Germany. Weather cloudy. Visibility fair. A six man dismounted patrol flushed six Germans from the woods. No prisoners were taken. After the patrol returned, we put several concentrations of artillery and mortar fire on the area.

B Company of the 41st Armored Infantry Regiment became attached to Bn at 1600.

24SEP1944 BATTALION DAILY REPORT

A dismounted patrol made a foot reconnaissance to the NE at 1430 consisting of Staff Sgt. Livengood and nine riflemen, entering the woods at Hahnbusch. Along the edge of the woods the enemy had prepared fox-holes, machine-gun emplacements and mortar sites with sufficient positions to take care of two infantry battalions. The enemy had evidently been driven from the position by artillery fire as there were 15 dead and numerous articles of blood-stained clothing. There were great quantities of abandoned small arms ammunition, bazooka ammunition, and rifles along with large quantities of clothing. Footprints showed to be very fresh. There was no evidence of enemy tanks. The patrol returned at 1700 without having contacted the enemy or suffering any casualties.

Another patrol started out at 1800 to investigate buildings in the vicinity but returned about dark when they came under friendly artillery fire and enemy small arms fire.

24SEP1944 LETTER HOME

All's well. A dismal rainy day and another Sunday, but unable to get to mass.

No longer am I just a replacement. I now belong. Here is my new address, although I do not as yet know the company I will be with, start using this address:

66th Armored Regiment 2nd Armored Division
A.P.O. 252, c/o PM.
New York, NY

They say that as soon as you get to an outfit the mail starts reaching you. I've heard it takes about 10 days for a letter to arrive from the U.S.

Getting rather cool, and light begins to fail earlier. Tomorrow I may go up to a company, and that will be it.

25SEP1944 BATTALION DAILY REPORT

0900 a four man patrol was sent out to Hahnbusch Woods. Enemy had removed its dead and destroyed or carried away abandoned material.

At 1700 six TDs were sent out to destroy, by burning, two tanks of 2nd Bn that had been left there as the result of enemy action. 102 rounds of High Explosive (HE) were expended. *(The tank destroyer crews probably used the already wrecked tanks for target practice—FCB.)*

Harassing fire was placed on the woods by 81mm mortars with 15 rounds at 2100, 15 at 2400 and 15 at 0330.

Three separate patrols searched their own sectors during the night and contacted no enemy.

26SEP1944

I was assigned to Company I, a medium tank company of the 66th AR, 2nd AD, to replace a tank platoon leader who had been either wounded or killed. I do not know what happened to him.

When I was introduced to my platoon sergeant, we shook hands, and I said to him, "Sergeant, I don't know just how to express this to you, but I am perhaps as well-schooled a first lieutenant as you will ever meet, *but* I have never been shot at in anger, so I want you to 'watch' me; you've been there." He looked at me with a bemused look. That was it.

A plus to this assignment was that Captain Henry Chatfield, commanding officer of Company

Dragon's teeth were a very effective device that stopped tanks from advancing. There were many thousands of these along the entire length of the German defensive line. Once covering fire from German pillboxes was suppressed, engineer units would set demolitions to destroy the teeth or fill over them with dirt to allow tanks to cross over their top. (U.S. Army Photo)

I, asked me whether I wanted the liquor ration of the lieutenant I was replacing, consisting of a fifth of Scotch and half a bottle of Gordon's Gin. Guess what I said. Well, it cost me eighteen Marks—all of $1.00 U.S. This liquor was through the courtesy of the British Officers' Corps. My initial introduction to the war did not fit the picture I had imagined of my first combat command.

This day saw twenty-six battalions of American artillery from the XIX Corps, the 30th and 29th Infantry (operating on the 30th's left, or northern, flank) Divisions, and the 2nd AD open up a four-day barrage to knock out pillboxes along the Siegfried Line in the XIX Corps' eleven-mile sector between Geilenkirchen and Aachen. As the advancing infantry of the 30th Infantry Division (30th ID) was to find out, though, the massive artillery barrage was for the most part ineffective, meaning that the infantry would have to get close with flamethrowers and hand grenades to take out the pillboxes.

The Siegfried Line, Germany's West Wall, ran 390 miles from its northern right flank on the Lower Rhine at Nijmegen to its southern left flank on the Swiss border. More than eighteen thousand bunkers, tunnels and tank traps had been constructed to protect the German homeland.

26–29SEP1944 BATTALION DAILY REPORT

Gillrath, Germany. Weather cloudy to rain. Visibility fair. No patrols during the day. Night patrols with no enemy contact made. Spasmodic artillery and mortar fire fell in the area.

Heard movement in the Hahnbusch Woods and laid down a concentration of mortars; six jerries ran out of the woods into the open field to our front. We sent out infantry to try to capture them but were unable to do so. In a last effort to keep them from getting back to their own lines we laid down a heavy mortar barrage. To the best of our knowledge all six enemy were killed.

28SEP1944 Letter Home

Somewhere in Germany

Today we had the sun with us, surely felt good. Hope it sticks with us. We are eating well and sleeping well.

I helped (very willingly) eat four rabbits that a couple of the men from my tank crew had "procured." I had three legs; very good. They were rolled in rough German flour and fried in a kitchen stove in a house the civilians had evacuated. I'm sitting in such a home now; methinks the housefrau would not wholly approve of our methods of housekeeping. We're harming nothing, but, of course, the woman's touch is not at all present.

As yet I haven't had what you would call actual combat, only a couple of experiences with artillery. Under censorship regulations we are permitted in some cases to mention individual experiences 14 days after they've occurred. It is funny how I feel about this. All will be well. I know.

Because of my many transitions, it has been more than a month since I received any mail, but that is to be expected.

01OCT1944 Battalion Daily Report

Battalion moved at 0600 NE to the vicinity of Hagg, Belgium completed at 1030.

01–05OCT1944

Brunssum, Holland

Several of our units maintained contact with the enemy, in support of the 117th Infantry Regiment's (117th IR) assault on the Siegfried Line at Übach-Palenberg, twelve miles north of Aachen. However, most elements of the division moved back to an assembly area near Brunssum, Holland, and Hagg, Belgium, to perform maintenance on vehicles and weapons. We were preparing to move through the breach in the line being made by the 117th IR, whose slogan was, significantly, "Break Through."

The breach the 117th IR opened at Palenberg was ten miles east of our assembly area. This would be a first step to enter the so-called Aachen Gap, an area of flat terrain beyond the Rhine with few natural obstacles. Once we cleared Aachen, our tanks could utilize their speed and numbers to attack the Ruhr industrial region, which was crucial to Germany's war efforts.

Troops of the 117th IR, 30th ID, with German troops captured near the Siegfried Line, Palenberg, Germany, October 1944. The 2nd AD was in support of the 117th IR in this action. Note the U.S. soldier to the left in the leather tanker's helmet. He and his tank would not have been involved in guarding prisoners, but perhaps to give credit to the tanker's assistance, he was invited to stand in the photo. He certainly is not watching the prisoners. (Photo courtesy of the 30th Infantry Division Association)

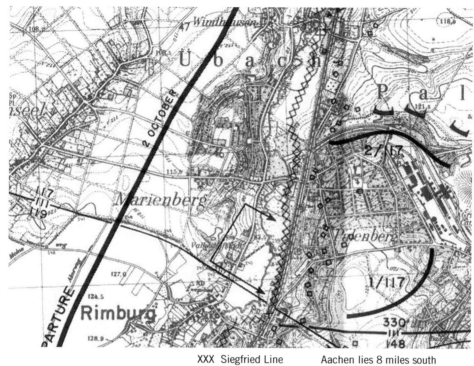

2nd Battalion, 117th IR (2/117) swung to the north of the breach.

Palenberg: The 2nd AD would attack between the two battalions of the 117th IR.

1st Battalion 117th IR (1/117) swung to the south of the breach.

XXX Siegfried Line   Aachen lies 8 miles south

(Courtesy of U.S. Army Map Service)

While in the assembly area, our infantry spent time getting reacquainted with flamethrowers, which were going to be needed to take out the pillboxes embedded in the Siegfried Line.

Ubach, Holland

We had some time off before the advance. I welcomed it to get to know my platoon better, but I soon realized that the time off was more important for the veterans, who had not had much relief in the last four months. One treat for all of us was the opportunity to get showers at a nearby coal mine. We even had movies and a live band.

01OCT1944 Letter Home

Another Sunday and another one without mass. You'd be surprised how well I get along with my scanty knowledge of German, I haven't talked to any Germans yet except to say

Practicing flamethrower technique for reducing pillboxes. (U.S. Army Signal Corps Photo)

"*Verboten*" (forbidden). But I did have an opportunity just once to use it in Holland. I made the acquaintance of a farmer in whose orchard we were bivouacked. He noticed one of my bars (lieutenant insignia) sticking out from under my coat and asked, "Lieutenant?"

"*Ja*," I answered.

He invited me to his house, where I met his wife and son. Swell people. I showed them your picture, Dad, and Helen's. Asked me how old I was. "*Funf und zwanzig*," I answered. Commented on your solid build and that that was very good.

They told me of the treatment they had received from the Germans. It's first-hand stuff and surely makes the blood boil. They had to hide their radios, cars, nothing seems to have been safe. One of the men in my crew told me of seeing the people of one town which had just been liberated carrying radios covered with dust from being hidden so long. At least 20 inhabitants in one little town came out with radios, while the Germans were only driven about 400 yards from the town, with artillery still falling on the town. Happiness all over their faces.

I, however, wished I had remembered more of the German Fr. Enzweiler had taught us. We did get by. It's wonderful to see how the Hollanders accept us.

Keep the prayers a-pouring. With what is before us, we shall need them.

The farmer gave me this large medal of Sancta Teresia, which I still have. (FCB)

One of the crews from I Company. Note the tank in the shadows to the left and the truck in rear. (FCB)

My tank in the farmer's orchard. One of the sergeants had named it *Illona*. Each tank in a company had a name that began with the company's letter. Naming seventeen tanks differently beginning with "I" was not easy. (FCB)

My tank *Illona*, name stenciled in white just above the middle bogie wheels. (FCB)

04OCT1944 BATTALION DAILY REPORT

```
Reconnaissance (recon) platoon, in preparation for the advance, reconnoitered the
right (Combat Command A—CCA) and left (CCB) columns' route to the bridge over the
Wurm River at Marienburg, Germany. Also received one company of the 116th Infantry
regiment, 30th Division. On 30 minute alert as of 0510 05OCT.
```

B would lead the assault through the breach in the Siegfried Line that had been made by the 117th IR of the 30th ID on 2 October. CCA was to follow. Once through the breach, CCB would swing north while CCA would turn to the southeast. My company, Company I, was in CCA, which was commanded by Lieutenant Colonel Parker, 1st Battalion commanding officer. Lieutenant Colonel Stokes, commanding officer of the 66th AR, led the left column of CCA.

What we did not realize at the time was that CCA was the northern part of a hook along with the 30th ID that was to attempt to circle south around Aachen to link with a unit of Hodge's First Army Group circling north. The aim was to cut Aachen off from its supplies and gain the propaganda value of U.S. forces capturing a major city in Germany.

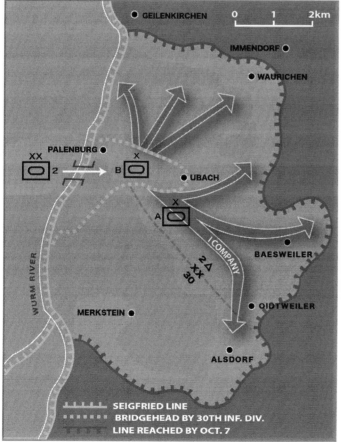

The plan had CCB turning north and CCA turning southeast.

] CCB

] CCA

Company I moved in the area between Baesweiler and Oidtweiler and turned southwest to Alsdorf, a distance of about three miles. The lower arrow pointing south follows our movement.

(Map by Gerry O'Neill)

The advance started off in the late morning of 5 October. This was to be my first combat action.

I Company easily crossed the narrow and shallow Wurm River just west of Übach-Palenberg and advanced three miles east to the outskirts of Baesweiler despite tough resistance. On 6 October, we moved southwest about three miles to take the high ground north of Alsdorf.

Moving forward on 5 October, we encountered many civilians, most of them claiming, "Ich ben ein Holländer, nicht ein Deutscher!" ("I am a Hollander, not a German!") At one point I was facing a large group of civilians, and, in exasperation, I got tired of their protestations and asked in a not exactly friendly tone, "Where the hell are the Germans?" My German was good enough that they understood. There was instant silence and the scuffling of feet.

We had not asked their nationality, but it's probable most were not German. However, at that point it was aggravating, and they were no doubt nervous, as we were very close to the Dutch-German border. Add to that I was looking down at them from the top of a tank.

Until we got closer to the front lines, where the platoon would need to spread out, I led my platoon of five Shermans in column. I was partly exposed as I looked out the turret's hatch in order to direct the platoon. As we approached a field to the east of Ubach, I stuck my arm out to the right to move the platoon

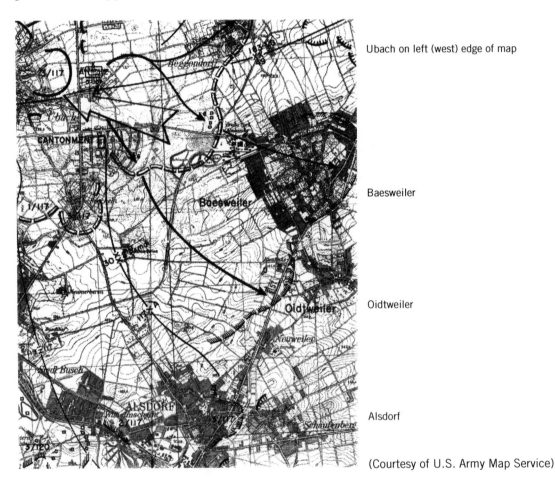

Ubach on left (west) edge of map

Baesweiler

Oidtweiler

Alsdorf

(Courtesy of U.S. Army Map Service)

from column to a line when … BING. A rifle shot rang off the turret, and an instant later incoming mortar fire exploded twenty to thirty feet to the right of our tank.

My exposed right hand was hit by what felt like a hot sting. I pulled my hand in, took a look, and was surprised to see a scorched hole in my glove. I took the glove off and saw a small wound dripping a bit of blood in the palm of my hand. A shell fragment from that explosion had burned a hole in my glove and nicked my hand. I suppose I could have gotten a Purple Heart for this, but it was so minor, I would have been embarrassed. I do remember saying to myself, "Hmm, my first attack and already I've been hit."

The wound was extremely minor, although it was a very hot fragment, and I remember almost chuckling to myself. The fragment was so small, but I kept it. A fragment from the same explosion, about three inches in size, sliced into my musette bag tied to the outside of the tank. I picked that fragment out and saved it, too, but I lost both fragments when my tank was hit and burned at Kaldenhausen.

We crossed the field, my tank on the far left of the platoon and fifteen-tank company line, with a wrecker following close behind us. We heard the wrecker as it contacted the company HQ, reporting a German soldier in a hole in front of him, adding that small arms fire was not accomplishing anything. HQ responded, "Bury him."

That night, I posted the platoon in a perimeter inside a cemetery; there were trees for cover, and the cemetery was on the top of a hill, so we had a good field of fire if anything came at us.

Someone from the rear came up, saw our position and ordered us out of the cemetery. "We are not going to desecrate holy ground with our presence," or something like that.

So I pulled the tanks out and repositioned them as best I could. Once the officer had been gone for a while, I ordered the tanks to move back to their previous positions, which were much safer than the ones outside the cemetery.

I could have gotten in big trouble, I am sure, if that officer had come back—maybe even lost my command—but he did not, and I did not want to jeopardize the safety of the platoon over sentiments for the cemetery.

The battalion took thirty-five prisoners (POWs) this day.

06OCT1944

This was going to be one helluva day. Supported by two companies of infantry from the 116th Infantry Regiment (Stonewall Brigade) of the 29th Infantry Division (the Blue and Gray Division), we were to take the commanding high ground to the north of Alsdorf and remain there until Alsdorf had been taken, which it was in early afternoon.

We were pulled out of line, relieved by elements of the 30th ID and swung back around to rejoin the column, with the objective of seizing the high ground just west of Oidtweiler.

An anti-tank ditch ran along the far side of the road we were on. As we moved along the road, our platoon approached a tree line, and we fired into it to see whether we got any response.

I radioed back to company that we would be changing our line of approach in order to cross the long and deep anti-tank ditch. I dismounted to find a way across the ditch. I found a way, went back to my platoon, and directed it over the ditch. After we passed the ditch and secured the area, one of the guys in my tank came up to me and said, "Lieutenant, you take too many chances; you ain't going to last very long."

On 6 October, the front-line positions generally followed the road shown here running from Oidtweiler off to the right of the photo to Alsdorf and to the left of the photo to Baesweiler. (U.S. Army photo)

Late that same afternoon, having taken our objective, our tanks and accompanying infantry were ordered to swing around to the south of Oidtweiler to gain the commanding ground south of the town.

Soon after the battalion moved, it started receiving heavy anti-tank fire. Two Shermans in F Company were knocked out, one of F Company's platoon leaders was killed in action, a second platoon leader was wounded in action, and that night, the third platoon leader was relieved due to battle fatigue. All three platoon leaders in Company F were out of action.

We kept moving and reached a ridge but were stopped by the same anti-tank gunfire that had decimated Company F. I moved the platoon to the right to work around the flank of the enemy position, but as we moved, we came under heavy artillery and mortar fire, and our infantry support took several casualties. While we were under fire, the platoon sergeant of our infantry support came to my tank to report to me, his officer having been either wounded or killed. He climbed up on my tank, looking very pale, and said to me, "I'm sorry, Sir, I have to leave. I've been hit." Can you imagine that? He was apologizing. His name was Kirk.

The attack continued. I halted the platoon in line at the edge of a large field that was bounded by a wood line at the far end. It looked to me the perfect spot for an ambush, the far woods offering cover for an anti-tank gun and giving it an open field of fire. Sure enough, I saw a gun blast through the trees. I radioed HQ and explained the situation. The commanding officer ordered one of the other platoons to swing around to the right and take the wood line in flank. A self-propelled 75mm gun was taken in flank and destroyed.

I am certain I got some points from Captain Chatfield for this, but, more important, my confidence increased, as I realized that all my training was very useful and paying off.

At another point, we were stopped, and I was using binoculars to see what was out in front of us. Within seconds, I saw a black dot flying through the air in our direction, and it kept getting bigger and bigger. I had no idea what it was. I continued to watch, and a second dot came toward me, this time a little lower. After a third one passed even closer, I suddenly realized, "Hey, they're *shooting* at *me*."

I yelled down to our driver to back the tank up the slope we were on, and we lurched to the rear, but this last shot was on target. The enemy's armor-piercing shot hit our tank low and took out the port-side final drive. We all realized that if we had not reversed up the slope, the armor-piercing shell would have hit us higher, possibly penetrating the turret and caroming around inside the crew compartment.

As it was, the armor-piercing shell gouged a long ragged groove that followed the downward curve of the bow armor, jarring the final drive mechanism, and passing into the ground under our tank. We were only able to move in reverse, so we backed out of there fast, parked the tank for pick-up by the recovery team and switched to another tank. I did not realize that one could see shells coming straight at you until that experience. We did not train for that.

The hatch on our tanks had a field expedient using bolts that allowed the two-part hatch to fold over the top of the tank commander's head like a tent. This provided cover against overhead bursts and had the added advantage that tank commanders could see much better than through the small slit built into the turret or the periscope.

Toward the end of the day, the entire company was in line with my platoon on the left, and I had the hatch folded over my head, observing to the front. We came to a ridge with a swale behind it. We crossed both and entered a field beyond which lay our final objective, a group of houses. We could tell that there had been some fighting in the area, so we approached the objective slowly. As we came out of the swale, we came to the edge of a slightly elevated, long, narrow sugar beet patch, which I duly reported to the commanding officer. We moved up and were told to hold at the edge of the patch.

I kept observing the field when suddenly up popped a head wearing a German helmet, right in the middle of the sugar beets. I turned to my gunner, Rocio, and asked, "Do you see what I see?" He said, "Yes," and I told him, "Give him a high burst of machine gun fire." He fired a burst from the coaxial machine gun, and the head dropped. The head popped up again, and my gunner fired the machine gun again.

Next we saw two hands come up, rocking back and forth indicating that the soldier was probably clambering out of a hole.

I radioed my platoon not to fire and motioned the German forward. He stepped out with hands up but crouching a little, looking as if he expected a bullet in the belly. He drew within about ten feet of my tank, and, all of a sudden, German hands and heads started popping up through the entire length of the field. I am sure I did not even see all of them, as my vision right and left was limited by the hatch halves. Most had dropped their weapons, but several carried weapons over their heads before dropping them. Many carried Panzerfausts, the German version of our bazooka and an efficient, dangerous anti-tank weapon. By the time all the Germans came out of the field, seventy-five soldiers had surrendered. I watched as they walked past us and pivoted behind my tank where they gathered as a group to my rear. I expect they were escorted back in column by our infantry and taken to a POW cage.

We then got the order to continue the advance and drove through the field, where I saw some well-camouflaged holes and dropped weapons. The sugar beet patch was no doubt policed for weapons by the following infantry, two platoons of I Company, 116th Infantry Regiment.

Sherman tanks in sugar beet fields near Baesweiler. (U.S. Army Signal Corps Photo)

I reported that we had reached our objective, and we were ordered to dig in and establish all-around security. We bivouacked around one of the houses that had been our last objective for the day.

I revisited our approach to the sugar beet field to learn what I could from what had just happened. The result was no doubt the best possible for both sides, but I was not sure how we got to that result. The Germans were probably ready to surrender, but if we wanted a fight, they were no doubt fully armed and ready to give us one. The soldier who raised his hands was probably "volunteered" to test us and see whether we were dead set on fighting it out with them. Our first burst over his head sent a certain message, as did the second. Once he climbed out of his hole, my motioning him forward encouraged the others in the field to surrender.

The Germans had to have realized that they had the firepower to knock out my entire platoon, but they also knew that two tank platoons were off to their left, and a lot of infantry was coming up behind us. The only thing I was certain of was that my training had given me an edge in assessing the situation, keeping me from overreacting to the raised arm of that German soldier.

Also, the experience and training of the tankers in our platoon were evident when they held their fire despite the imminent threat plainly visible to their front.

Years later, I read through the battalion report and noticed that our platoon did not get credit for the capture of the prisoners; rather, the infantry behind us did. Given the scheme of things and the outcome, it certainly doesn't matter.

06 OCT 1944 BATTALION DAILY REPORT

Approximately 20 bazooka teams were dug out of an anti-tank ditch by our attached infantry. I Company destroyed the self-propelled 75mm gun from the flank. Previously I Company had received fire from this weapon that penetrated the final drive but the tank was not rendered useless. Enemy casualties are unknown, but 128 PWs taken of which 20 were bazooka teams. 2 SP 75mm guns knocked out and 1 thought to have been knocked out. Six 81mm mortars and 18 large German bazookas were destroyed.

There was nothing to be done about inaccuracies in the daily reports, as we were never asked to review them before they were submitted. There were more important things to do.

That night, the platoon leaders met with Captain Chatfield, our commanding officer, behind his tank. Referring to the tank I had lost earlier in the day, I said, "Captain, I'm sorry I already lost one of your tanks so soon after joining the company." He responded, "Don't worry, Lieutenant; it happens all the time." The captain had five tanks knocked out from under him during his service.

At the end of what had been my second day of combat as tank platoon leader, I got a sense from the platoon sergeant and the men that I had been accepted. I had proved to them that I maybe knew what I was doing and wouldn't get them hurt through my mistake. I learned over time that the experienced combat soldier can judge when a commander is a phony, be he enlisted noncom or commissioned officer. I knew I had been accepted. I felt rather good about that, but it is true.

Back at the platoon area, I celebrated our wedding anniversary! Our platoon's bivouac was around a house that was untouched by any battle action. I told the crew to check out the house, and they reported that it was loaded with perfume, silk stockings, all sorts of loot from Paris, a lot of Nazi stuff, plus a store of wine! Knowing that the Germans had looted all this material, I told them it was an open house. They brought me a bottle of champagne on account of my anniversary. So there I was, sitting on the ground with my back against the tank's engine compartment hatches, sipping on a bottle of bubbly. I am sure I didn't finish it, as it was not smart to drink it all under the circumstances, and we had been ordered to resume the attack at 0700 the next morning.

Two bombing attacks were carried out that night at 2000 and 2200 by not more than ten planes. The attacks were not concentrated and consisted of antipersonnel "butterfly" bombs and one-hundred-kilogram bombs. One Sherman and two mortar half-tracks were hit, and several men from the mortar platoon were wounded. It had been quite a day.

I believe I speak for all of my fellow tankers when I say I have nothing but a very profound admiration and respect for the, as we tankers of the 2nd AD usually spoke of them, "doughs." There are several conjectures on how U.S. infantry got the nickname "doughboys," one tracing it to the American Revolution, but the nickname was certainly in active use during the European campaigns of World War II.

A neighbor and friend of mine was with the 30th ID; he was a platoon sergeant during the war and eventually retired as a colonel. We worked with the 30th ID many times; in fact, I am sure we were teamed with them more than with any other infantry unit while in action in the European Theater of Operations.

Every time we met, he greeted me with a hearty "Hi, Hell on Wheeler!" In swapping stories, we learned that we were at least as close to each other as perhaps the length of a football field during at least one of our attacks.

I told him one day that we often referred to the infantry as "those poor bastards." He cocked his head and said, "Funny, ya know that's exactly what we said about you tankers!"

I remember an incident when we were in column moving slowly on a narrow road and a single column of doughs was marching on each side of the road. My driver, sitting high in his seat, called to one of them, "Hey soldier, would you like a ride?" The dough replied, "You couldn't get me in one of those incinerators for anything!" We were always very happy to have "ground pounders" with us at night, giving us good all-around protection.

07OCT1944

The weather was fair with excellent visibility. The 2nd Battalion was to attack Oidtweiler from the north, F Company from the east, and I Company from the high ground to the south of town. The town fell quickly, although F Company lost two more tanks, one going up in flames. We dug in and organized for defense, one crucial activity being the zeroing in of our guns on road intersections. Five tank destroyers were sent to us from the 702nd Tank Destroyer Battalion, but they were to be kept in reserve, not to be committed unless we came under too much pressure. We were again on the receiving end of heavy enemy fire.

08OCT1944 BATTALION DAILY REPORT

```
Further improvement of positions and firing of artillery missions by forward observ-
ers from 65th and 14th Field Artillery. Medium and light artillery still coming
into the area of the forward troops. A thorough search of all buildings and dugouts
was made. One wounded German in uniform was found; two German soldiers in civilian
clothing were found and turned over to the Division Prisoner of War Cage.
```

I learned that night that our sister F Company had taken a real beating, losing all three platoon leaders and at least four Shermans. The company as a whole had not suffered that many casualties, but the 2nd Platoon had been severely mauled.

The battalion commanding officer called me in and asked whether I would be willing to transfer to F Company to rebuild the 2nd Platoon. I know Captain Chatfield of Company I liked what I had done while with the platoon, even though I had only been with him for just under two weeks. I could only guess that they picked me for this job because I was the new guy on the block. Evidently, Henry Chatfield had given me a good report. I really think I could have turned it down; at least that is the way I interpreted the "order" or "request." I told the commanding officer, "Okay, but I want back to Company I when I feel the F Company platoon is ready." He agreed, so I was transferred from I Company to F Company.

09OCT1944

I Company attacked south toward Schaufenberg and encountered only light small arms fire. However, I was not in this attack, as I was getting ready to transfer to F Company. I got word that my I Company gunner, Sergeant Philip M. Bylewski, was killed in the attack. He was the first man I knew personally who had been killed in action. I also realized that I probably would have witnessed his death had I not transferred.

10OCT1944

I got a kick out of a memo that I found while conducting research at the U.S. Army Heritage and Education Center in Carlisle, Pennsylvania. It's addressed to the commanding officer of the 2nd Battalion, 66th AR, from the commanding officer of the 66th AR via the regiment's S-3 (training and operations officer), Major Long. It was discovered that the radio operator/gunner in the regimental commanding officer's Stuart tank had never fired a 37mm gun before. Major Davis "nicely" demanded that a gunner from A

Company provide this man immediate intensive training in the firing of the 37mm gun that day, to include target practice. One has to assume that this training took place right away.

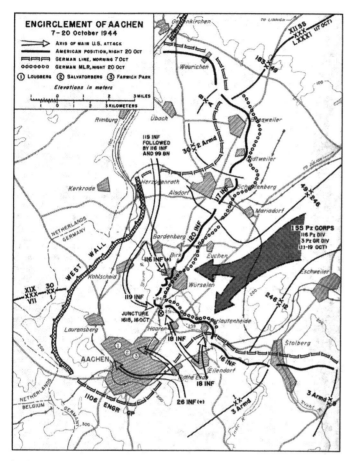

The 29th ID and the 2nd AD moved north for rest and refit during the latter part of the battle.

The 30th ID continued the drive south, eventually linking up with the 1st ID to cut off Aachen from the rest of Germany.

The 30th and 1st IDs met here on 16 October 1944, sealing Aachen off from any help from the east.

The 1st ID had driven north to link with the 30th ID. The battle was now for Aachen itself and to hold off German rescue attempts from the east.

Aachen had been incorporated into the Siegfried Line, the battle for it lasting from 2 October to 21 October 1944. It was the first major German city to fall into Allied hands and was held tenaciously by the German forces. It was the gateway to western Germany and the industrialized Ruhr River basin. (Courtesy of U.S. Army Map Service)

12OCT1944 LETTER HOME

All's well! I received the first letter since I've been with this outfit from Helen dated Sept. 1. They should start rolling in now. Morale booster. There just isn't the time or opportunity right now to write &, second, the topics cannot be mentioned—obvious reasons.

Wish you could see me right now—shaved yesterday first time in don't know how long & I left a few hairs under my nose. It's doing quite well, thank you. Just something to be doing something different than the "job" we have here. Haven't had my shoes off for, well, a lot of time but strangely doesn't bother me.

4

Company F to Merzenhausen

14OCT1944

Completed transfer within the 1st Battalion from Company I to Company F, where I was assigned to the 2nd Platoon. I met my new commanding officer, Captain Ed Fawks, who had been in command of Company F since 11 August 1944.

A platoon at that time consisted of twenty-five men in five tanks. When I got to Company F I found I had some twenty-three men who were new to the platoon, including a new platoon sergeant who had

been a tank commander and was just promoted to platoon sergeant. This was Bill Harris, who proved to be an excellent tank platoon sergeant. After the war Harris became the first sergeant of Company F. He was a good, steady man, solid. He went home earlier than I did, and he promised he would call my wife and mother when he got home . . . and he did.

There was one other "old timer": Tank Commander Sergeant Weinert.

I was under the impression that the replacements coming into the 2nd Platoon had all gone through advanced basic training, which supposedly made tankers out of them. I could not do anything about the lack of experience, having to take what they gave me, but at least they had the foundation, and that I could work with.

An unforeseen plus of the transfer was that I received one of the platoon leader's liquor rations.

On learning where I was from and hearing my accent, one member of the platoon said, "Oh, geez!

Sergeant Bill Harris with Sergeant Weinert to the right, who certainly does not look to be an "old timer." (FCB)

65

We finally got a Yankee!" Realizing that the 2nd AD worked closely with units like the 116th Infantry Regiment (a descendant of regiments in the original Stonewall Brigade) and the 29th Infantry Division (the Blue and Gray Division), out of Virginia, this comment made a lot of sense.

15OCT1944 LETTER HOME

Germany

Today is Sunday. So to mark the day I shaved, even washed my neck. I have left the stuff under my nose; gonna see how it turns out. It's interesting to note how well you can get along wearing the same socks, shorts, etc. for not just past days but weeks. And here we are all on the same level; we "blend" together nicely.

At this moment, I am sitting in the turret of my tank. A cool day, a little cloudy but not unpleasant. My pockets bulge with necessities, and I could live fairly well out of my pockets.

I carry a toothbrush and powder in a pocket, and I can whip it out at any opportunity. My advice to anyone coming overseas is to forget the frills and extra clothes. Those things can, when really needed, be obtained. We all carried too much. I have nothing with me now but a musette bag and bedroll, and that's all I need. My blouse and other stuff are all stored in the company supply vehicle. (We'll probably have to break the blouse out for the V-Day parade, whenever that might come.) The war could end any day and then again drag on and on . . . here we just go from day to day, each day being very separate from the previous day.

Guess I'll have to get my Good Book out and have my own Mass today.

The entire company was near Oidtweiler, Germany, where we had been positioned on 5 October. The first and third platoons were on the front line, and my reforming second platoon was placed in reserve just behind the front line. Although we caught occasional mortar and artillery fire, we were afforded enough time to get to know each other, pull together and develop a viable, working tank platoon. I found that my experience and training at Camp Chaffee came very much into play here.

Despite the heavy rain during these first days in line, and the ground being nothing but mud, our defensive line was still very active. German aircraft bombed us during the night, and incoming mortar and artillery fire was nearly constant. Topping this off, a railroad gun was firing at our lines and rear area from what could have been up to nearly forty miles away. The 560-pound shells sounded like jeeps flying over our heads. It is likely it was a Krupp 28cm Kanone 5 (E).

The most notable individual action of our time fighting around Aachen, Germany, was that of Captain James Burt, commanding officer of Company B of the 66th AR, who earned the Congressional Medal of Honor. He was the only soldier from the 2nd AD to win the medal during the war.

(Wikimedia Commons)

His award is unique in that he was given the medal not for a single act of valor but for his actions during a ten-day period as we fought around Aachen. News of his Medal of Honor traveled quickly throughout the division, giving a real morale boost to all of us. I met Jim after the war—quite a guy. It turned out we had a lot in common besides being company commanders, as we both ended up having long careers in the paper industry. Sadly, his brother Zeke was killed in action in Normandy in October 1943.

James Burt and I at a 2nd AD reunion. Captain Burt is on the right. (FCB)

OCT 1944

Oidtweiler, Germany

We lived in a line of houses, and behind the houses was a series of rabbit hutches with thirty-three big, fat white rabbits. Some of the men came to me one day and said, "Lieutenant, as far as we can see nobody is taking care of these rabbits. We should do something about that . . . like eat 'em! They're gonna die anyway."

That sounded like a good idea to me, and we had some country boys who knew about such things. They scrounged up some potatoes from the cellars and augmented the meals with the best of our regular rations. We enjoyed excellent rabbit meals in different forms every day and were living "high on the hog," or rather "rabbit." I tried to eat with a different tank crew every meal.

We finally got down to the last rabbit. It had bald spots, sort of limped, had runny eyes; he was a sad, sick picture. We watched him for a few days, and, finally, someone said, "What the hell! Let's eat him too!" And we did. It was good.

Being unfamiliar with the men, I censored each of their outgoing letters carefully, as per regulations. After I got to know them all, I just signed the envelope and let it go at that, but that was after I really got to know them.

I set myself up to censor letters in a house on the end of our row of houses and got comfortably seated on a couch at a fairly long table, with the pile of mail to censor in front of me. I felt quite safe, probably because there was a picture of the pope—Saint Pius X, I think, or it could have been the current pope, Pius XII—on the wall. Hanging on the wall across the small room was a crucifix. I felt safe, snug and comfortable.

Captain Fawks, company commanding officer, drove up in a jeep, came into the room where I was censoring the mail and asked me whether I would like to take an inspection tour with him of the other two platoons that were on the line. I said, "Sure," and since the men of my platoon were scattered throughout the buildings working on radio procedure and other chores, I just left without informing anyone.

As we walked out of the building, we heard incoming artillery. We both hit the dirt, and one shell exploded somewhere near us, but we were safe and never looked back. We got in the jeep and drove up to the 1st Platoon, commanded by Lieutenant William E. Trinen, recipient of a battlefield commission.

Lieutenant William E. Trinen, commanding officer of the 1st Platoon. (FCB)

We took the stairs into the attic of a building that had one wall partially blown out and found Trinen, who was acting as a forward observer for the artillery. He immediately warned me not to go up to the opening in the wall but to stay back, for it was likely I would be seen. We talked a bit and then left, driving back to the company command post (CP), which was just across and a short way down the street from my platoon.

As I approached the building where I had been censoring the letters, I noticed that the brick wall behind the couch where I had been sitting had a huge hole in it. The shell Captain Fawks and I had heard hit the room I'd been in. I walked into the house, and the couch was piled high with bricks. Men from the platoon were digging through the bricks, but when they saw me, they came running over shouting, "Hey, Lieutenant, we was looking all over for you, thought at first you were under those bricks!"

Interestingly, the pile of letters I had been censoring was still piled neatly on the table. The picture of the pope that had been over my head had disappeared.

Captain Fawks's CP was in a building with very thick walls, at least eighteen inches of stone, maybe more. Fawks and I were sitting at a table in the corner room one day when the battalion staff came in—five officers in all, who were usually posted to the rear. I do not remember why they came in, but just after they entered the CP, mortar shells began falling just outside the building. Fawks and I remained sitting at the table as if nothing was happening while each of the five officers literally hit the floor. We got a big laugh as they each got up and fell over one another running down the steps to the cellar. We were used to the mortar fire.

Mortar incoming is not like artillery, as mortar rounds give little or no warning. They just fall out of the sky at a very high angle right on top of your position. We felt quite safe in that room and never thought about what might have happened if a shell had come through the roof, but there was at least one other floor above us—maybe two. I am not sure whether those floors would have protected us, but we acted like they would.

A replacement came to the CP one day and was dropped off at the door. The jeep drove away, and a mortar shell came in. The poor guy never even got a chance to report into the company.

The colonel came up one morning and entered the CP. We had a bottle of Scotch sitting on the table, left from the previous night. The colonel grabbed it and started drinking! Ed and I joined him so that he wouldn't drink it all.

2nd Platoon, Company F, in front of an entrance to a fairly elaborate German dugout; one tank crew missed the photo. Kneeling (left to right): Steffy, Skovira, Manzetti, Cignetto. Standing (left to right): Brierly, Hanson, Ferring, Conner, Harris, Weinert, Green, Butler, Gentile, Jutras, Villagecenter, Kello, me. On the tank (left to right): Merritt, Gradelmi, Stewart. (FCB)

After working with the platoon and training them to work as a team, I really felt that this was my platoon. They had worked well together and had good attitudes.

I requested to the battalion commanding officer that I be allowed to stay as their platoon leader, and he agreed, so that was it. I never regretted making the request, although Captain Chatfield, I found out later, was miffed at me because I did not come back to Company I.

I didn't find out he was displeased until almost the end of the war. But well after the war, we found each other and cleared it all up. Henry and I quickly became good friends.

May 5, 1985

Dear Fred,

I do recall your being transferred to F Company. To your credit, I was annoyed to lose you. You had learned a lot in I Company and were doing a fine job.

I always had a low opinion of F Company. They never could put it all together. Their COs were weak and vacillating. Beginning in July 1944 on into November 1944, I Company led almost every attack that 1st Battalion was supposed to launch. Lt. _____ was a sorry excuse for Company's F's CO, and Captain _____ was one of the most indecisive dilatory officers I have ever met.

Your transfer from I to F is typical of how Lt. Col. Parker [1st Battalion commanding officer] would depend on I Company to get the job done. I don't recall exactly when F Company got so severely "mauled," as you put it, but it doesn't surprise me.

It was great to hear from you. It brought back old—and happy—memories. I wouldn't want to go through it again, but my World War II experience is something I shall always cherish and never forget.

Yours in the 66th AR
Henry Chatfield
CO, Company I

His opinions of Company F were very emotional. There was more to his reaction at the time than I was aware of, but he knew that my staying with Company F had nothing to do with him and that I had come to think of the 2nd Platoon as really my baby. I never regretted my sticking with my new platoon.

17OCT1944

Passed through Heerlen, Holland.

18–19OCT1944

Entered Germany and moved into Übach-Palenberg.

22OCT1944 Letter Home

Quite comfortable right now—sitting in an evacuated house, candle light now. Our set-up at present isn't at all bad—not much I can say about anything for security reasons. But we're eating well and sleeping well—does get annoyingly noisy at times, seems as if there are "those" who do not appreciate our presence here.

23OCT1944 Letter Home

Mail today. One dated Aug. 15, another Aug 13 and one Oct 7. And then my absentee ballot . . . which, by gum, I am certainly going to use. How ya votin', Dad? Lemme know how you see it. The immensity of the A.P.O. job—they do a very good job.
    Wish you could see my platoon C.P. (command post)—real class. Sitting there now very warm and cozy.

25OCT1944 Letter Home

Yesterday I removed the growth beneath my nose—the mustache is no more.
    Today for lunch we are going to have fried potatoes, string beans, meat and beans (from our regular issue C rations) with onion added, G.I. coffee, dill pickles, pickled onions and G.I. bread. My tank crew is preparing it now on a stove in an evacuated house. We have been able to add quite a few supplements to our regular G.I. items. We will also have some canned pears. Eatin' well!

28OCT1944 Letter Home

Today we can actually see patches of blue sky, a welcome sight. This is a move day, and good weather makes our task shorter. We can work much better, and those air corps men can really work Jerry over!

Took a couple of pictures today—I've got four left in the camera—have two rolls completed, but I don't know where, when or how I'll get them developed. I know film is hard for you to get, but I wish you would (I'm racing darkness) take pics every chance you get and send them to me. Nearly every man here has a big stack of photos of the things he loves.

29OCT1944

1st Battalion moved to Merkelbeek, Holland.

30OCT1944

1st Battalion placed in division reserve and moved to Neerbeek, Holland.

Letter Home

All is well—having real spicy football weather. What I wouldn't give to see a Bears game with you all. Saw the movie Cover Girl *again. We saw it in Louisville, remember? With Rita Hayworth and Gene Kelly. Also, I had a bath! The first real bath in more than a month. It surely felt good.*

Mass and communion yesterday at 4:00 p.m. in a nice church; it even had a steeple. Altar boys with red cassocks served for our Chaplain. It was good to be able to go.

02NOV1944 LETTER HOME

We spend most of our days maintaining and winterizing our vehicles. Tonight is beautiful with a dark sky and stars. We have a very good set-up now. We're well-established in the living room of a Dutch farmer, and I have four officers with me. Mom, how would you like five bedrolls spread in our living room and five pairs of muddy boots on our floor every night at 2210 North Lamon Avenue? We attempt to scrape the boots clean, but . . .

We're eating very well. Tonight we had pork chops, mashed potatoes, peas, pudding, bread and coffee with some vitamin pills. What more could we ask for? Even pills we got!

Went to mass and communion yesterday on All Saints Day. It's a real holiday here; the locals all dress up as though it were Sunday. (These "Joes" with whom I am living are carrying on a loud and disturbing bull session right now.)

We just finished censoring a stack of mail. Now we are just sitting around: one is sewing, one reading and smoking, one fooling with a radio we found in an evacuated, ruined house, another just sitting, and me writing to you, but you know that. Dug out my air mattress from the supply truck and will be sleeping on air again. Plus a rebroadcast of Hit Parade *is just coming on the radio. This is a good night.*

04NOV1944

Rained today. We listened to a rebroadcast of a Fred Allen show followed by *Duffy's Tavern.*

07NOV1945 LETTER HOME

Sitting on my cot on top of my bedroll; have the radio playing. I just finished a cup of cocoa and am now working on a second cup. Saw the movie Wintertime—*not very bad. Just bad.*

First a big roar. Then I saw it—a flying bomb. It was quite a distance away, but still loud. All I could see was a streaking black object moving on its dirty mission.

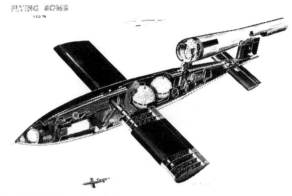

(U.S. Air Force Photo)

Left: The V-1 flying bomb was the first in the V series of "vengeance weapons" (*Vergeltungswaffen*). The initial V-1 launches were aimed at London beginning on 13 June 1944, a week after the Normandy landings. Weighing more than two tons with a length of twenty-seven feet, this jet propelled rocket carried a 1,870-pound bomb up to 160 miles, but its efficiency was poor, reaching and hitting its target only 25 percent of the time. Thirty thousand of the rockets were manufactured. Still, that's an estimated seventy-five hundred targets hit. (Wikimedia Commons)

I was able to get two postcards made of me in my new field coat. Both postcards made it home to Helen and my folks in Chicago! The photographer had only three plates left. I did not want to hog them all, but I probably should have had a third photo without the helmet. (FCB)

07NOV1945 LETTER HOME

Somewhere in Holland. Today I had a couple of pictures taken, will get them Saturday. I hope they turn out. Paid a Guilden a piece (approx. 40 cents in our money).

We were dispersed in different houses and directed to give classes during the day. This seemed like a waste of time to me; rest and relaxation seeming to be more in order. I set up a man on watch in case anyone was checking up on us, and sure enough he spotted a staff officer coming toward the house. I got everyone together, threw a map on the wall and started talking map coordinates. The officer entered, looked around and congratulated us on the best class he had seen that day! As soon as he was out of sight, we reverted to R&R.

11NOV1944

1st Battalion released from division reserve and designated as part of Task Force A under CCA control and commanded by Brigadier General John H. Collier.

Letter Home

Eight o'clock, squattin' on bedroll by candlelight (very well blacked-out). I just finished censoring some mail and also getting those pictures in the mail. I was able to make arrangements to get them developed. I cut pieces of cardboard to fit the regular air-mail envelope and sent one set of 3 pictures in each of 3 envelopes. They should arrive without being too bent. They'll show you what type uniform I've been wearing.

13NOV1944

Near Oidtweiler, Germany, where we had our first of three consecutive days of rain.

14NOV1944

Two troops of British Squadron B, 1st Fife and Forfar Yeomanry (1st FFY), with flame-throwing Crocodile tanks, were attached to us 15–24 November 1944. Crocodiles are Churchill tanks redesigned as flame-throwers, with each Crocodile towing a trailer containing napalm.

Photo of me taken in Holland on 11 November 1944. It was printed on a postcard so that I could send it directly to Helen, which I did. (FCB)

15NOV1944 LETTER HOME

Hope you receive the Christmas card which the division had made. It's really a very nice one—expresses Merry Christmas in the languages of every country in which the division has spent time.

We've been having hotcakes almost every morning. They are so good that the men complain when we don't have them. Cooked on field ranges and out in the field under a large fly . . . and winter is now on us. We've had a little snow—the wet kind—also sleet.

I'm sitting under the kitchen fly now—the stoves throw a little heat around, and the sound of the stoves has a good psychological effect. One of the men just walked past the kitchen and yelled, "Hot cakes tomorrow?" This morning we did have eggs. Powdered, but they do a good job of fixing them up.

Before I left England I put in a good stock of woolen socks. They serve me very well now.

(FCB)

(FCB)

16NOV1944

The offensive began at 1245 on 16 November 1944. Our jump-off point was the eastern edge of the bridge-head near Oidtweiler that we had secured in October. We were to break out of the bridgehead, cross the Roer plain and reach the Roer River ten miles to our east. The assault was to be essentially a straightforward frontal attack. The ultimate goal was for the 29th Infantry Division advancing to our south to capture Jülich (just off the map below to the lower right) and secure a Roer River crossing there.

While elements of CCA were to pass through Setterich and immediately circle north to attack Gereonsweiler from the southeast, our elements of CCA were to advance on the division's right following an eastern course. Our objectives were to pass through Setterich; take Freialdenhoven, two miles east of Setterich; advance four more miles through Merzenhausen; and move in the direction of Barmen, which was just above the flood plain of the Roer.

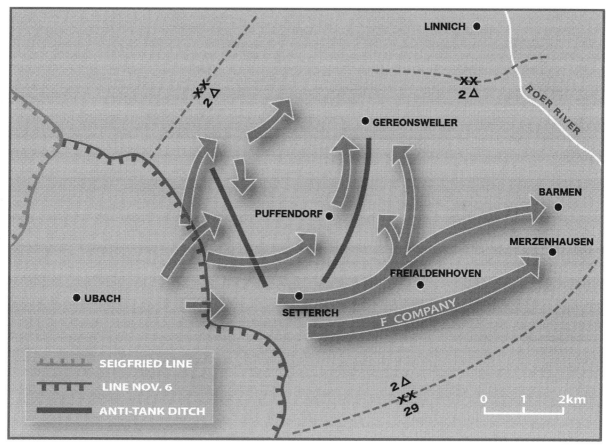

(Map by Gerry O'Neill)

The Roer plain was open agricultural land, and our line of sight was very good. Sergeant Ed Huckaby, commanding officer of one of our platoon's tanks, spotted a Royal Tiger tank (a Tiger II) crossing our front from left to right at thirteen hundred yards out. It was rare to see a Royal Tiger in the first place, but to see any German tank offering its vulnerable side armor and open tracks to flanking fire was unheard of, but there it was.

Sergeant Huckaby fired three shots from his 75mm gun in quick succession. Either his first or his second shot hit the turret's rim just where it met with the body of the tank. The shot crimped the turret's armor into the body of the tank, keeping the crew from rotating the turret to fire at us.

The Tiger crew could still swing the entire tank to bring their 88mm gun to bear on us, but Sergeant Huckaby's next shot took care of that possibility as it hit and broke the right track, one of the few spots where we could do any damage from this distance. Combined, these two hits put the Royal Tiger completely out of action.

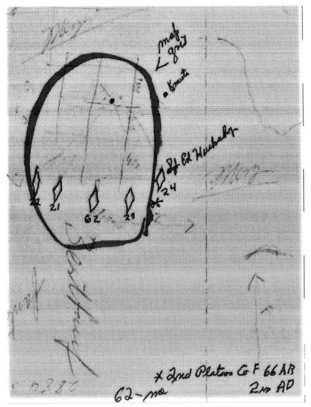

This sketch, made immediately after the action, shows our tanks' positions when we saw the Royal Tiger. In the middle of the formation is the platoon command tank (62). Sergeant Huckaby, in 24, was on the right point of what was a somewhat inverted "V" formation. It is possible to see the grid lines from the main map that I wrote on the paper to mark the exact location where this took place. (FCB)

Through my binoculars, I watched the crew bail out, and I heard Sergeant Huckaby say over the radio, "Beautiful." Two of his three shots hit! Great shots, each taken while the Royal Tiger was on the move at over a thousand yards.

As we moved up, I watched one of our M36 tank destroyers come up, stop close to the Royal Tiger and put a 90mm armor-piercing shot through its turret! To our chagrin, the crew of that M36 got credit for the kill, even though it was already dead. I believe this was the first Royal Tiger destroyed by the Ninth Army, although I am sure there is some discussion about that. There certainly is discussion about who knocked it out.

The two hits that knocked the tank out are seen here, the first at the turret ring and the second at the front end of the track. The shot from the M36 can be seen directly above Huckaby's shot at the base of the turret. I am fairly certain that is one of Huck's crew climbing onto the tank. (FCB)

From this angle, the wrecked track is more evident, as is the shot at the turret line. Note the open escape hatches on the top and rear of the turret. (FCB)

The top hole was made by the M36 armor-piercing shot. The M36 had a 90mm gun, which accounts for the difference in the size of the holes. The M36 was new to us, seeing its first action in October 1944. It was tasked with replacing the under-gunned M10 TD with its 3-inch (76.2mm) gun.

Ed's lucky (but still very good) first shot from his 75mm jammed the turret by twisting the turret ring into the tank's body, as seen here. Recall that our tanks had howitzers, so Ed's shot was not on a level line to the target, but Ed had to account for a looping trajectory.

One of Ed's other shots had to have hit the track. No matter what, the tank was not going to move anymore, and with the hit jamming the turret, the tank was out of the fight. (FCB)

Sergeant Ed Huckaby commented, "We just got a lucky shot. It was about thirteen hundred yards away, and I cut loose with three quick shots. I got in one shot in a hundred, hitting and locking the turret so it could not turn. When the turret would not turn, the crew bailed out." I am not sure he knew he had hit the track.

The passage below is from *A History of the Second United States Armored Division 1940–1946*, page 117, giving credit to the tank destroyer for its destruction. Also note that the passage erroneously refers to the tank as a Panther tank. It is the same Royal Tiger as in the previous photos, only from the front.

(U.S. Army Photo)

> *A German Mark V (Panther) [sic] tank knocked out by Tank Destroyer fire in the fighting near the Siegfried Line. The point of penetration can be seen as a small hole on the left side of the turret. Many of the men of the division rated this the best tank the Germans possessed.*

The hole from the tank destroyer shot is visible on the left side of the turret in the top photo.

If you got the drop on Tigers and fired the first shot, it was okay, but we could not stand and slug it out with them. We knocked out some Tigers because our crews took better advantage of terrain, and sometimes we overwhelmed them with numbers of Shermans and tank destroyers. Our

(U.S. Army Photo)

Sherman tank was not in the same class as the Tiger; the Tiger had six inches of frontal armor and thirty-four-inch treads, allowing it to travel through terrain that would bog us down.

The Royal Tiger's twenty-one-foot-long 88mm gun fired a high-velocity shot, meaning the gun was more accurate since its shot followed a straight course to its target. The Germans also used smokeless powder, making the tank more difficult to locate. The Tiger was a very dangerous tank, but the guys in my platoon still thought the Panther Mark V a better tank.

Captain Fawks said afterward that getting a Tiger was 75 percent luck and 25 percent marksmanship.

The bottom photo followed the one above in the book. No mention is made of the shell hole where the turret meets the body of the tank or the broken track, both clearly visible here.

This photo gives a sense of the size of the Royal Tiger. I have been unable to identify anyone in this photo, but there are five men, so one could assume they are the crew from Sergeant Huckaby's tank. A blowup of the photo (right) still does not provide sufficient detail to identify these men. (FCB)

A photo that appears in Steven Smith's *2nd Armored Division: Hell on Wheels* is almost certainly a close-up of the turret of the Royal Tiger that Sergeant Huckaby knocked out. The photo suggests that units coming behind us took some pot shots at it as well, perhaps wanting to see what impact their guns would have on the tank's armor or just for practice.

Target practice, the impact is marked as a 90mm shot; note that it did not appear to penetrate the armor of the Tiger, perhaps as the tank fired from some distance away.

The impact of the "kill" shot that I saw taken by the M36's 90mm gun at extremely close range.

Two shots circled here; the one to the left has been marked as a shot from a 76mm gun (would have been from the 76mm gun of an M10 tank destroyer). Note that it too did not penetrate the armor. The hole to the right is Sgt. Huckaby's shot that struck just above the tank's turret ring. That shot was from his 75mm howitzer but is mislabeled as a 76mm shot.

(U.S. Army Photo)

Photo of Ed Huckaby (circled) with Company F at Fort Benning, Georgia, taken 6 April 1942. (EH)

Ed Huckaby at the 2004 2nd AD reunion. (FCB)

Soon after knocking out the Royal Tiger, Sergeant Huckaby was promoted and transferred to command C Company with its light tanks.

019NOV1944

Our units easily passed through Setterich and attacked two miles east toward Freialdenhoven. We took our objective, which was the high ground to the south of the town, but we could not enter the town due to a very extensive minefield that ran across the entire front of our line. From the high ground, we were able to cover the town and support the infantry as they went forward.

20NOV1944

We prepared to move forward off the high ground at 0900, but the move was delayed, so we waited. At 1000, we got the word to reconnoiter farther south of Freialdenhoven, but it was slow going through thick mud. We reached our first objective but encountered another large minefield. Company I lost two tanks in the minefield, so we contacted the engineers. They informed us that they had cleared a path through the field during the night. We found the path and started into the minefield in column formation, our tanks slowly following one another across. Despite the cleared path, one tank to the rear of the column hit a mine, even though it had followed in the tracks of the tanks to its front. There were no casualties, but the tank's track was broken, which is a tedious but fairly quick repair.

We discussed it later and figured that either the mine had been buried deeper than the others and detonated after several tanks passed over it, a trick we had encountered before, or the engineers just missed one.

Battalion figured that the entire ground in front of us was mined, so we were ordered to move even farther to the south to see whether we could skirt the minefields. We finally got away from the mines and started to move forward again when we were slowed by a long and deep irrigation ditch that acted like an anti-tank ditch. Probably the ditch was the reason there were no mines in this area; the Germans figured

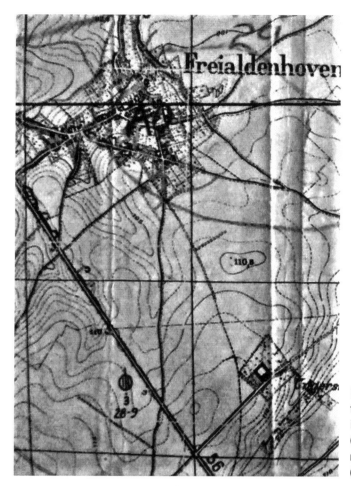

Highway 56 crosses this portion of the map from the middle left to the lower right. The circle indicates about where we crossed the road. (U.S. Army Map Service with author's marks made during swing south around Freidaldenoven.) (Courtesy U.S. Army Map Service)

the ditch would stop us or at least slow us down. It did. Working our way across the ditch took a while, but we finally got across. Once on the other side, it was a clear path to our next objective, which showed on our map as Highway 56.

When we reached Highway 56, we observed loosened bricks in the road bed, a good indication that the road had been mined. On orders from our battalion commander, we sent a tank from my platoon to definitely establish whether the road was mined. I told the tank commander not to tell his crew what they were about to do. I did not want them to tense up and possibly be injured. The tank had not been on the road for more than a few minutes when I heard an explosion.

The tank commander came on the radio immediately and reported, "We found what we were looking for." I informed battalion that indeed there were mines on the road.

I personally thought this was an unnecessary waste of a tank since we had seen the loosened bricks and already knew that the entire area had been heavily mined. The crew got out, shaken but uninjured, and went to the rear for another tank. Maintenance towed the disabled tank to the rear to replace the track and repair the suspension system. The tank was back with us in two days.

We crossed the highway and halted about 1330, taking up positions in a large field east and somewhat south of the town. We had a platoon of tank destroyers attached to our company that moved into position to our south to protect our flank. Part of our company moved to a position directly east of Freialdenhoven to cut off the Germans in the town.

A force under the control of the commanding officer of the 2nd Battalion, 119th Infantry Regiment, was ordered to enter the town and start clearing it up. When darkness fell, about a quarter of the town had been taken over; the clearing of the town continued through the night.

We expected much-needed fuel to reach us that night, and we got our orders for the next day. Company I was detached and sent to envelop Edern, a town due north of Freialdenhoven.

21NOV1944

Fuel did not get up to us that night as expected, so we were unable to gas up. The fuel trucks got there just after 0900, the time we had been ordered to start our advance. While we were busy refueling, battalion kept radioing us to get moving, thinking we had gassed up the night before. Excuses did not cut it with battalion. Finally, in answer to their insistence that we "get moving," we radioed, "We are moving," and continued gassing up until we were done. That completed, we really set out about 1000.

Our next objective was the high ground south of Merzenhausen. The original route selected to reach our objective was over a relatively flat, open area; however, after a close map study of the contour lines, our company officers determined that there was a protected approach that ran through a small valley that had covering ridges on both sides. We proposed this to battalion, and they accepted. On the original map at battalion the contours indicating the valley were easily recognizable, although it is not as clear on my map.

We learned we would be facing contingents of the 246th Volksgrenadier Division led by a capable battalion commander, but the going looked like it would be fairly easy. I was wrong.

Our task force was made up of the 1st Battalion of the 66th AR, the 2nd Battalion of the 119th Infantry Regiment and elements of the 41st Armored Infantry Regiment. A troop of one Churchill and four flame-throwing Crocodile tanks from Squadron B, 1st FFY of the British 79th AD, would be joining us.

We were to make a two-pronged attack against the village. A troop of flame-throwing Crocodiles would be attached to each prong. At our planning session the night before, we were told just the sight of these tanks would make white flags appear in abundance as this had been the result of previous Crocodile attacks.

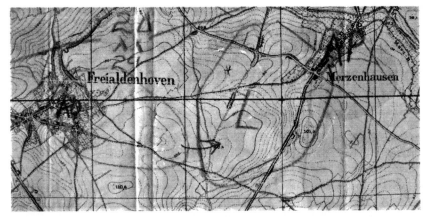

The arrow in the middle approximates our well-concealed advance. Again note the division boundaries in the upper left. Note that we are *not* within our assigned boundary. (Courtesy of U.S. Army Map Service)

Our company moved out at 1000 following the valley to the high ground south of Merzenhausen.

As we advanced, the company line spread up both sides of the valley with our 2nd Platoon on the left. As we had hoped, the Germans did not see our advance up the valley, or maybe they just decided not to respond to our movement. We reached the high ground at 1330 without meeting any resistance. Infantry moved up to us and consolidated our position. Our platoon was assigned to back up the 1st and 3rd Platoons.

The 1st and 3rd Platoons moved to our right and took up positions along the high ground facing the town. My platoon remained on the left flank of the company positioned in an old gravel pit that had been dug into the south side of the ridge. I moved my tank down into the middle of the pit with two tanks of the platoon on either side of me.

We made sure each of the five tanks was positioned below the crest of the front edge of the pit to stay out of sight of German anti-tank crews.

The two tanks on my left straddled a dirt road that led up and over the ridge, while the tank on the far right was in contact with the flank of the two platoons that had moved into position to our right. The 1st and 3rd Platoons immediately came under fire from the town, but no fire came our way. Our position in the quarry was keeping us out of sight of German artillery spotters.

Soon after we were in position, a deer ran run across the face of the front slope of the gravel pit. The entire platoon opened up with their machine guns. What was left of the deer was retrieved and hung behind our line.

Later in the afternoon, I heard that there would be a "shoot" into Merzenhausen, and I wanted to see whether we could get in on it since we had been sitting inactive for a while. I told my crew that I was going to dismount and run up to the company's CP, located in a small cave in the forward wall of the quarry seventy-five yards directly to our front.

I remember setting my canteen cup on the breach of the tank's gun; we had just brewed up some coffee, and I wanted some when I got back. I pulled myself out of the hatch. No sooner had I touched the top deck when I heard an artillery shell coming in. We had been getting intermittent fire all day, but this sounded like it was coming right at us. I literally flew off the tank, hit the ground and scrambled for a nearby covered slit trench. There were four GIs in the hole already, protected by light overhead cover; I had not known they were even there. The shelling went on for a bit; Ray Stewart remembers two rounds passing directly over his tank, *Frances*, which was located to our right front.

I stayed in the hole until the shelling ceased. I stuck my head out of the trench and looked at my tank to see whether it was okay, but I was alarmed to see that all the hatches were open. I called out, but there was no answer. I looked forward to the CP and saw my men at the entrance to the cave, one of them beckoning me to come to them.

I ran to the CP and found my crew in a daze, all standing there except for Martin, my gunner. I went up to them and shouted, "Where's Martin! Where's Martin?" My stunned crew could only shake their heads. I asked again, but this time one of our platoon leaders nudged me with his elbow and pointed to the backs of the uniforms of my crew. Their uniforms were covered in blood. I then knew where Martin was.

As I slipped out of the turret, Martin did exactly what he was supposed to do. It was standard operating procedure. Martin picked up the binoculars, moved to the position I had left just seconds before and lifted his head in order to observe the terrain to our front and flanks. He did this just as the incoming high-explosive round hit the top of the turret. The blast struck the hatch ring, blew it completely off the turret and split Martin's head in two. While I was hunkered down in the hole for cover, the remaining crew had bailed out. Doing his job had cost Martin his life.

I left the HQ with my first thoughts being to go back to the tank to retrieve my maps and other equipment I would need since the tank would have to be retrieved and taken to maintenance for repairs. I was thinking that a hit like that could have seriously damaged the gun support or the gear system. Thinking only about the mechanical damage to the tank, I was not prepared for what I was about to see.

Illustration of a hatch ring on a Sherman used to support the two half-hatches. The shell hit the front of the hatch ring as Martin looked out of the tank. (U.S. Army Photo)

I climbed into the tank, the first thing I spotted being my canteen cup still sitting on the breach of the gun. I looked around the inside of the turret. Martin's body was curled around the gunner's seat with his scalp sitting right on the seat . . . a full set of hair, like a toupee, very dark and very thick. On the floor just in front of the where I had been sitting was a full set of teeth, uppers and lowers. The entire compartment was covered in Martin's blood and body parts. I later found the hatch ring that had hit Martin in the face. It had been blown twenty feet behind the tank.

Martin was a fine young man. He never knew what hit him. And people wonder why we cannot easily forget or let go of the experiences we had as rather young and impressionable men. This was certainly one experience I have never forgotten.

I grabbed my maps, personal gear and equipment and switched to another tank in my platoon while my crew went to the rear to get a replacement tank.

I later determined that I had unknowingly placed my tank on a map grid line. No doubt the Germans had figured that enemy units might use the gravel pit and had noted various coordinates that allowed them to fire indirect, harassing artillery at specific spots on the map. They never saw us, but they caused so much damage.

Casualties sustained 21NOV1944
Cpl. Manuel R. Martin KIA
From Winters, California

Martin is officially listed as KIA (killed in action) on 23 November 1944, but he died on 21 November 1944. Graves Registration did not receive his body until 23 November. They had no time to spend verifying dates.

I was disappointed that I was unable to locate the gravel pit when I visited in 1968, as a lot had happened while we were there in 1944. Martin's death was just the beginning.

I needed to get my head back into my responsibilities. From my new command tank, I concentrated on a ridge running roughly east to west at the grid line on the map that I could see was exactly two thousand yards from my position according to my map.

While scouting the ridge through binoculars, I spotted a man standing on top of the ridge holding a map. Soon, a couple more men appeared. I radioed the platoon and told them to hold their fire, adding, "It looks like they are planning a party or something; we'll fire with range set at two thousand yards." I advised the tank commanders to adjust their fire based on where our shell landed and then fire at will.

As we waited to fire, I continued to watch as the group of German staff on the ridge got even larger, finally totaling seven men. I assumed the soldier standing in the center holding a map had to be a commanding officer.

I told my new gunner to lay the crosshairs on the guy in the center.

What I did not specify was whether the fuse on the shell should be set for direct or delayed. In my tank, as a matter of choice, I always kept the fuses at delay, which meant the shell would hit the ground and ricochet into the air, creating an airburst, which was very effective when firing on infantry. A shell on delay could also penetrate a building and explode inside.

The other option was to set fuses on "super quick," which meant the shell would explode immediately on contact with its target. How the fuses were set was left up to the tank commander, who always had the option to change a shell's setting when giving his firing order. What I did not know was that the tank commander of the tank I had just taken as command tank kept the tank's fuses on "super quick."

I could not understand why the group of men on the ridge had not taken notice of us; we were out in the open, and they must have seen our tanks. All I could think was that they thought we were knocked out, as there was no movement outside our vehicles, our crews all being inside the tanks, and we had no infantry with us yet. Either that or they arrogantly thought we were lousy shots.

I was watching the group through my binoculars as I gave the command, "FIRE!" The gunner fired, and what I saw was unbelievable. The projectile made a direct hit on the man with the map and exploded instantly on contact.

The young gunner turned and looked up at me. These are his exact words: "I don't mind shooting at them, Sir, but I sure don't like to see them fly apart like that!" His face was drained of all color.

I radioed the tank to my right on the ridge above me and asked, "Two-Four, did you see what I saw?" The tank commander's response was, and these are his exact words, "Did I? You bet! It was beautiful. Arms and legs and heads flying all over the place!"

No other tank in the platoon needed to fire another shot. No further comment.

Infantry moved up to help us consolidate our positions, and the actual attack on Merzenhausen did not start until 1400 when the force under the commanding officer of the 2nd Battalion, 119th Infantry Regiment (2/119), was ordered to move into the village from the west and clear it. However, at the same time, six tanks, reported to be Mark VI Tigers, were spotted entering Merzenhausen from the northeast, taking under fire any target they saw. Fire from the two forward platoons to our right knocked out one tank and damaged another, but the remaining four moved into the town. Our air observation patrol called in artillery fire, forcing the four tanks to move constantly in the village. The force under the commanding officer of 2/119 quickly came under heavy fire and was stopped three hundred yards from the village. It immediately consolidated its position for the night.

22NOV1944 MORNING

Due to rain and poor visibility, our attack on Merzenhausen, scheduled to start at 0900, was postponed. It was to be a two-pronged advance: the force under the commanding officer of 2/119 to again work its way from the west and enter the village, while a platoon of tanks from F Company with attached tank destroyers moved around to the east of the village to take it under fire. We were expecting the troop of flame-throwing Crocodile tanks to join in the attack as well.

The Crocodile was a converted Churchill tank that towed a highly vulnerable trailer filled with napalm. (Wikimedia Commons)

The 2nd Platoon remained in a support position in the gravel pit when, at 0900, a British major in command of one Churchill tank and four Crocodile tanks came up along the secondary road that ran between our two tanks on the left flank. (Some reports have the troop with two Churchills and three Crocodiles.)

I was outside my new tank when the major jumped out of his tank and walked toward me, saying, "I say, Chaps, what's the situation up ahead?" He quickly followed this up with something about a flame-throwing mission. We knew that one troop of flamethrowers was to accompany each prong of the attack.

I told him every time we exposed our turrets above the front rim of the gravel pit to fire into the town, the "people over there shot at us and were very unfriendly."

That was it. He had heard all he needed to hear. He did not ask about our attack's timing or whether it was still on. It was 0900, the time originally set for the attack to begin. He thanked me, waved his arm, turned around and mounted his tank. I had no idea what his orders were or what he planned to do, but I could not believe my eyes as he moved his five tanks up over the ridge on the dirt road to our left, and to make matters even more amazing, he went over in column formation rather than spread out in a line, which would have made the vehicles harder to hit.

Within minutes all five tanks were hit, the napalm exploding and catching fire. I believe all five tanks burned. We could hear the cries of the crews, but we could not offer any assistance until nightfall, when, under the cover of darkness, we were able to help evacuate those few who had survived. The enemy had that front slope too well covered to risk doing anything during the light of day. This all happened shortly after 0900. The major, attacking without support, did not survive. Nor did most of his men.

To my knowledge, this is the only known photo of the attack by the Crocodiles at Merzenhausen, taken while I stood next to my tank. The burning Crocodile just beyond the crest of the gravel pit is clearly visible. The "smudge" to the left of the road is the last tank of the 2nd Platoon securing our left flank. The Sherman on this side of the dirt road is clearly identifiable. (FCB)

In September 1945, we took part in a joint British-American live-fire demonstration in front of a large group of dignitaries, including, I heard rumored, Winston Churchill. As I walked along the rear of the line of departure, I came to parked Churchills that had the same escutcheon as the tanks at Merzenhausen. I looked up to question a lieutenant standing on one of the tanks.

"Are you the unit that lost the flame-throwers at Merzenhausen?"

"YES," he replied and added immediately, "The bloody bastard always said he was going to die in battle, but he didn't have to take so many good men with him!"

The two troops of Squadron B, 1st FFY (British), had a valiant history with us. They were recently attached to our unit and took part on three occasions in the advance between the Wurm and Roer Rivers on 18–22 November 1944. One troop of Crocodiles achieved some success in the direct assault on Freialdenhoven, but the accompanying infantry did not close rapidly enough after the edge of the town was flamed. Despite this, the town was occupied and cleared on schedule on 20 November.

Another troop aided greatly in the capture of Gereonsweiler to our north later that same day, as this time the infantry advanced with the tanks. Before entering the town, the tanks flamed haystacks as German tanks would take cover in them and ambush tanks as they passed.

Entering the town, the Crocodiles shot a hole in each building with the tank's 75mm cannon and aimed the flamethrower through the hole. Soon, white flags were popping out of every window and door. Flank protection was afforded the Crocodiles by our division's Shermans.

But on this third occasion, the troop of Crocodiles that was committed in column over an open slope in the assault of Merzenhausen on 22 November was a complete waste of good men and equipment. A debacle.

I found out later that we had been on the same operation together at another time and that they had been very near us; in fact, we had seen his unit but did not recognize it at the time.

The "Tommy" standing on the tank was the lieutenant who called the major "the bloody bastard." (FCB)

(FCB)

22NOV1944 AFTERNOON

At 1300, Company I came back under control of the battalion and was immediately ordered to move as quickly as possible to the west and north of Merzenhausen and push as aggressively as possible into the village. Company I did not draw much fire as it maneuvered, and it was able to advance through orchards on both the western and the northern edges of town. However, Company I started receiving stiff resistance from enemy infantry. The Company I commanding officer called for infantry from the 2/119 to come forward and clean up the enemy to the front of his tanks. Slowly, the infantry were able to push forward, and they reached the edges of Merzenhausen before darkness fell. The Germans continued the fight into the night with infantry infiltrating our lines and setting booby traps in the orchard.

The ongoing and intense pressure applied by the enemy prevented our troops from taking any further action that night. The infantry gathered around the tanks as they consolidated their gains, but the entire force had been hit hard. From as far away as the gravel pit we heard a German tank moving back and forth in the streets of the town all night long. The daily report inaccurately concluded that the mission had been accomplished.

As darkness fell, I called for artillery to cover the entire ridge where the German staff had been standing from end to end. We had lost our infantry support, and tankers feel uncomfortable without some infantry dug in around them at night. Knowing we had artillery support made us feel more comfortable, and I hoped showing the Germans that the ridge was zeroed in would prevent any attack from that direction.

I checked in at the battalion CP and was sent to battalion HQ to report our company's situation. When I entered the CP, I immediately saw the commanding officer of Company I sitting at the table with his head in his hands, crying.

23NOV1944

I knew I had a grim task to perform the next morning. The tank that had been hit in the gravel pit was drivable and had been taken a short distance to the rear and parked in a farmyard where it would eventually be picked up by Ordnance for cleaning and repair. Martin's remains were still inside. On a map that had been taken from some captured Germans, the word "gut" was written by that particular farm. We had learned that the "gut" indicated good water.

We drove our jeep back to the farmyard, even though we were receiving incoming fire. We passed a GI in a covered position along a brick wall, who yelled, "You're going to get yourself killed, Lieutenant." Funny thing—I never felt that way.

I yelled back, "Don't interfere, soldier. I'm here to get my driver; he's just been killed."

There were five or six GIs in one of the farm buildings. I asked for a volunteer to help me lift Martin out of the tank. No one moved. I shouted at them that I needed assistance getting a body out of my tank. Finally one fellow moved to help. The two of us lifted Martin out of the turret and laid him in some hay in the barn.

When we left, we passed the first GI, and I apologized to him. He said, "I understand, Lieutenant."

When we eventually got the tank back, the cleaning crew had neglected to clean under the tank's floorboards where blood had collected. The tank compartment reeked. The crew had the jolting but necessary job of removing all the remains below the floor before being able to use the tank.

I made sure First Sergeant De Pratt knew where Martin's body was. Martin is buried at the Luxembourg American Cemetery in a plot very close to General George S. Patton's grave. I visited Martin's grave in 1986. Corporal Gentile (my driver) and one other tanker visited the young woman Martin had been seeing. Everything about this was so sad and tragic.

When I got back to the platoon, I learned we were moving out. We formed in column, and our company drove through Merzenhausen on our way out of the area. I recall seeing an American 2½-ton truck carrying the bodies of many German soldiers. On one side of the street, wooden landmines had been stacked, no doubt by our infantry or engineers. We had to be extremely careful on the narrow turn to avoid scraping the piles of mines.

There was no sign of the enemy tanks. We wondered whether the German tank noisily moving back and forth all night in the streets of the town had done that purposely to mask the sounds of retreating tanks.

23–25NOV1944

Baesweiler, Germany

The regiment moved into its assembly area, and we did maintenance on our equipment. We also tried to rehab ourselves.

26NOV1944

Track extensions were installed on the treads of each of the tanks, widening the tracks to make them work more efficiently in snow.

Track extensions, also known as "duck bills" because of their shape, were an on-the-spot fix manufactured locally in France and Belgium to provide better traction in snow. Note the tread is rubber, adding to the tank's efficiency on ice. (U.S. Army Photo)

27NOV1944 LETTER HOME

Some of the letters we censor say, "I haven't got much time to write," and then they write for 10 or 12 pages. As it is termed, these were real "snow jobs" where they were trying to impress, that is "snow," some gal.

Without you back there keeping our little family together, praying for me, and just being there, well, I wouldn't have any reason for going on at the very unpleasant "work" we do. You are doing your share, and it's a great one. A nation is only as strong as its homes—its families.

28NOV1944

The 1st Battalion received Battle Honors on 6 October 1945 for our efforts on 18–28 November 1944.

29 NOV–20 DEC 1944

Baesweiler

The 2nd Battalion and the Reconnaissance Company maintained defensive positions near Freialdenhoven, while the rest of the regiment was in assembly areas around Baesweiler. The 66th AR's strength as reported for this date showed 132 officers and 2,257 enlisted men.

03DEC1944

The regiment minus one company of light tanks reverted to CCA control. I got a forty-eight-hour pass and headed to Belgium.

04DEC1944

Of all the letters that I sent home, this seems to be the only one that had been censored. I have no idea what I said that deserved the black ink, although I am pretty sure I mentioned the town I was in. I should not have done that.

I met a Lieutenant Jackson and found out we were both from the Midwest, so we window-shopped together. I was able to send a surprise package to Helen with some lace, perfume and a collar and some lace and a vase for my folks. Two movies were available, and we took those in: *Sensations of 1945* and *The Hairy Ape*, which were not bad. I stopped by the very welcoming Red Cross center and picked up stationery (FORM 539A) for this letter.

A troop of Belgian Boy Scouts held a parade and sang as they marched. The scouts had been suppressed during the occupation, and all were wanted by the Germans to join the Nazi youth organizations. With the Germans gone, they were free to parade; however, when the Nazis left, they took the scouts' musical instruments with them. All the children asked us for "chew gum." I was also able to pick up some film for my camera.

An officers' mess had been set up by the division, where we ate and were able to get real coffee. Jackson and I decided to celebrate and bought a bottle of champagne to share with the owners of the house we were staying in.

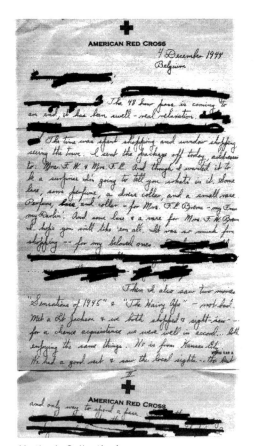

(Author's Collection)

How I appreciated walking down a quiet, peaceful street, something I realized at the time that I had always taken for granted. After a very relaxing time, I headed back to the unit and made it within the forty-eight hours' allotted time. It would be the last relaxation we would have for a while.

07DEC1944

The operations plan for the Roer River crossing was received. Our 1st Battalion was assigned to Task Force C along with our Reconnaissance Company, one platoon of Company A, 702nd Tank Destroyer Battalion and one platoon of Company A, 17th Engineer Battalion.

08DEC1944

We had a command inspection.

16DEC1944

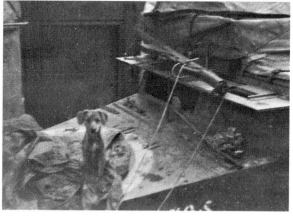

The Maintenance Company's pup in Baesweiler. (FCB)

Many of us expected, or more accurately hoped, that the war would be over soon. We were all surprised by the news that the Germans had attacked with a very large force through the Ardennes Forest to our south.

Here is a note sent from S-3 with our first warning that Germans dressed in American uniforms were infiltrating our lines to cause whatever disruption they could. The note reads:

"From Master—150 American speaking Germans from 150 Panzer Brigade are behind Master lines. They are in American uniforms wearing dog tags riding 4 to a peep.

Their instructions are to destroy HQs. and lines of communication to check on movement and supply. From S3, 66 A.R."

[The message was confirmed.] *Recd 192000A from Warren (?) S-2-3*
(Original in the author's files)

Intel had also been gathered from several field artillery units and sent out by Captain Lana, 256th Field Artillery, informing us that enemy paratroopers were being dropped in specific map grid squares and again that the Germans were wearing U.S. uniforms with U.S. dog tags. They were also riding around in jeeps.

17DEC1944

A light tank company was alerted to be ready to move to any part of the division zone to combat German parachutists that might be dropped.

18DEC1944

We were on three-hour alert status, meaning if the order came to move, we would have three hours to get ready to move.

19DEC1944

Colonel William S. Triplet assumed command of the regiment. Colonel Stokes became the commander of the CCR (Combat Command Reserve).

19DEC1944

I was mentioned in an article in the *Chicago Herald American* written by Jess Krueger, the *Chicago Herald American*'s war correspondent. He quoted me as saying I was one of the few graduates of De Paul Academy in Chicago who had not played basketball but then went on to say that I was "proud of a recent feat" of spotting seven Germans over two thousand yards away and eliminating them all with one shot from our main gun. I am not sure why Mr. Krueger inserted the word "proud" in that final paragraph, as I know I did not use it. I am not sure what the right word is for how I felt about that shot, but "proud" certainly is not one of them.

20DEC1944

Still at Baesweiler, continuing on three-hour alert status.

21DEC1944

The regiment was alerted to be ready to move at daylight, then it was delayed to 1400 and then again to 2400. Billeting parties were sent seventy miles southeast of Baesweiler to the general vicinity of Havelange, Belgium, to prepare for the arrival of the entire division. Unknown to us, this perched the 2nd AD directly on the northern flank of the attacking Germans.

Our part in the Battle of the Bulge was about to begin.

Major General Ernest Harmon, commanding officer of the 2nd AD during the Battle of the Bulge, with Colonel John "Pee Wee" Collier, commanding officer of CCA, 2nd AD, during the Bulge. (U.S. Army Photo)

5

The Battle of the Bulge

The winter of 1944–1945 was the coldest, wettest winter that western Europe had experienced in thirty years. It was with this advantage as a backdrop and cover that the Germans launched their attack through the thickly forested Ardennes, sweeping in an attempt to drive west and north to the port city of Antwerp. We called this massive struggle the Ardennes Counteroffensive, but the press called it the Battle of the Bulge after the shape the attack took on the maps. That name stuck.

16DEC1944

The Germans had mustered more than two hundred thousand men, close to one thousand tanks and assault vehicles (including more Royal Tigers) and nineteen hundred artillery pieces. A full two thousand aircraft, including Messerschmitt Me 262 jets, were ready to provide ground support. Between 16 December and 19 December, the Germans penetrated forty miles into the U.S. lines, one-third of the way to their objective, the port at Antwerp.

The initial assault split Bradley's Twelfth Army Group in two, with the entire U.S. Ninth Army and the bulk of U.S. First Army in and to the north of the German bulge. Commander Bradley was completely cut off from those troops, as his headquarters was south of the bulge in Luxembourg. Command of Ninth Army and First Army

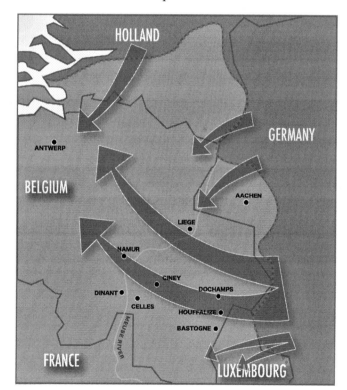

The German plan for Unternehmen Wacht am Rhein (Operation Watch on the Rhine), the German name for the Ardennes Offensive. This was Hitler's last gamble. (Map by Gerry O'Neill)

forces in and north of the Bulge quickly became a real problem for the allies. British General Sir Bernard Montgomery being the nearest army group commander north of the bulge, Supreme Allied Commander General Dwight D. Eisenhower made the decision four days after the Germans had begun their offensive to temporarily transfer command of Bradley's two U.S. armies to Montgomery's 21st Army Group.

We were stationed in Baesweiler, Germany. I remember walking down the street and seeing my Lieutenant, a guy by the name of Brems. We did not salute out of fear of snipers at this time. I asked him about the Germans, and he said, "When I hear anything, I will let you know." —Bow Gunner Sergeant Ray Stewart, F Company

20DEC1944

Lieutenant Don Critchfield transferred from E Company to F Company. He had seen action in North Africa during Operation Torch and in Sicily in Operation Husky. During the Normandy invasion, his unit was sent to assist the 101st Airborne that had parachuted into Normandy predawn on June 6. He said that he had never seen so many dead, before or since. The 101st had landed in the middle of a German Panzer Grenadier division. At Sainte-Marie-du-Mont, Don had two tanks knocked out under him. He had seen it all and was a veteran in every way. He was also an avid photographer. We were to become close friends. For better or for worse, he joined us just in time for the Battle of the Bulge.

Mike Skovira's short snorter has our platoon in Aachen on 21 December 1944. I was only in Aachen once, and it makes sense that we would have been passing through Aachen at this time. Perhaps we had been prepositioned in Aachen in preparation for the march south. Our march south to Havelange, Belgium, to join in the Battle of the Bulge started that night.

21DEC1944

A realignment of commands was going on that we were not at all aware of. Our division was removed from the Ninth Army to the First Army and

I am standing by my tank with 2nd Platoon tanks and crews stretched down a street in Aachen. (FCB)

Aachen: compared to Berlin and Frankfurt, which we entered after the war, Aachen was in good shape. Some buildings still had roofs. (FCB)

attached to the VII Corps (commanded by General "Lightning" Joe Collins). The order came down from Collins that the entire 2nd AD was to move seventy miles to an assembly area in the bend of the Meuse River near the town of Havelange, Belgium, and we must roll before midnight. We just moved where and when we were told to go. With fourteen thousand men, three thousand vehicles, and four hundred fifty heavily armored mobile units on a single road with vehicles separated by at least the regulation fifty yards, we made a column more than one hundred miles long.

Besides the new command arrangement, someone higher up (perhaps the 2nd AD's commanding officer, General Harmon) had decided all units of the regiment were to be reorganized into three combined-arms "task forces." Each task force had armor, infantry and artillery to call on whatever we encountered.

Any attacking force's movement would be constricted in the Ardennes due to the rough and thickly wooded terrain and the narrow roads and trails. Tactics would be determined by the nature of the situation. Mixing types of troops meant that each

General John "Pee Wee" Collier
(U.S. Army Photo)

task force could apply the elements it needed to any tactical solutions. Company F was detached from the 1st Battalion and attached to the 2nd Battalion, forming Task Force A along with companies A, D and E and various other units, all under the command of General John "Pee Wee" Collier.

General Harmon's confidence in the 2nd AD led to a daring move. The plan was for the division to make a night march on bad roads in winter weather and arrive on the north rim of the bulge, all the while keeping clear of the fighting so the Germans would not know we were there. We were then to watch and wait for the right time to hit the enemy with everything we had on their northern flank.

Rather than be stretched out on a single road, the 2nd AD was to take three separate routes, the muscle on two routes east of the Meuse River with the supply column paralleling the advance on the west of the river. All military identification on vehicles was obliterated in the interest of secrecy.

Task Force C consisted of the remaining companies of the 1st Battalion, Companies C and I, as well as the reconnaissance company. Task Force B included the rest of the regiment. All three task forces comprised Combat Command A (CCA). The recon company of Task Force C led the move to Havelange, departing at 2230 21 December. Task Force A with our platoon followed, with Task Force B behind us.

It was at this point that Company F disappeared from the daily report of the 1st Battalion. Our absence was noted on the 1st Battalion's report as "minus Company F" or with a little "-" next to the 1st Battalion symbol on a map. Lieutenant Colonel Parker had no idea where we were. We also did not appear on the 2nd Battalion's report, probably because during the confusion of the next two weeks I did not submit any written reports to anyone, nor was I asked for one. All I knew was that Company F was under the command of the 2nd Battalion, and it fell to Captain Fawks to keep in contact with 2nd Battalion HQ and relay orders to his platoons.

When we started out, the night was pitch black, the roads slippery with sleet and ice and clogged with traffic. There was an unremitting icy drizzle . . . and the weather worsened as the night progressed.

I stood in the turret of our Sherman, my face getting pelted by sleet and my hands sticking to the metal hatch ring. I was covered by a poncho that I'd draped over the turret ring in an attempt to keep the sleet from invading the inside of the tank. In spite of the cold sleet hitting my face, I still had trouble staying awake, almost dozing off a few times, causing me to jerk my head to an upright position. We did not have maps, but the division had posted MPs (military police) and band members at each road intersection to provide hand signals pointing the way. The driver had to keep his eyes on the moving shadow of the vehicle in front of us, probably a tank, which was visible only by two small green lights that the snow kept blotting out of sight.

I radioed the driver and told him to take a break and let the bow gunner relieve him for a while. He responded, "No, Sir, Lieutenant, I'm taking my baby all the way!"

At the price of approximately sixty thousand gallons of gasoline, our units starting arriving in and around Havelange at midday. Task Force C pulled into its assembly area, the Bois-et-Borsu, at 1330 on 22 December. Our Task Force A arrived at the village of Borsu, four miles east of Havelange, at 1520, and Task Force B arrived at 1745. We had traveled seventy miles in fourteen hours in terrible conditions. We set up roadblocks and secured the area. A force of light tanks and infantry was set up in each task force to combat any parachutists that might drop on us.

General Harmon considered this road march a great accomplishment for the division. Not one vehicle lost its way and all but eleven vehicles arrived at their assembly points with their units, all eleven having slipped off the ice-covered roads.

On the afternoon of the twenty-third, in the cold and snow squalls, Task Force A was ordered to move southwest to occupy the town of Ciney, placing ourselves on the northern flank of the German penetration and putting us in a position to cut off the Germans' lead elements. The night march had paid off. I don't think the Germans knew we were there. That was probably the greatest accomplishment.

Once Ciney was secured, CCA was ordered to keep on moving to the southeast, with our next objective being Buissonville, fifteen miles away. We

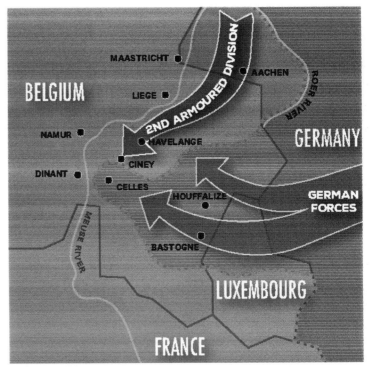

Map of the 2nd AD's move on the night of 21 December 1944. (Map by Gerry O'Neill)

moved at night, General Collins's idea, starting out at 2330. Two miles southeast of Ciney, our lead elements ran into a small force of Germans that was quickly dealt with. Another mile on, they ran head-on into a German column around midnight. That column was taken care of as well. We then stopped for the night.

24DEC1944

The skies cleared for us. CCA continued to move east toward the Lesse River while CCB moved west toward Celles. Fifteen miles separated the two combat commands, a risk to be out of supporting distance of each other, but it turned out to be worth taking.

The next morning, we mounted up and moved out through Haid. At a crossroads a mile south of Haid, the platoon of tank destroyers that was with us from Company A of the 702nd Tank Destroyer Battalion knocked out a Mark V Panther.

It is likely that the photo below is of the Mark V Panther destroyed outside of Haid. The weather had cleared, as the photo indicates, and my notes say the tank was destroyed before Christmas.

We were starting to see evidence that the quality of the steel being used in the German tanks might be suffering. Usually a hit from an armor-piercing round made a clean hole, but the size of the holes in the Panther and their jagged appearance made us think that perhaps the steel they were forced to use was subgrade and very brittle. We later learned that in the summer of 1944, the Germans experienced a shortage of manganese and had to switch to using high-carbon steel alloyed with nickel, which made the armor on their tanks quite brittle.

We were redirected to Forzee, a mile short of Buissonville. We entered Forzee unopposed and were now eight miles from Ciney, where we had started.

It was cold. The decision to wear the wool cap or the helmet liner or the steel helmet was up to each tanker while in the tank. But outside the tank, even back from the lines, we were all supposed to wear the steel. Many tankers got chewed out on the spot by meandering staff officers who happened to spot the wool cap, easy to see from any distance. One young gunner in the light platoon attached to us was constantly in trouble for this, but he continued to wear the wool. Getting chewed out did not seem to faze him.

A good German tank—kaput! Captain Fawks, commanding officer of F Company, with a knocked-out Mark V Panther tank with two jagged holes that we were not used to seeing on damaged German tanks. The Panther had also thrown its track (again, an old cavalry reference, as in a horse "throwing its shoe"). (FCB)

25DEC1944 (CHRISTMAS DAY)

Christmas Day started out clear and very cold. CCB headed southwest at dawn and took Celles by 1700. While we stayed in Forzee, part of CCA night marched the four miles to Humain and took it early Christmas morning, rested a bit and then started out again at 0730.

It was now our task force's turn to be reorganized. Two companies, D and E, were attached to the 2nd Battalion under Major Herbert Long and named Task Force Long. At 1515, Task Force Long moved south out of Forzee, but we ran into a minefield and were ordered to stay in Forzee for the night.

26DEC1944

About three miles east of our position, my old company, Company I, was attacked just before dawn by a strong force from the Panzer Lehr Division at Havrenne, Belgium. Fifteen Panther tanks and a battalion of grenadiers from the 10th Panzer Grenadier Regiment riding in armored half-tracks had been ordered to protect the right flank of the leading 2nd Panzer Division, and we were a threat. Captain Chatfield and his company stopped three attacks, knocking out five of the Panthers and seven of the half-tracks. Henry received the Silver Star for halting this German counterattack.

We moved southeast toward Rochefort, ten miles distant, and headed directly at the center of the German penetration. Task Force A succeeded in occupying a key road junction west of Humain.

To our west, CCB succeeded in surrounding the lead German elements of the 2nd Panzer Division in a pocket at Celles. Mark V Panther tanks and Mark VI Tigers struck south to punch a hole in the pocket to escape, but Typhoon aircraft stopped them cold.

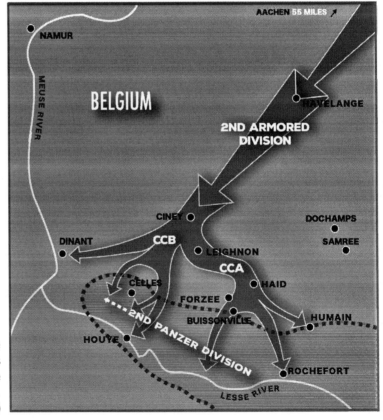

The 2nd AD struck the north edge of the Bulge from several points. My platoon was on the arrow leading to Rochefort. Note the pocket forming around Celles. (Map by Gerry O'Neill)

27DEC1944

Both task forces attacked south and southeast to occupy road junctions in order to cut supply and support routes crucial to the German advance.

Somewhere near Rochefort, our platoon was halted at the edge of a wooded area and told to establish a base of fire in support of an infantry battalion that was pinned down by heavy machine gun and small arms fire to our front.

I lined up the platoon's tanks to provide suppressing fire into the woods to our front and on the edge of the town to our left. Our fire was returned immediately by volleys of Nebelwerfer rockets, what we called "screaming mimis!" The rockets were more annoyingly noisy than accurate, but they did add an unnerving screeching to the din of the small arms fire.

I radioed the commanding officer of the light tank platoon, located to my right, that his Stuarts should fire canister rounds into the woods to their front. Canister rounds were very effective against infantry, acting like shotgun blasts with numerous projectiles spreading out soon after they left the gun.

There was no response on the radio to my request, and none of the light tanks fired, so I radioed again. Still there was no response. Figuring that their radio communication was out, I climbed out of my tank and ran to the command tank of the light platoon and ordered them to fire canister into the woods. They promptly did, and the small arms fire stopped, as did the fire from the Nebelwerfers, which were either knocked out or, more likely, pulled out. Either way, we were relieved to get rid of the "screaming mimis."

Once the firing settled, the lieutenant of the light tank platoon left his tank and began to walk in my direction. As he came up, I asked him where he was going. All he could say was "I can't take any more of this." Trying to get through to him was useless, so I ordered him to go back to headquarters, and he trudged to the rear. A minute later, his platoon sergeant came to my tank and told me that the radio had worked fine—both times—but that the lieutenant

German 15cm Nebelwerfer 41. (Wikimedia Commons)

had just ignored my calls. I told the sergeant to take command of the platoon, and I thought that was that.

Later I learned that the lieutenant had put in for a Purple Heart for combat fatigue. On hearing this, I immediately wrote a letter to headquarters describing what had happened and that, in my opinion, he did not deserve a Purple Heart. I never did hear what became of the lieutenant or his Purple Heart.

I also found out that the young gunner in the light platoon who had insisted on wearing only his wool cap when he was outside the tank had been killed. He'd been shot in the mouth. As it turned out, a steel helmet would have done him no good.

The Combat Command Reserve (CCR) under Colonel Sidney Hinds retook Humain, as the Germans had moved back in after CCA took it on Christmas Day. The British 1st Fife and Forfar Yeomanry, the unit that had lost an entire platoon in front of our eyes at Merzenhausen, sent in Crocodile flamethrower tanks, lit up one tree as an example, and gathered in all the Germans as they surrendered.

By the end of the day, the 2nd AD had complete control of the north bank of the Lesse River to Rochefort. Our three days of fighting put a real crimp in the 2nd Panzer Division's attempts to reach the Meuse River. We had accomplished a lot, much of it due to General Harmon's planning. We did not know it at the time, but the 2nd AD's surprise attacks from the north had blunted and stopped the German attack. General Harmon's carefully laid plans to strike the German advance at multiple points along its stretched northern flank opened up many opportunities to break through the flank, get behind the Germans' leading units and disrupt supplies and reinforcements, leading to the encirclement of the 2nd Panzer Division in what is called the Celles Pocket.

The 2nd Panzer Division's units marked the deepest penetration of Unternehmen Wacht am Rhein, getting within four miles of the Meuse River bridge in Dinant. In the end, the Germans were forced to break out of the Celles Pocket on foot and turn east to Germany. They were forced to leave all their vehicles behind.

None of us on the front lines had any idea all this was taking place. We just did what we were told to do, and we made it happen.

28DEC1944

We all stayed in place for a rest and refit. We needed to be ready to go back into action.

30DEC1944

Each of the task forces moved to assembly areas fifteen miles to the north near Achet and Porcheresse for maintenance and rehabilitation. Since going into action on 23 December, the 66th AR had knocked out 7 Panther tanks, 23 artillery pieces and 113 other vehicles. Our losses for the entire period were 5 killed, 132 wounded and 1 missing.

01JAN1945

The weather closed in again with snow, then rain, followed by a hard freeze, putting a glaze on the roads and the trees. And then another layer of snow dropped on top of the ice. It took the entire division three days to move thirty miles to a town twenty-five miles due north of Bastogne. It was at this point that General Harmon ordered our steel treads to be changed out for rubber.

02JAN1945

The regiment was ordered to move east and southeast about fifteen miles to new assembly areas. After eleven hours on the treacherous roads, our Task Force A assembled near Ny, Belgium, ten miles northeast of Dochamps.

03JAN1945

Our next objective was Houffalize, where we hoped to link up with Patton's Third Army coming north and cut off any German troops to the west. To make this happen, we attacked south on an eight-mile front on what would be nearly two straight weeks of tough fighting. Our ability to see what we were driving into was limited by the heavily falling snow. Large snowdrifts slowed our advance, as did our own minefields, which had been laid by our troops as they retreated at the beginning of the German attack. Laid so quickly, these minefields had no time to be mapped. Even worse, some of the mines were made of plastic and could not be detected until the ice melted or constant traffic put enough pressure on them to make them explode.

At some point while we were moving toward Dochamps, our platoon received one of the new Sherman "Easy Eights" (the M4A3E8) with the 76mm rifled gun that fired at a higher velocity and a flatter trajectory. The 75mm guns on our older Shermans were smoothbore and fired in a parabola like a howitzer. This new 76mm gun could fire directly at a target. The 76mm barrel was rifled, with spiraling grooves in the barrel that put a spin on the shell, and longer, giving the shell greater velocity and striking power. Thinking of the comparison between a knuckleball and a fastball pitch is an easy way to visualize the difference between our 75mm gun and the new 76mm gun. The company received only the one Easy Eight at this time, and Lieutenant Cornelius Aebi in my platoon got it.

Soon after we got the new tank, the company was moving forward in column, with my platoon in the lead. I was looking out of my turret and to my right spotted a German self-propelled gun at the corner of a building. I was not sure whether it was manned, but I radioed down the column for Lieutenant Aebi (codename "two-six") to take the vehicle under fire.

Aebi fired the combined high-explosive, armor-piercing round with that new 76mm gun and completely

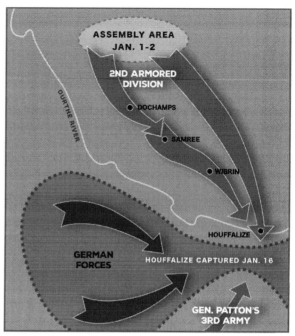

(Map by Gerry O'Neill)

Sherman Easy Eight with 76mm gun; photo taken at Teuven, Belgium. Unit is unknown, but the tank commander is Sergeant Edgar Cameron. Numbers of Easy Eights started arriving in Europe in December 1944. Photo taken 22 February 1945. (U.S. Army Signal Corps Photo)

destroyed the target. As the German vehicle exploded, the entire company cheered, definitely more for the effectiveness of the gun than the hit, which was a sure thing. We all were thinking that now we might have a weapon that would level the playing field with the German tanks. We loved it! We wished each crew had one.

04JAN1945

Company I led its task force in the attack that secured Beffe. The next day, the task forces remained in position.

06JAN1945

General Collier again launched a night attack and captured the town of Devantave by noon.

Company F command tank *Fawks Family* and Sergeant Weinert's tank, *Faith's Fancy*. (FCB)

07JAN1945

Again attacking at night due east of Devantave; this time Dochamps fell.

Well after the war, I received the book *The Bitter Woods* by John S. D. Eisenhower. I fanned through the index looking for Dochamps, not really believing it would be mentioned. There it was, with three page numbers listed after it. On page 416 there is this sentence: "The 2nd Armored took the important town of Dochamps." At the time we had no idea this small village was important.

On the morning of January 7, my platoon, the 2nd, was leading the company column southeast out of Ny.

Sergeant Rose took the lead with his tank. I radioed him to turn the lead over to the second tank in the column a number of times, but he requested permission to stay put.

He seemed to relish the challenge. Being the lead tank in a column was a nerve-racking spot to be in, as every turn in the twisting road presented the

A closer look at *Fawks Family* with its crew: Wawers, Riddle, Kapsha and Bezes. (FCB)

possibility of running into hidden enemy fire. This put great pressure on the lead tank's commander and crew, but at his request, I let him stay.

I was the third tank in the column. All five tanks of the platoon were present, one of those tanks being that new Sherman Easy Eight (the M4A3E8) with the 76mm gun. The company entered the town of Amonines, Belgium, from the northwest and at the T intersection took the road to the left to Dochamps, my platoon staying in the lead.

I stopped my tank and was on the ground talking with Captain Fawks on the eastern edge of Amonines looking southwest overlooking an open field. Suddenly, German infantry broke from the woods to our left and ran to our right across the open field. My gunner fired our machine gun at them, joined quickly by the gunners in the other tanks.

As we fired, a German tank came out of the woods to our right. The German tank commander either was surprised by the sight of us when he came out of the woods

Sergeant Rose. (U.S. Army Photo)

or was trying to draw our fire off the infantry, as his tank immediately turned 180 degrees on a dime and drove back into the woods. We did not have any time to take a shot at the tank with our main gun, and I am not certain whether our fire hit any of the enemy infantry, but what appeared to have been an attempt at a paralleling attack by the Germans dissolved, perhaps as a result of our fire and presence. We

believed that the tank and infantry presented no threat to us, as they were going in the opposite direction.

This encounter really pointed out an advantage that the German tanks had over ours. They were able to brake one track and pivot on the other track. The Sherman had to turn with both tracks moving forward, forcing us to move in a wide semicircle to turn around. The tank that popped out of the woods turned in place and got out of there a lot faster than we would have been able to.

My platoon continued southeast on the road to Dochamps while Captain Fawks, the commanding officer of Company F, and the rest of the company stayed just east of Amonines.

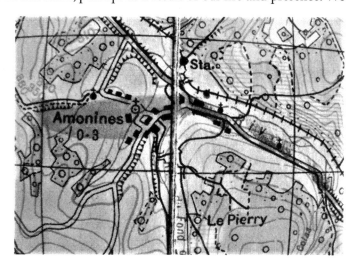

Close-up taken from the map I used during the operation. We entered Amonines on the road from Ny, on the top left of the map, and continued to Dochamps on the road that trails off to the lower right of the map. (Courtesy of U.S. Army Map Service with markings made by the author)

Ours was a cautious probing column. All of us were uncomfortable, as a road-bound column is the least effective way to employ tanks. The proximity of the trees to the road made us even more vulnerable. The road twisted and horseshoe turned over numerous culverts, always dangerous, as they made good positions where the enemy could hide and ambush the column. On those narrow roads, any hidden anti-tank gun taking out the first tank would halt the entire column.

About a third of the way to Dochamps, a jeep from the company came up to my tank and gave me the message that Captain Fawks had been wounded by shell fragments from a high-explosive mortar round. I turned the platoon over to Second Lieutenant Aebi and hopped into the jeep. I returned to Amonines and managed to say only a few words to Captain Fawks as he was being loaded onto a truck for evacuation.

Without any orders or direction, I just assumed command of the company, probably thinking it would fall to me, as both Trinen and Critchfield were second lieutenants and I was a first lieutenant. It is possible Captain Fawks had directed that I take command since the company jeep came to get me, but it is also very possible that I just did not think at all.

I climbed into *Fawks Family*, the command tank, and knew that my first job was to keep the company in motion toward Dochamps. Sergeant Rose was still leading the column. However, after I took command of the company, I ordered him to turn the lead over, which he did, turning the point over to Sergeant Merritt's tank *Frances*. This made sense, as

The Amonines-Dochamps road in 2014. The road to Dochamps was narrow, made more so by the trees skirting the road's edge. In 1945, the trees on the left side of the road were as close to the road as the trees on the right side are in this photo and they were all covered in thick snow. The telephone poles on the left were not there in 1945. (FGB)

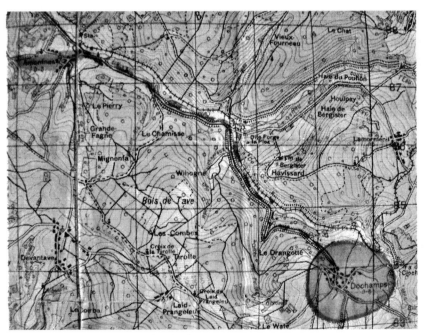

(Courtesy of U.S. Army Map Service)

Frances was the only tank in the company that had rubber treads, giving it better traction on ice. General Harmon had ordered rubber tracks up for all his 2nd AD tanks, but we did not receive enough for more than the one tank. With us off the daily reports, perhaps they did not know where to deliver them.

The platoon's progress was still very slow, as we expected anti-tank fire at every turn, and there were many turns to negotiate.

I radioed Lieutenant Jones, the forward observer for the artillery attached to assist us, and asked him to drop some artillery into Dochamps. He responded, "As soon as I dry my feet and put my socks on!" When he'd finished doing that, he forwarded the request to the artillery, who responded that Dochamps was in friendly hands, to which Jones responded, "Well, if it is in our hands, how come they are still shooting at us?"

We backed the command tank off the road, and I stood on its back deck to get a better look at the situation. I had a microphone in hand and was talking with HQ, Lieutenant Jones and the other tanks in the unit all at once. Apparently I was gesturing as I received the numerous and continual radio transmissions. Doc O'Neill came up in his jeep, looked up at me and told me that I looked like a traffic cop in downtown New York City.

With darkness settling in, we moved into a defile for cover, and the darkness afforded by the thick woods blocked out what little light remained. I radioed battalion that we had stopped. They approved, but within ten minutes they radioed that we must continue and secure the town of Dochamps that night. We were to proceed at once. We learned we were part of a larger night attack, a tactic General Collier had brilliantly pulled off just the night before at Devantave two miles to our southwest.

Sergeant Merritt's tank *Frances*, with Bow Gunner Ray Stewart, Gunner Conner, Driver Clements and Assistant Gunner Mike Skovira, led the way into Dochamps.

The T48 rubber nonreversible chevron tread was manufactured by Goodyear, Firestone, Ohio Rubber, U.S. Rubber and Goodrich. This link was the longest in production of the rubber-tread types. Each link weighed twenty-eight pounds; a full track weighed over two tons. Tracks were not easy to replace. (Photo courtesy of http://the.shadock. free.fr/sherman_minutia/tracks/vvss_tracks.html)

Frances. The location and date of this photo are unknown, but it was before *Frances* entered Dochamps. *Frances* was the one tank we had with rubber treads as we moved to Dochamps. It is difficult to determine whether the treads in this photo are steel or rubber. Both treads had the chevron pattern and were only slightly different in appearance. (RS)

It was almost dark as Merritt's tank followed the iced road into Dochamps. The road made a slightly uphill turn to the right as it entered the town. Merritt carefully approached the first building of the town, located to the right front, his head sticking out of the turret just enough to observe what he was driving into.

As the tank rounded the last turn into town, a sniper at the rear of the second floor of the first building on the right fired at Sergeant Merritt, the bullet hitting right next to Merritt on the top of the turret, knocking snow down the hatch. Merritt dropped down and ordered Conner to traverse the main gun to aim at the rear corner of the building and fire a high-explosive round. It was a direct hit, and the rear portion of the building was destroyed.

It is likely that the sniper escaped in the short time it took Conner to turn the turret, aim and fire the 75mm, but Sergeant Merritt and his crew had bigger things to worry about.

Assistant Gunner Mike Skovira relates what happened:

This was the first building Merritt saw as he took *Frances* into Dochamps. (FGB)

Sergeant Merritt kept his head out of the hatch, watching the buildings ahead. An infantryman came by and offered liverwurst sandwiches to our crew, the sandwiches having been found in a German vehicle. I gladly took one and planned to wolf it down. After taking just my first bite out of the sandwich, Conner yelled, "Mike! Look alive!" I saw a huge flash in front of the tank and heard the slam as a shot hit the turret above Bow Gunner Ray Stewart's head. A second shot immediately followed and ricocheted off the front slope plate, gouging the armor and throwing out steel shavings that struck

The newer masonry indicates the repairs made to the building at the spot Merritt's shot hit over seventy-five years before. (FGB)

Sergeant Merritt around his eyes! That second hit also wounded Conner pretty badly in the back as he had bailed out after the first shot. We lost track of him, as he had dove into a ditch, took cover until everything quieted down and made his way to a farmhouse. None of the other crew members were wounded. Still, we all were shaken by the severe concussions from the hits. The rest of the crew jumped out of the tank. After the first shot, I stayed inside the turret attempting to release the spring-loaded release to close the cage—it was easier for me to get out that way—but the release was jammed. I got down under the gun as the second shot hit the tank. I felt slivers of steel coming off the inside of the tank and hitting my helmet!

Gunner Conner. (FCB)

A German anti-tank gun had been set up to the right of the church tower under the tree. The German crew probably was not manning the gun at the time Merritt came around the curve into town, as the weather was cold. In addition, the Germans were not used to the Americans attacking at night. If the crew had been at the gun, they most likely would have fired as soon as *Frances* came into view. The gun crew was possibly alerted to the presence of Merritt's Sherman by the sound of the sniper's shot but most certainly by the firing of *Frances's* 75mm gun. The armor-piercing rounds that hit Merritt's tank, located fifteen yards back from where the photo below was taken, came directly down this street. The sniper had fired from the opposite end of the house on the right.

Driver Clements. (FCB)

Things then quieted down. I am sure the Germans decided the tank was no longer a threat, as it had no crew. I jumped off the turret into the snow, landing on a blue-eyed GI—dead. His tongue protruded from his mouth, and he had a bullet hole in his forehead, perhaps killed by the sniper who had fired on us. I did not see Conner at the time or know that he was wounded.

I ran like hell down the road we had just come up and encountered a GI who had a head wound. A jeep came up and the driver asked me to put the GI in the front seat so he could take him to the rear for treatment. I helped the GI in and jumped in the back seat, holding him so he would not fall out. I also wrapped my scarf around his head and put his helmet on to apply pressure on the wound. At the aid station, medics helped the fellow out of the jeep.

There was a group of prisoners there. I walked over to them, and one handed me a beautiful diamond ring—not sure why—but I

The German anti-tank crew had a straight shot down the street at *Frances*. (FGB)

gave it back immediately. Maybe he thought we might shoot them, and he was trying to buy me off.

First Sergeant De Pratt led me into a nearby house for the night. Some of the other guys from the company were also staying there. An officer offered me his sleeping bag, and I took it, settling in the kitchen, but sleep was not possible because of the cold. I later found out that Ray had helped Sergeant Merritt down the road as the blood from his facial wounds was entering his eyes and blinding him. Conner was eventually found in a farmhouse he had crawled to and was taken to the aid station. The rest of us managed to get back safely to the rest of the platoon.

Assistant Gunner Mike Skovira. (U.S. Army Photo)

We were all played out by this time; I know I was. But we had our orders. We discussed the situation with an infantry company from the 41st Armored Infantry Regiment attached to the 2nd AD, which had just come up to support our attack. Three tank destroyers came up as well, accompanied by five Stuart light tanks.

We decided to form three teams, two to take strategic points at opposite ends of the town from our present position and one to secure the point directly to our front. The tank destroyers, with their rubber tracks, were sent to the opposite sides of the town. Soon I received radio reports from the teams that each had reached its position without incident.

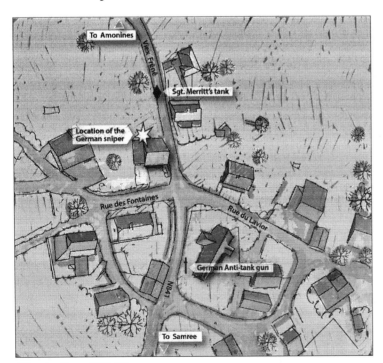

To Amonines

Voie Frênê

Sgt. Merritt's tank

Location of the German sniper

Rue des Fontaines

Rue du Lavior

N841

German Anti-tank gun

To Samree

(Map by Gerry O'Neill)

I made radio contact with Lieutenant Aebi in the Easy Eight with the 2nd Platoon, which was part of the team securing the point directly to our front. His tank had reached the first position just inside the town. He radioed back, "It's so quiet down here we could hold a marshmallow-wiener roast!"

Almost immediately after he said, "Out," I heard a gun firing from his direction.

Aebi's Easy Eight was hit by an armor-piercing projectile fired by a German tank that had backed into a building for cover. The tank had held its fire until the other tanks of the platoon passed its position. The shot penetrated the turret where Gunner Vincent Villagecenter sat, passing

Lieutenant Aebi before entering Berlin. (FCB)

The Easy Eight version (M4A3E8) of the Sherman at the 1st Infantry Division Museum, Chantilly, Illinois. (FGB)

through his chest and killing him instantly. The shell ricocheted around the walls of the inside of the turret, seriously wounding the loader/radio operator, driver, and assistant driver/bow gunner.

Aebi said all he got was "a bum wrist," but there was more. He wrote me from the hospital:

Hi Brow,

I want you to know I'm lonesome. I didn't get hurt much other than a few holes and a rotten wrist and ankle. I'm sorry I lost the best tank you had, but that Jerry was waiting a long time to hit me. It was too bad about Chief.

Left to right: Gentile (my driver), Jutras (my gunner), Vincent Villagecenter, and Conner. Conner would be wounded again at Kaldenhausen. A tough cookie, he rejoined the company before we went to Berlin. (FCB)

It has caused me to dream a lot. The other two boys won't be back for a long time. I'm not the kind to say I told you so, but remind Trenton I said that Jerry might come back in there. He did too.

Keep my mail there, and save a little of the Scotch for me. Any packages I get, open and use before they ruin. Tell Critch I'll be back to collect because I lead a charmed life. I saw in the Stars and Stripes you got that town [Dochamps].

Well, I hope that the Jerry didn't get any more of us that night. I warned the others. It's not good to see a guy you like get cut in half like Villagecenter was.

If I ever get in again I'll never let a Jerry soldier surrender to me. Be good, Boy, and say hello to the old grouch Trent for me and also Mac and Crist. Good luck. Whatta hell of a way to make a living.

Niel Aebi

None of Aebi's crew ever returned to the company. Lieutenant Aebi, after returning to duty, asked to be transferred to an infantry (armored) unit attached to the division. He ended up with reconnaissance. Vincent was a Native American known as "Chief" by all the men and officers of the company. He was especially liked, and his death deeply saddened the entire command.

08JAN1945

Early the next morning Platoon Commander Lieutenant Trinen and I went to Sergeant Merritt's tank at the entry to the town. To our surprise, *Frances*'s engine was still running, and it could still move. We determined that the anti-tank gun that had fired at *Frances* had long since moved out. Trinen and I backed *Frances* down the road and parked it, turning it over to Bow Gunner Ray Stewart and someone from maintenance. Stewart told me that Sergeant Merritt was not seriously wounded, which I was very relieved to hear. They were able to drive *Frances* back to the Maintenance Battalion.

At about the same time that we were moving *Frances*, the M10 tank destroyers that we'd stationed on the other side of Dochamps spotted a number of enemy tanks crossing a field to their flank. They rushed to take them under fire with their main guns, but their turrets had frozen. Unfortunately, there was no time to pivot the entire M10 using its treads to bring their guns to bear before the Germans got away.

(FGB)

In the summer of 2014, my son Rick visited Dochamps with two friends, Mark Storella and Wayne Stoios. Here is what they encountered:

We stopped in Amonines first, just to get a lay of the land. A map of the town and local road net was situated in a display near the railroad tracks. I had a photocopy of Dad's map and compared the current road network with what had been there in 1944. There was virtually no difference. This was going to make our search for sites Dad mentioned easier.

While we were reading the sign, two young local men came up to us and, in perfect English, wondered whether they could assist us. We told them that we were retracing the route my dad had taken during the Battle of the Bulge and that he had served in the 2nd AD. We spoke a little more and then we moved on to the next sign. Soon, one of the young men approached us again and very sincerely said, "Please thank your father for us." This was the start of what would turn out to be a very emotional day for the three of us.

We followed the road to Dochamps and just outside of town looked for the open area where the German infantry had been sighted and where the tank had come out and made the quick U-turn, but we were unable to locate any ground that looked like that. The trees have grown in heavily along the road since then.

As we entered Dochamps, we saw what had to have been the first house of the town, where the sniper had hidden. We decided to knock on the door. Within a few moments, Monsieur Simone Gregoire answered the door, ninety-one years old but still spry. We introduced ourselves.

Mark has good French, so we were able to make ourselves understood. He translated as I recounted what I knew of the approach to town by Sergeant Merritt's tank, that there had been a German sniper in his house who had fired upon the tank and that the tank had fired at the

As we got back into the car, I saw this building across the street and realized that Dad's tank had to have rolled right in front of it. A true "witness building." There are many of these in this area, but, for some reason, this one became personal to me. (FGB)

Monsieur Gregoire in front of his home. (FGB)

section of the house where the sniper had been. We asked whether we could see that part of the house.

Monsieur Gregoire willingly showed us into the house. We quickly learned that this had been his family home during the war. He led us down a set of stairs into an earth-floored two-story building that served as a barn, the earthy smells thickening the air as the chickens scattered. We entered a room toward the far end of the barn, and Monsieur Gregoire began to gesture emphatically while pointing to the ground. I assumed he was telling me to watch my step, as there was a fairly high stoop, but Mark said, "He is saying, 'This is the spot! This is the spot!'"

We followed him over the stoop into the passageway between a row of stalls and a stone wall, the passageway leading to an outer door. We could clearly see the stress on his face and in his suddenly red-rimmed eyes.

Fighting back tears and anger, Monsieur Gregoire related that the Germans had told the residents to clear out of the town since an American attack was expected, but his mother, brother and sister decided to stay and took shelter in the barn's lower level. They hunkered down along the wall seen on the right side of the passage in the photo above, thinking they would be safe this far back from the outside wall and door.

(FGB)

The family may or may not have known about the sniper above them, but they probably heard the shot, considering that they were almost directly beneath the sniper's location . . . and then the tank opened up.

There was too little time for them to distinguish between the tank firing and the explosion of the shell, certainly no time for them to react. The high-explosive round detonated with tremendous force, blowing the upper part of the building away, shattering the wooden doorframe in front of the family members and sending shards of wood and splinters along the wall, killing all three instantly. Word was sent to Monsieur Gregoire, who was two hours away. He got home as quickly as he could, only to see his family lying where they had been killed, his sister decapitated and his mother with a huge splinter embedded in her head. "This is the spot! This is the spot!"

Monsieur Gregoire went on in an angry voice about a U.S. Army officer who had come to the house and ordered him to have the three bodies buried within twenty-four hours. He was incensed then, and he was still angry now, stating that if he had had a gun that day, he would have shot the officer.

Until we knocked on his door and told the story, Monsieur Gregoire had thought his house had been hit by a bomb dropped randomly from an airplane. He did not know about the German sniper in the house *or that the sniper's fire had drawn the shot from the tank. He had no idea that it was the blast from a high-explosive round fired from an American tank that had killed his family.*

Mark, Wayne and I were truly shaken by this encounter, wondering how Monsieur Gregoire had lived with this pain that was obviously so close to the surface and no doubt revisited every time he passed that spot. Every time he stepped down the stairs to the barn he reimagined the horrible sight that had been his family. We wondered whether perhaps we brought him some small solace, as he now had an explanation of what had actually happened, albeit over sixty years later. Perhaps it helped him to know that the loss of his family was not as random an event as it appeared. Or perhaps our visit made it all the worse for him. We continued on to Bastogne, but everything else we saw that day paled after Dochamps.

One can see the extent of the explosion and the way the shock worked down to the doorway, now rebuilt. (FGB)

I am certain that neither Sergeant Merritt nor any of his crew knew about the collateral consequences of their shot at the sniper, and I did not know about this until Rick told me on his return. So many "what ifs?"

I am also certain that the U.S. officer who approached Monsieur Gregoire and informed him he had to bury his family within twenty-four hours was an infantry officer following up and making sure the town was secure. Although his action can be seen as cruel, the officer was doing his job, guarding the health of both the troops coming through town and the citizens of Dochamps. He was carrying forward with another necessity of war.

09JAN1945

Dochamps, Belgium

Our orders were to move due south out of Dochamps toward Samrée, so it made sense to establish our CP in a house along the road that led in that direction, but the road climbed and curved up a steep hill that was now plastered in a thick layer of ice. We watched in frustration as drivers took their tanks gingerly up the ice-sheeted road, only to see them slide backward and sideways as they neared the top of the hill. The steel tracks acted like ice skates, and we had no solution.

While our attention was drawn to the debacle on the icy road, General John H. "Pee Wee" Collier, CCA commander, stormed unexpectedly into our CP. I mean no disrespect to General Collier with that nickname. He was known throughout the division as "Pee Wee" and respected as a man of small stature but all soldier.

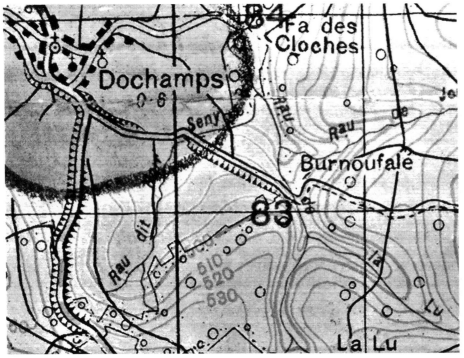

The contour lines indicate how steep the roads out of Dochamps were. The closer the lines are to each other, the steeper the incline. Until we got those rubber tracks and installed them, we were going to be stuck here.

Co. F Command Post was located along the road to Samrée.

To Samrée   (Courtesy of U.S. Army Map Service)

Before he had even completely entered the front door of our CP, he barked, "Who's in command of these tanks?"

I answered immediately, "I am, Sir."

His next question was worded very differently but was something to this effect: "Why after all this time have your tanks not moved out of the town?"

I asked the general to please come to a window facing up the road and said, "That's why, Sir."

We were supposed to be well on our way to Samrée, but the general could plainly see our tanks crawling up the icy road, with several awkwardly tilting off the side of the road.

"Dochamps—slippery slopes for tanks of the 2nd AD." The men here are most likely from CCB, which followed us through Dochamps but took the eastern road toward Samrée. I do not remember seeing any Signal Corps photographers joining us, but they were pretty much everywhere. It should be noted that CCB had rubber treads on its tanks. (U.S. Army Photo)

The general said nothing more to me, rapidly took in the problem, turned, walked to our radio, and immediately contacted someone in the rear. I was not privy to what he said, but as soon as he got off the radio, he left our CP. He never said another word to me.

Only hours later, we received a load of rubber tracks. There is no doubt in my mind that it was "Pee Wee" who was responsible.

Each tank had a track jack, but changing the track was always a difficult job even in the best of circumstances. Each track literally weighed a ton. The cold and ice added misery to our crews' work.

Unlike other armored units that were able to pull two tanks back every day to change the tracks, we had to change the tracks of each tank in the company in one day. We were out of the fight for now.

Some days earlier I had accompanied our new regimental commander, Colonel Clayton J. Mansfield, on a short reconnaissance. He had been the division chief of staff and requested a combat position. We walked up a narrow path through fairly high grass, and as we moved along, the colonel found a German belt buckle inscribed with the familiar "Gott mit Uns" (God [is] with us)." He said to me, "This will be for my son."

Changing tracks on a Sherman tank in the Ardennes, January 1945. Changing a track was time-consuming, knuckle-breaking work. (U.S. Army Photo)

Changing a track in the cold weather. (Photo by Luke Bolin)

A half-track, a Sherman tank and a medical jeep in Dochamps; again, these would be from CCB, which followed behind us and turned east toward Burnoufale to get to Samrée. The church where the anti-tank gun that hit Merritt's tank was located directly up the road to the rear. (U.S. Army Signal Corps Photo)

As we stepped through a tree line to get a clearer view, Colonel Mansfield moved forward out of the cover of the trees. I jokingly said, "Colonel, I wouldn't even want a second lieutenant to do what you're doing." He was out in the open, exposed dangerously. He turned to me and smiled, and we went back to my company.

Days after my recon with the colonel—the same day we were changing the tracks in Dochamps—General Harmon came up and pinned a Silver Star on Colonel Mansfield's tanker jacket. Five minutes later, Colonel Mansfield went forward to get a firsthand view of the area around Samrée.

He was standing outside the tree line, as he had when I was with him, when the fog and haze lifted momentarily. The Germans immediately put an artillery airburst over his position, killing him instantly. When his body was recovered, the Silver Star was still pinned to his jacket. He was a good man and a fine officer. Although I met him only

I stepped out of the CP to take this photo of the steep hills that were keeping us in Dochamps. The photo is looking southeast at the road CCB took toward Burnoufale. I am standing on the road to Samrée that went off to my right. Ruined buildings were plentiful in the town, as the 30th AD had been hit hard by strong German forces on 20 December at the beginning of their advance. This is the only photo I had time to take while we were in Dochamps. (FCB)

that one time, I had taken an instant liking to him. His death brought the shot we'd made at Merzenhausen to mind.

I have often wondered whether his son ever got that belt buckle.

Lieutenant Colonel Stokes, freed up from command of the Combat Command Reserve, reassumed command of the regiment.

08JAN1945

Both CCA and CCB were ordered to attack and capture Samrée. F Company's assignment was to attack south from Dochamps to Samrée with CCA circling to the west and CCB to the east, attacking Samrée from three directions. We were an important element of the attack—hence General Collier's impatience.

All roads to Samrée were as narrow as the road we had taken into Dochamps or worse, some being only tracks through the woods, nothing like they appeared on our maps. Thick fog and deep snow made the going rough for both CCA and CCB. General White's CCB had pushed southeast on our left, moving through Burnoufale to arrive to the east of Samrée in order to attack the town's eastern and southern exits.

Simultaneously with CCB, CCA had moved out of Dochamps to the west on the roads to Le Wate and Em de Banasse. The tanks, unable to get through the woods on either side of the road beyond Le Wate, were road bound. The Germans were waiting in ambush with some ten tanks on the edge of the woods, well concealed by trees and snow. The first Sherman in the column was immediately destroyed, and with no room to maneuver around the flanks of the Germans, the column withdrew. The other column—made up of infantry, as the track they were assigned was too narrow for tanks—ran into German infantry and two

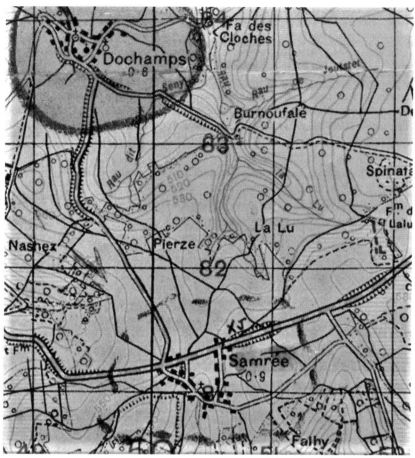

Burnoufale and the road to the La Roche-Vielsalm Road

The LaRoche (off to the west/left in the photo) to Vielsalm (east/right) road passes through Samrée.

CCB's attack straddled the La-Roche-Vielsalm road, advancing on Samrée from the east (from the right) and the southeast. Resistance was stiff, the German forces numbering an estimated three hundred infantry and five Mark V Panther tanks. Realizing they were threatened from any direction, their defense was circular and strongly dug in behind minefields and strong roadblocks. If the other two prongs of our attack had succeeded in getting through to Samrée, the Germans would have been attacked from all sides. (Courtesy of U.S. Army Map Service)

Mark IV tanks in the woods east of Em de Banasse. They knocked out one of the tanks with bazooka fire. Farther on, however, the fog lifted momentarily to reveal five Mark V Panthers only four hundred yards to the front. The Panthers pulled out, but darkness was settling in. The two columns of CCA consolidated for the night, having been taken out of the fight for Samrée by the bad weather, poor roads and the German ambush.

CCB secured Samrée on 10 January 1945, overcoming a stout German defense that was desperate to hold the vital La Roche-Vielsalm road open, the line of retreat for their troops in this sector.

Our company finally got the rubber tracks onto the tanks, and we were able to leave Dochamps.

We were not needed in Samrée, as the battle there was over. We received orders directing us northeast of Dochamps for a refitting and rest.

U.S. vehicles moving through Dochamps. This photo could easily be of CCB as it proceeded through Dochamps to Burnoufale on its move to encircle Samrée from the east. Our company tried to move out on the road leading directly to Samrée, located on the far side of the church. (U.S. Army Signal Corps Photo)

Again, this is the road to Burnoufale. Since vehicles are heading in both directions, indicating no sense of urgency, the photo was probably taken sometime after the attack on Samrée and during the advance toward Houffalize. (U.S. Army Signal Corps Photo)

Sometime after our departure, two infantrymen moved through Dochamps along the road to Samrée. The west side of the church and the tree that provided cover for the anti-tank gun are clearly visible. (U.S. Army Signal Corps Photo)

A tank and jeep of the 2nd AD during the advance to Samrée. These vehicles were probably from CCB on the road heading east of Dochamps. (U.S. Army Signal Corps Photo)

Photo identified as 2nd AD tanks advancing to Samrée, again probably CCB moving to the east of Dochamps. (U.S. Army Signal Corps Photo)

Below: When the skies were clear, aerial reconnaissance was able to provide us photographs of where we were being ordered to go. We all received this photo of Samrée at our planning meeting. The photo looks southeast. The black smudges mark explosions of German artillery fire from the early days of the offensive, the trails of black in the snow indicating that the fire came from the east (left) as the Germans moved west toward the Meuse River. The heavy snows would have covered these craters by the time CCB attacked on either side of the road coming from the left (east). F Company's assignment had been to approach Samrée using the road coming out of the lower right corner (heading south). CCA, also part of the plan, was to have come in from the right side (west) of the photo. Neither F Company nor CCA made it to Samrée. (U.S. Army Photo in the Author's Collection)

11JAN1945

We assembled two miles away from Dochamps near the towns of Lamormenil and Freyneux, to rest and maintain our vehicles. More than anything, we dug in against the cold.

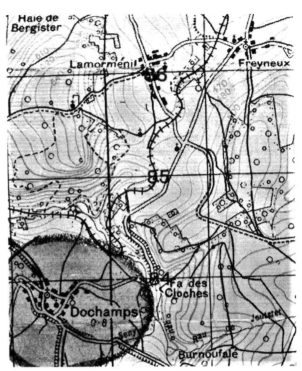

Lamormenil and Freyneux. (Courtesy of U.S. Army Map Service)

"The weather we endured. I shiver to think of it." Second Lieutenant Don Critchfield with his tank *Fearless Fosdick* in the Ardennes. (DAC)

The trees provided good insulation, so we backed into the branches as far as we could go, allowing our guns to face front. Doc O'Neill came up in his medical jeep, visible here on the right, with some paregoric, as we had a few tankers with bum stomachs. Good ol' First Sergeant De Pratt came up with cold fried chicken. (FCB)

One of the company's M4A1 76W Sherman tanks with a 76mm gun. These were first used in September 1944 by Patton at the Battle of Arracourt against Panther tanks. Their success against the Panthers led to their being accepted by the tankers as replacements for the 75mm M4 Shermans. A drawback was the gun's tendency to throw dust and smoke into the tank's vision when it was fired, making it hard to track a shot and correct on it. The Easy Eight added a blast deflector to rectify that. (FCB)

Sergeant Peter Ubereauga came up from maintenance to help work on the tanks. (FCB)

13JAN1945

Our next objective was Wibrin, which was almost due south of us. We were directed to go on a compass course through the woods, cross the La Roche-Vielsalm road and continue south to secure a bridge on the Wibrin-Chabrehez road. We were then to take that road into the town. My map showed two bridges. We were to take the southern one, which was closer to Wibrin. Still attached to F Company were the infantry from the 41st Armored Infantry Regiment, the platoon of light tanks, and the tank destroyers. All remained under my command.

A series of phase lines identified by colors was assigned to the map so that we could report our progress to battalion. Another task force also heading to Wibrin was some distance to our right, perhaps on the road south out of Samrée. Our progress through the woods was slow with the ground covered with eight to twelve inches of snow. I was constantly getting radio messages from battalion that we were falling way behind the unit to our right. Each time they called, I gave them our position and tried to get across to battalion that we were moving as fast as conditions would allow.

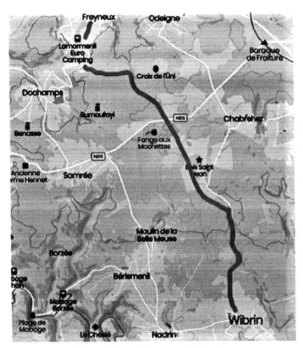

(FCB)

Then, as dusk approached, we got a message from battalion that our sister company to our right had just reached Phase Line Orange, which we had crossed a while back. I reported that we had just crossed Phase Line Red and was immediately told that we were now way ahead of everyone else and were sticking out like the proverbial sore thumb. The unit to our right, for unknown reasons, was well behind us. I never learned why.

Night caught us still some distance from the bridge we were to secure, so the company went into a "covered wagon" formation, circling the tanks and spotting the infantry around the circle. We radioed in the coordinates of the bridge to the artillery and had them fire one round. By the sound of the explosion, we determined that we were headed in the right direction.

I sent out a patrol, and it returned with a prisoner, a member of the Volkssturm ("people's assault"). The Volkssturm was a national militia organized in October 1944 and made up of conscripted males ages sixteen to sixty. The prisoner was carrying a message from one of the bridges to the other: "Wo bist [where are] . . . Amis' panzers [the Americans' tanks]? We heard them, but don't know where they are."

The old guy was shivering and kept saying, "Ach, Krieg ist nicht gut!" ("War is not good!")

His heart was obviously not in this fight, but I foolishly asked him, "Why the hell are you fighting us then?"

He just kept repeating, "Krieg ist nicht gut!"

This sounds cruel, and I guess it was, but I put my .45 against his head and asked, "Wo ist die Brücke?" ("Where is the bridge?") He pointed in what we had figured was the direction of the bridge. The old guy just confirmed it.

I would not have shot him if he had given me the wrong answer, but he did not know that. Poor guy. I truly felt sorry for him. We left him in the care of the infantry.

14JAN1945

At daylight we moved out and arrived at the road right at the point where we had been directed. The bridge and Wibrin were to our right. My time as an Eagle Scout and the merit badge in orienteering paid off in this very unexpected situation.

We were in for what should not have been a surprise. The Germans had blocked access to the bridge by cutting down many trees, felling them to fall in a tangled, crisscrossed mess on the road. Placed in, under and around the trees were box mines like we'd seen at Merzenhausen.

Before we could hook cables from the tanks to the trees and pull them off the road, the mines had to be removed. In addition, the retreating Germans had sawed halfway through the standing trees along both sides of the road. When we tried to anchor cables to pull the trees off the road, the weakened trees could not support the weight and came crashing down.

We scouted the woods to see whether we could go around the trees and mines, but the surrounding forest was too thick and the terrain too rough for tanks. There was no other option than to take the time to remove the trees and box mines. Fortunately, the mines had not been booby-trapped or linked, so moving one would not set off any others. Once we were finished, we could not believe the pile of mines we'd removed.

While we were tackling these roadblocks, battalion was constantly calling me on the radio, questioning our progress. I tried to explain the situation, but the messages kept coming. I just could not get them to realize what a big problem we had.

I began to have evil thoughts about those serving in the rear when Colonel Hinds, our combat commander and a good man, came up to check on what was going on.

The Schü-mine ("shoe-mine") 42, also known as the Schützenmine 42, was a German anti-personnel mine used during World War II. It was a simple wooden box with a hinged lid containing 7.1 ounces of TNT and a detonator. Sufficient pressure on the lid caused a pin to trigger the detonator. The mine was cheap to produce and was deployed in large numbers. It was difficult to detect since the only metal present was a small amount in the detonator. Somebody got the idea to use pitch-forks as mine detectors, and that idea worked out well. (U.S. Army Training Manual)

Downed trees were used as roadblocks on the road to Wibrin. We had to pull each of them off to the side of the road. The shadows indicate that the sun was out—briefly. (FCB)

I asked him, "Colonel, will you get battalion off my butt? I cannot get them to understand our situation, and they keep calling me."

The colonel got on my tank, picked up the mike, and these were his exact words: "These vehicles do not have a flying capability. They must clear the road of these downed trees and landmines! OUT!"

Needless to say, battalion went silent until I reported we were on our way.

Thinking that the Tank Battalion HQ personnel were a bunch of jerks is not a fair remark, but it seemed appropriate at the time. HQ troops often had little knowledge of what was actually going on along the front line or what the actual conditions were and did not seem to trust our judgment. However, I knew it was their responsibility to push the attack. And they were getting pressure from higher up.

By the time we cleared and crossed the bridge, it was starting to get dark, and it was completely dark when we finally reached the open fields on the outskirts of Wibrin, but our orders held to continue the attack. A few buildings in the town were on fire. I formed all of our tanks into line, and we began to move toward the town, firing rounds at targets of opportunity where the enemy might be sheltering.

Looking through my binoculars to check the effect of our fire, I realized that the figures I saw silhouetted against the light of the fires in the buildings were wearing American helmets. I radioed the company to cease fire, but we continued to move forward and ran into American infantry already in the town.

Fortunately, the few rounds we had fired did not cause any casualties, or at least none of the infantry we talked to said a thing to us about anyone being hit. It was obvious that these were combat-wise doughs who knew what they were doing and had the situation under control. Battalion had not known the status of the situation, and so it could not inform us, but Task Force B had taken the town earlier that day. The infantry we met were from Company F, 41st Armored Infantry, a sister company to the infantry attached to us.

Now we could stop for the night. We moved into some barns and a few houses in Wibrin. One large barn soon became our temporary CP.

We were called, appropriately, Polar Bear A. This was our original CP. The tank is *Fawks Family*, which was now my tank. Notice our "stuff" that we used to make ourselves as comfortable as possible piled in front of the barn door. (FCB)

F Company tankers gather to chat. (FCB)

Unfortunately for us, we were ordered to leave the houses to the infantry (which regrettably made sense) and move to the surrounding woods just outside town.

First Sergeant De Pratt told me that the infantry had kindly left their tents for us. We all had pyramidal tents complete with straw on the floors. The lodging was very comfortable in contrast with our days and weeks before. At least one tent had a steel wood stove. For sure the company CP tent had a stove.

This attack on Wibrin ended our action during the Battle of the Bulge.

In the morning a couple of members of my old 2nd Platoon came to the CP and said to me, "Lieutenant, we have a visitor in our area; we'd like you to come meet him."

Inside the CP tent with the makeshift stove. The grim-faced fellow peering over the pitcher of coffee is First Sergeant De Pratt. (FCB)

The visitor turned out to be a large, very distinguished-looking man. He was easily over six feet tall and wore a dark blue uniform . . . and he was frozen stiff. I recall tapping on his chest; it was like a rock. The man's face showed a dark bruise, as if he'd been hit by the butt of a rifle. We radioed battalion and told them what we had found. A couple of officers from either civil affairs or intelligence came to our bivouac with a sled. We laid the body on the sled, but the sled was too short, and the man's legs hung over the end. There was nothing to be done. I can still picture the men from HQ pulling the sled down the snow-covered road with our visitor's feet sticking out over the back.

Battalion did the research and let us know that the visitor had been the chief of police of the City of Liège, which was nearly forty miles due north of us. He apparently had been captured by the Germans at some point and killed. Liège had been liberated by the British in September 1944, so it is possible he had been their prisoner for several months.

The weather was still very cold. One of our platoon commanders kept his engine running to keep the tank warmed up. He did not realize that an infantryman was on the ground close behind his tank, trying to stay warm by the tank's engines. The lieutenant backed up, not knowing the infantryman was there. The lieutenant was never the same after that and soon transferred out of the company.

An abandoned German Sd.Kfz.251 half-track near Wibrin, where F Company found itself at the end of the Battle of the Bulge. (FCB)

A knocked-out Mark V tank. Originally designated the Panzerkampfwagen V Panther, on 27 February 1944, Hitler ordered that the Roman numeral "V" be deleted. We called it a Panther tank. Officially a medium tank, it weighed in as a heavy tank at forty-nine tons. Its crew of five relied on a 75mm gun. Although it was the same size as the Sherman's gun, because of a large propellant charge and the long barrel, it had excellent armor-piercing qualities. We always said it was the best German tank with perhaps the most powerful gun of the war. (FCB)

On one very cold and dark day, we passed this knocked-out or abandoned German Panzer IV, officially a Panzerkampfwagen IV Ausf F.2. medium tank. We'd encountered this type numerous times before. Its long-barreled KwK 40 L/43 anti-tank gun was introduced to counter the Soviet T-34 tank. (FCB)

A crater caused by a bomb dropped by a buzz bomb or an airplane. It tore deep into the ground, destroying the house. Note the truck in center rear. (FCB)

On the way north to our rest and refit area, we stopped in a small town in Belgium. I don't believe I knew its name even then. I recall standing in the center of a room in a small house when I heard the, by then, familiar sound of a buzz bomb going overhead and simultaneously heard .50 caliber machine guns firing.

Suddenly the windows shattered, the glass blowing into the room.

Fortunately, I was far enough from the windows and escaped being hit by the flying glass. I later learned that the .50 caliber machine gun firing I had heard was from the tanks of our company. They had actually hit the low-flying rocket bomb, and it plunged into the field close to the tanks and the house we were occupying, exploding on contact.

We often heard what we called "buzz" bombs fly over. We would listen and wait, hoping that the sound wouldn't stop—the continuous sound comforting, as it indicated the bomb was still in flight and would not be coming down on us. Most of those we heard at this time were probably on their way to targets in and around Liège.

Very soon after, a German aircraft came in low over our tanks, and everyone who could get to the tanks' .50 caliber machine guns fired at it. The plane went down, plowing into a field close to where the buzz bomb had exploded. The exuberant tankers rushed out to the plane as the pilot climbed out, some of them shouting, "We got him! We got him," as they ran across the field.

When they reached the pilot, the German said to them, in perfect English, "Sorry, old chaps, but I just ran out of petrol."

16JAN1945—0930

Elements of the 2nd AD, driving south, linked up with Patton's Third Army moving north in a field northeast of Houffalize, trapping any German troops to the west still trying to retreat to Germany. The Battle of the Bulge was, except for scattered mopping up operations, over. The division moved to a defensive line to the west of Houffalize.

Looking back, I realized that we had been a part of a massive effort that accomplished a great deal in the last month. We did not know it at the time, but the 2nd AD had blunted and stopped Unternehmen Wacht am Rhein.

Major General Harmon was promoted at this time and left the 2nd AD for command of a corps. Our new commander, Brigadier General Isaac D. White, took command of the division.

General Isaac Davis White. He was nicknamed "Mr. Armor" by *Army Magazine* when he retired. (U.S. Army Photo)

17JAN1945

The three task forces were dissolved.

20JAN1945

F Company was reattached to 1st Battalion and would now reappear on its after-action reports. We moved to Fraipont, Belgium, thirty-three miles to the north, to refit and, of all things, to train.

25JAN1945 LETTER HOME

Sleeping in a farm house now. A good set-up. Snow is all gone, and in its place we again have King Mud. The words army and mud should be synonymous. Last night Lt. Critchfield and I had a fine gab-fest on the houses we are going to have when we get back home. He has many good ideas. His dad is in the construction business. He, too,

Several of us stayed here at the Villa Ghislain a couple of nights while in Fraipont. (Postcard from Fraipont, 1945, in the Author's Collection)

wants a rambling house, a large fireplace, a large kitchen (no pantry), a good-sized bathroom (shower and big tub) with the commode separate from the bathing room. It was fun. ¾" floor boards are a must, he says. He said, "Let me build your house." It's so good thinking of our future. I do it all the time. S'wunnerful.

28JAN1945 LETTER HOME

A good quiet day. It snowed this morning, piled on a couple more inches. Nice powdery stuff.

Went to a civilian mass today. At 1000 in the little church in the nearby village. It was very fine. The sermon was, of course, in French. I caught the words "American soldiers," and after mass I asked one of our men who understands a little French what had been said. The gist of it was this: "Today we have some American soldiers in church with us. We are very pleased to have them. They are setting an example for the entire world by going to mass at every opportunity and up to the last possible moment before going into battle." He went on to say that after mass the American National Anthem would be played, and he requested that everyone stand at that time because it would please us and affect us deeply. They did just that, and it was a wonderful gesture on their part. Belgium is a fine little country.

03FEB1945 LETTER HOME

The Company went on a hill (mountain) climb yesterday, and I snapped some pictures despite the foggy weather. It was rugged, but what a beautiful view. The Vesdre River and the Fraipont bridge were below us in full view.

On the way down I took a rocky trail and, while scrambling along, a red fox jumped out of the bush. A beautiful little animal. The climb was worth the effort. The exercise was part of what turned out to be an easy training routine.

Photo of most of the company. The lighting was poor, so it is hard to identify individual faces, but it is possible to see that many are smiling. So far, so good. (FCB)

03FEB1945

We moved twenty-two miles north to Teuven, Belgium, our next assembly area. We were now twenty miles west of Aachen. Our convoy traveled under strict security conditions, with patches and vehicle markings covered.

04FEB1945

The regiment assembled around Teuven, Belgium, where we camouflaged our tanks and, to strengthen our tanks' defenses, put logs and sandbags on the sides and fronts of our tanks, a practice that Patton deplored and would not allow in his units. Our commanding officer had no problem with those additions, though. Maybe it was only in our minds, but the extra protection made us feel safer. We also appreciated the rest and time to warm ourselves up, knowing that we would be on the move again soon. We were kept sharp by a training schedule designed for us by those at regimental headquarters.

There were several reasons why the Germans lost the Battle of the Bulge, but the three perhaps major contributors were (1) the Germans never had enough fuel to make it to Antwerp without capturing many U.S. supply depots, which they did not; (2) U.S. resistance at a number of key road junctions, roadblocks on narrow icy roads and important terrain features disrupted the entire schedule of the German advance; and (3) the weather started to clear on 23 December, allowing Allied aircraft to devastate German columns of troops, vehicles and supplies. To achieve its objectives, Unternehmen Wacht am Rhein needed every piece to fall perfectly in place.

"My beat-up tank. Sandbags and logs for protection against bazookas."
Quote and photo from platoon commander Lieutenant Don Critchfield.
The photo is of his tank *Fancy Pants*, taken not too long after the Bulge,
probably in Teuven. Track extenders are still attached, so snow had been
in our recent past. Notice the helmet and gear on the ground in front of
the tank. (DAC)

At its deepest penetration, the 2nd Panzer Division got within four miles of the Meuse River bridge at Dinant, a key point. Crossing that bridge would have gotten the Germans into open tank country all the way to Antwerp. The Allied forces, General Harmon and the 2nd AD made sure that they did not get to that bridge.

F Company had driven and fought for two hundred miles since the 21 December night march south from Baesweiler twenty-six days before.

6

Operation Grenade: Schiefbahn

04FEB1945

The regiment moved from the Fraipont area and assembled twenty kilometers to the northeast around Teuven, Belgium. The 1st Battalion settled in three miles east of Teuven in Terziet, Holland. We were in our old stomping grounds, only eleven miles west of Aachen.

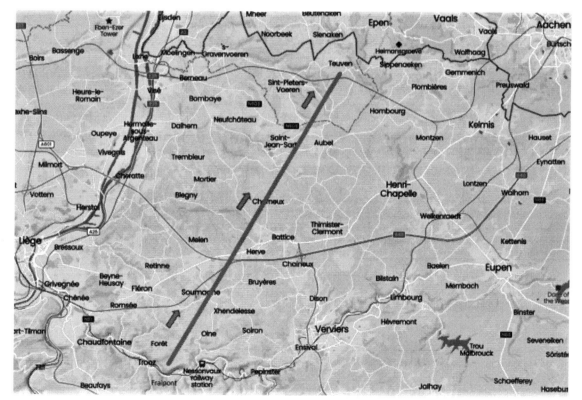

(Base map © OpenStreetMap, see https://www.openstreetmap.org/copyright)

We were to be here until 23 February 1945. The regiment gave us plenty to do to keep us sharp during our period off the line with a full training schedule that called for gunnery, driving and map reading practice; vehicle and weapon maintenance; new vehicle identification; radio procedure and fraternization instruction; first aid and venereal disease lectures; bivouac security procedure, military courtesy and discipline review; platoon tactics practice; and current events briefings to bring us up to date on what was happening in the world. Our battalion also seemed to do road repair in our area every day, preparing for any move forward we would be making. Weather was mostly overcast with rain and only a bit of sun.

07FEB1945

Colonel Henry Zeien replaced Colonel Parker as battalion commander.

Captain Henry Johnson, previous commanding officer of F Company until he was wounded on 11 October 1944, returned to the company during this time. When Captain Johnson arrived, I relinquished command of the company to him. When Colonel Zeien asked whether I wanted to transfer to command another company rather than take what could be seen as a "demotion" back to commanding officer of my old platoon, I replied I would rather return to my platoon.

Lieutenant Trinen, commanding officer of our 1st Platoon, related to me afterward that early on, Captain Johnson had said to him that he thought I was too much by the book to be successful.

The 1st Battalion assumed its original organization with C Company (with new Chaffee M24 light tanks replacing the Stuarts), I Company and F Company. The major change was that we were now part of Combat Command Reserve (CCR). During our next operation, the 1st Battalion (minus Company I) was part of Task Force Anderson under Lieutenant Colonel Russell W. Jenna.

Here I am after having transferred back to my old 2nd Platoon. The photo was taken in Terziet, Holland, about two miles from Teuven, between 7 and 24 February 1945. There is no doubt that this is *Frances* again, as that is Ray Stewart sticking out of the hatch on the top right. I have missed a few names, but here is as close as I can get. I cannot guarantee that the names correctly match with the photo. Top of the turret (left to right): Cignetto, Stewart. Sitting on the tank: Hayfield, Joretsky, Gentile, Zabok, Jutras with two I cannot remember. Standing: Jenkins, Loss, Conner, Clymer, Ross, Kelso, Manning, Skovira and me. Kneeling: Weinert, Evans, Hanson, Marino, Sherffero, Manzella with one unknown. (FCB)

15FEB1945 LETTER HOME

Another beautiful day, and we made very good use of it. A knockdown-drag-out game of touch football. My platoon challenged Lt. Critchfield's 3rd Platoon, and it developed into a real contest. Neither team gave an inch. It ended in a 6-6 tie. Felt like school days or the games we played around the neighborhood. Even have a nicely bruised thigh . . . was clipped twice.

20FEB1945 LETTER HOME

Started a letter last night but got interrupted, involved a meeting and a peep ride. Returned in time to hit the sack. Just finished packing up a souvenir map showing the countries and routes which the division has touched. I've packed it in a cardboard cylinder which originally contained a bazooka shell. A re-broadcast of Charlie McCarthy is now on the radio. Just read a little article in Stars and Stripes. Frank Sinatra says that if he is inducted he would like to drive a tank or be on a PT boat. I'd like to have him on my tank. "Sing to me, Frankie Boy!" We could turn on the tank radio and entertain the whole outfit.

About this time, I received this in a note from my Boy Scout buddy Harry Staats just after he had spoken with my mother:

I called up your mom a couple of weeks ago to find out where the government had sent you. Found out. Your mom is taking your being in the Army very well. She told me: "I just pretend he's away at Boy Scout camp."

I kept the note that Harry gave me from my mother and read it often.

Frederick,
Do what conscience says is right,
Do what reason says is best,
Do with all your mind and might
Do your duty and be blest.
Your loving Mother

(Author's Collection)

23FEB1945 BATTALION DAILY REPORT

COMBAT EFFICIENCY: 90%

The battalion completed all preparations to move out, including camouflaging vehicles. From 24–26 February 26, we moved east through Gemmenich, Belgium, closing on Aachen on the evening of 26 February. 27 February found us in a wooded area southeast of Jülich, Germany. We were placed just behind and in support of our fellow XIX Corps units, the 29th and 30th Infantry Divisions, who were on the jump-off line for our next advance.

08FEB1945–05MAR1945

Eisenhower's next push in his broad-front strategy was to advance four Allied armies, the First Canadian, parts of the Second British, the Ninth U.S. and elements of the First U.S., across the Rhineland, the flat plain between the Roer and Rhine Rivers. The objective was to converge along the banks of the Rhine River north and south of Duisburg, a city at the western edge of the Ruhr Valley, a coal-rich area where Germany had concentrated much of its industrial production. Speed was essential to capture intact bridges over the Rhine to allow for a strike into the Ruhr.

The advance was divided into two operations: Operation Veritable, with three hundred forty thousand British and Canadian troops in the north, and Operation Grenade, with three hundred thousand U.S. troops to the west and southwest. The Canadians were the first to step off, moving out at 0500 on 8 February from Nijmegen, situated at the angle of the Rhine and the Dutch frontier. They struck southeast along the left bank of the Rhine. The U.S. forces were to move forward on 9 February, jumping off from their lines along the Roer River and moving northeast with fifty miles to cover to reach the Rhine.

The XIX Corps was assigned to cross the flat Cologne plain. The combined operations became known as the Rhineland Campaign.

Sherman tank from the 2nd AD crossing a treadway bridge over the Roer River in Jülich on 26 February 1945; bridge courtesy of the 17th Engineers. Notice the engineers' vigilance. The bridge was under their constant inspection to make sure it did not fail. (U.S. Army Signal Corps Photo)

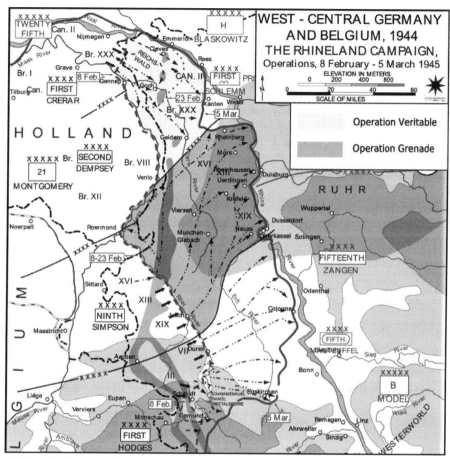

(Wikimedia Commons)

Operation Veritable (Canadians and British) in the north

The Ruhr, the industrial heartland of Germany. The Ruhr River flows into the Rhine River at Duisburg.

The starting point for Operation Grenade was the Roer River, with the main movement to the northeast toward the Ruhr.

The XIX Corps (29th ID, 30th ID, 2nd AD) was on the southern flank of a general advance northeast that began around Julich. The hope and goal was to capture intact Rhine River bridges anywhere north of Dusseldorf and advance into the industrialized Ruhr.

Schwammenauel Dam

The Allies knew that the Germans had prepared to blow the seven Roer River dams situated upstream to flood the Cologne plain in order to stall or stop any Allied attack, but the Allies' plan was for U.S. troops to capture the dams and prevent their destruction.

However, as soon as the Canadians stepped off, the Germans destroyed the sluice gates of the dams, inundating the Cologne plain. Both Veritable and Grenade were stopped cold.

The Schwammenauel Dam near Schmidt, Germany, one of seven dams located on the Roer River. The river flows north, which is to the right. (U.S. Army Photo)

The G-2 of the 9th Infantry Division, Major Jack A. Houston, had previously assessed the damage that could be caused by the dams' destruction: "By demolition of some of them [Roer River dams], great destructive waves can be produced which would destroy everything in the populated industrial valley [of the Roer] as far as the Meuse River [Maas] and into Holland" (*The Siegfried Line Campaign* by Charles B. MacDonald).

The flooding bought a valuable two weeks for German Field Marshal Gerd von Rundstedt, who, having been denied permission by Hitler to retreat behind the Rhine, did the best he could to prepare his defenses and his troops for the attacks to come.

23FEB1945

The floodwaters subsided, and the Ninth Army was able to cross the Roer River. The 2nd AD was to follow the 29th and the 30th Infantry Divisions, prepared to rush our tanks through any gaps the infantry might make in the German defenses.

28FEB1945

We moved out of the wooded area near Jülich at 1200, passed through the 29th Infantry Division and advanced to the northeast. We met little resistance, covering the eighteen miles to our objective Jüchen by 2000. Interestingly, we captured German tankers who were fighting as infantry.

The terrain of the Cologne plain was open and flat, perfect for tanks . . . when it was dry.

In the photo below are either CCA or CCB tanks, which were able to move very quickly across the open terrain of the Cologne plain. The speed of their advance cut off many German units to the west,

The photo is of 2nd AD Sherman tanks moving northeast toward the Rhine across the Cologne plain. The burning buildings indicate positions where the Germans fought delaying actions. (U.S. Army Photo in the Author's Collection)

Aerial photo of the same advance seen in the photo at left. This shot shows the terrain farther east, the smoke coming from the burning buildings shown in the previous photo. (U.S. Army Photo in the Author's Collection)

This is a close-up of the map I used at the time.

Schaan

I made the black line to mark the boundary between the 29th ID and the 2nd AD. The 2nd AD was to the right of the line.

Juchen

29th ID/2nd AD Boundary

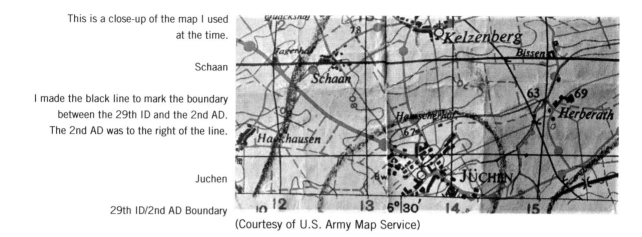

(Courtesy of U.S. Army Map Service)

which is to the left of this photo. Company F was in CCR, where we followed the left flank and rear of the two leading combat commands, protecting them from those cutoff units as they tried to return to Germany. We would encounter elements of one of the Panzer Lehr Divisions at Schiefbahn as it tried to cut through our lines in an attempt to make it back to the Rhine.

Colonel Jenna sent out elements of the CCR to set up a roadblock near Schaan on the Schaan-Jüchen road to the northwest of Jüchen. CCA and CCB were already well north of this point, having passed it during their rapid advance.

While constructing the roadblock, the troops were interrupted by German Panzerschreck rockets (a larger version of our bazooka) and small arms fire. The CCR troops held the Germans off, capturing a 75mm self-propelled gun and twenty-one prisoners. Units from the 29th Infantry Division moved alongside and took over the roadblock to allow CCR to continue to the northeast on the left flank of the 2nd AD.

Panzerschreck (Raketenpanzerbüchse 54) with blast shield. (Wikimedia Commons)

01MAR1945

We met light resistance as we skirted two miles east of the industrial city of München-Gladbach (now Mönchengladbach).

By 1630, my platoon had moved ten miles north of Schaan and halted in the town of Schiefbahn, where CCB had been seeing heavy action earlier in the day before they moved north to Willich. We hooked up with a platoon of tanks from Company H that was left to secure the city. F Company was ordered to cover Schiefbahn, and Captain Johnson set up three outposts on the main roads coming into town. Our platoon was ordered to move to the central marketplace of the town, located in front of Schiefbahn's main church, St. Hubertus. I directed the platoon to establish positions around the church.

Battalion HQ also set up one outpost with one medium and one light tank. Around 1800, Captain Johnson pulled his tank in front of St. Hubertus on the main west-to-east street of the town, Hochstrasse, and we reviewed what we knew of the situation. While I was standing on the street looking up at him in the turret of his tank, we both heard heavy fire as well as infantry small arms fire coming down the street in front of us.

Captain Johnson pulled his tank out immediately, and I got into my tank to make sure there was communication with the tanks in the platoon. To make sure everyone in the platoon knew what was happening, I got out and ran to each tank to talk to the tank com-

St. Hubertus, Schiefbahn, Germany, 1970 photo. (Courtesy Udo Holzenthal, City Archivist of Willich)

mander and position his tank to cover the nearby streets, intersections and each other. I decided to wait outside my tank to determine how the German attack was developing. Hochstrasse was long and straight for several blocks to the west and was being covered by a tank or self-propelled gun at the western end. Any vehicle crossing the street would be hit by large-caliber anti-tank fire.

Mike Skovira, assistant gunner in *Frances*, relates what he experienced at that time:

We were instructed to park the tank in the front yard (of the church) and take a look around. While standing outside the tank, we heard a shot and realized we were under enemy fire. We climbed aboard our tank and were soon given orders by Captain Johnson to proceed to the north side of town. Our tank driver, Sergeant Shafer, was about to cross over Hochstrasse when we spotted Lieutenant Brems standing at the crossroads frantically waving his arms and firing his .45 in the air to get our attention. Our tank commander, Sergeant Bibby Evans, immediately ordered Shafer to stop the tank. Just as we stopped, I saw a ball of fire coming from the left down the street. It hit an American half-track full of ammunition that had been sitting just to our right front by the church. I remember that first shot splitting the half-track's front axle in two. Another ball of fire quickly followed the first and struck the half-track full on, causing it to burst into flames. Lieutenant Brems had warned us in time about the danger lying up the street. His actions probably saved our lives.

The following anecdote about the exploding ammunition truck is from a compilation of German accounts of the action in and around Schiefbahn, pulled together in 2002 by local historian Ludwig Hügen. He used both civilian interviews and reports from units that had been involved in the fight. The sixteen-page article was translated into English for the first time for this book by former U.S. Army Intelligence Officer Jerry Whitaker, segments of which are interwoven below:

(Drawing by Dylan Soal)

Photo taken from the corner of Hochstrasse and Növergasse, the most likely position of the German gun. From here, the Germans commanded the main street of Schiefbahn, Hochstrasse, all the way to the main plaza in front of the church. Being in an overwatch position, they were aimed and set to fire immediately at anything that moved along or across the street. The positioning of the gun was well thought out. If it needed to retreat, it could back out and immediately turn north on Növergasse, the street immediately to its left and rear. (Photo courtesy Udo Holzenthal, City Archivist of Willich, 2021)

Reverend Kaiser had fallen asleep in the basement of the church but was awakened by a huge explosion. The five American soldiers who had been squatting on the floor of the basement with the civilians since dawn at first prevented Kaiser from leaving the basement, threatening him with their submachine guns, but after a short time he was allowed to climb the stairs and hallway, on his hands and knees the entire time. Out the door of the church he saw the flames of burning tanks and vehicles, like huge torches, reflected on the houses and church tower. The explosion had been caused by an ammunition half-track that had been hit in front of the Strucker house, the shells and tracer ammunition on the half-track exploding in quick succession. Reverend Kaiser heard the screams of women from the neighboring houses and the painful cries of wounded and dying soldiers.

Since the wind threatened to spread the fire to the adjacent houses, the reverend grabbed two buckets, filled them with water, ran across the street and frantically tried to extinguish the fire. On each of his six trips, he fell, and he could feel the fire's heat increasing. Exhausted, he rested in the protective cover of a hallway exactly when what was left of the ammunition exploded in front of the house. The clergyman considered any further rescue operations to be too dangerous, and he returned to the basement, where the American soldiers were still squatting in fear. . . .

Some neighbors tried to help fight the fire, but they soon realized that there was nothing they could do. Four of the city's firefighters, Herr Brocker, master baker Wilhelm Schmithuysen, his seventeen-year-old son Herbert Schmithuysen and fifteen-year-old Albert Rahm, were pressured by the occupants of the basement to set out and get the fire truck, located in a nearby schoolyard, and extinguish the fire at the Strucker house.

M3A1 half-track used to carry troops, ammunition, and other supplies. (U.S. Army Photo)

Gentile. (U.S. Army Photo)

The half-track's ammunition cooked off for much of the night, burning furiously, lighting up the entire area in front of the church, and probably causing the fire in the Stucker house. A medical half-track had been hit as well.

While heavy fire from tanks, anti-tank guns and small arms continued throughout the late afternoon and most of the night, we sat still around the church, having sighted in and loaded our main guns, listening to the sounds of battle and waiting. We had Hochstrasse, the main west-to-east street in Schiefbahn, blocked. Although the German gun at the top of the street controlled Hochstrasse itself, the Germans would have a tough time getting past us.

I made numerous visits to each of my four other crews. On one visit, I remember grabbing my driver, saying, "Gentile, grab a tommy gun and let's go!" He hopped right to it. I think that was the only visit where I had someone with me.

During one round checking on the platoon, I was running toward one of our tanks sitting along the side of the church. I slowed down as I got even with the end of the tank's gun barrel when suddenly my body was completely lifted off the ground by a tremendous explosion. I landed face down on the sidewalk and watched my helmet fly off and roll down the street. I lay there long enough to check my various parts, and I found, to my relief, that everything was still there. It ran through my head that German artillery or mortar fire had knocked me over or that a panzer had fired as it darted across the intersection up the street from my position. I never thought the blast had come from one of our own tanks. It turns out that that is exactly what had happened.

When I had pulled myself together, I got up, walked over to the tank and climbed up on the deck. I got right next to the tank commander, who did not see me, as he had his head down into the tank yelling, "You killed the lieutenant! You killed the lieutenant!"

The tank commander suddenly stood, turned, looked my way and did a double take when he saw me standing right next

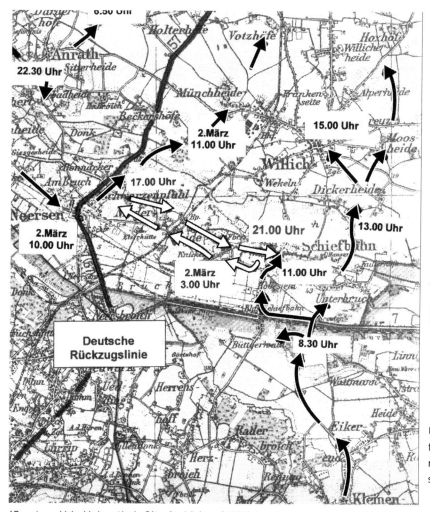

The clear arrows show the German attack from the west. The black arrows show the advance of CCR to the east of Schiefbahn and the advance into the center of Schiefbahn by F Company. (Map provided by Udo Holzenthal, City Archivist of Stadtarchiv)

St. Hubertus is located where the black and clear arrows meet.

The black arrow turning west and then north marks the path F Company took into Schiefbahn.

Until this chapter of the book was sent to Mr. Holzenthal, the archives had no report of the battle from the American side.

(Courtesy Udo Holzenthal, City Archivist of Willich; adapted by Gerry O'Neill)

to him on the deck. He immediately threw his arms around my neck and shoulders, yelling, "You're all right! You're all right!" The sergeant had never been very affectionate before. I don't remember what we said after that, but I know we talked about something. I climbed down to go on and check the other tanks.

I was figuring that the gunner had fired by accident, been inadvertently tapped on the head by the tank commander's foot (using the outdated but ingrained tap signal to fire the gun) or thought I was a German soldier coming down the street to attack them. It turned out that the gunner thought I had indeed been a German soldier, and he fired of his own accord.

It was the concussion from the firing of the tank's 75mm gun right next to me that had knocked me over, the projectile passing within inches of my head. Luckily I had no injuries, although my hearing was permanently affected. Ray Stewart was bow gunner in the tank and saw the entire thing through his periscope: me getting bowled down the street by the explosive force of the gun firing and the explosion as the high-explosive round hit a house down the street behind me.

I know I was very glad to be alive. If nothing else, this was a sure sign that everyone was tense that night.

That night was pitch dark except for the reflected glow of the burning ammunition half-track. With the firing continuing all around the area, it was difficult to distinguish sounds. While I continued to check on my platoon, I came along a brick wall and walkway that wound around the rear of the church. I followed the walk, and where it opened to the street, I spotted a German Mark IV tank that had pulled up, blocking the walkway's other end. A self-propelled anti-tank gun, perhaps a Marder, was positioned in front of the tank.

In 1986, I revisited the spot where I had gotten blown off my feet. I had not even been scratched at the time, but over the years I had a growing ringing in my ears that made hearing increasingly difficult, to the point that even hearing aids have not helped much. (FCB)

The walkway behind the church as it appeared in 1986. The German Mark IV was parked just beyond the end of the bushes where the walk came out onto the adjacent street. (FCB)

A German Marder self-propelled gun. (Wikimedia Commons)

A German Mark IV medium tank. (Wikimedia Commons)

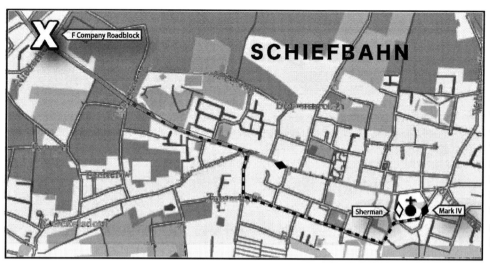

The X marks the spot where the roadblock had been; it may have been farther west (left). The dashes indicate what we figured was the route the two German vehicles had taken behind us to arrive at St. Hubertus. (Base map © Open StreetMap, see https://www.openstreetmap.org/copyright; adapted by Gerry O'Neill)

The German vehicles had to have worked their way around us to the south in an attempt either to flank us or to determine how deep into the town our defenses ran. After the action, we worked out that they had probably taken the side street that turned south off Hochstrasse and turned east on a narrow accessway, a lane that only showed as a dull black line on the map. A turn to the left on the main north-to-south road brought them to the east side of the church. We were on the church's west side.

I didn't want to risk announcing our presence by cranking up our tank engine. Even if I did, moving the tank to a spot where I could fire directly at the panzer would be difficult in the limited space we had to maneuver. Taking the chance was tempting, as the shot would have been a solid hit at this close range, no more than sixty feet. But I knew any panzer commander worth his salt would have heard us coming. If he knew what he was doing, and I had to assume he was a veteran, he would have followed the sound of our engine and aimed his gun down that walkway to fire just as we showed ourselves.

I needed another option. I ran toward a position where I knew there were some infantry. By luck, I found a bazooka team and told them to come with me. We crawled along the walk to within twenty feet of the tank. The Mark IV commander did not spot us and stood in the open hatch looking forward in perfect silhouette, but this close, the tank had to be our main target, not the commander. I whispered to the team to load and fire their bazooka, which they quickly did. The rocket struck the tank, but even in the dim light, I could see from where it exploded that the rocket had not done crippling damage.

I turned to tell the bazooka man to quickly reload and fire again, but he and his two buddies had scrambled out of there as soon as they fired that first shot. I wasn't too happy, and, more in frustration than anything else, I fired my .45, all eight rounds (one in the chamber), at and around the turret, even though the tank commander had already ducked inside and buttoned up. Not knowing what he was up against, he did the right thing. He was blocked from going straight forward by the self-propelled gun and certainly fearful of advancing around the self-propelled gun and entering the illumination given off by the still-burning ammunition half-track, so he backed out of there. I got out of there as well, and I assume the self-propelled gun backed out of there soon after his support left him.

When I got back to my tank, I could hear my crew talking inside, "Where is he? He's been gone a long time!" I found it gratifying that they were glad to see me back in the tank and safe.

Still not sure of the situation, I went out again to reconnoiter a couple of blocks farther west, hoping to find out what we were facing at the German end of the Hochstrasse. As I got to the second street west of us, I spotted something that I could not believe. A fire truck with lights on and bells ringing was racing up the street right toward Hochstrasse.

I held up my hand and stopped them, but they shouted at me, "Da ist ein Feuer!" I knew what they were saying, and I also knew that there was more fire out there than they could handle.

I tried to tell these civilians in my faltering German to stop there and not turn onto the street ahead. "Gehen Sie nicht on Strasse! Viel schiessen!" They insisted they were going to go around the corner, and they would not be stopped. This I understood mostly by their pointing and shouting. I reached for my pistol to threaten them into turning around, but before I could get my .45 out of its holster, they rushed ahead.

My immediate hope was that with their lights on and bells ringing they might be recognized as a local fire truck, but with all the confusion out there, I feared that this would not happen and that they had little chance of survival. I do remember thinking that firemen had their duty to perform, and come hell or high water, they were going to do it. What they did not realize was that they were in the middle of a battle.

Schiefbahn firefighters in 1937. The fire truck I saw that night was very similar, perhaps this very truck. (Courtesy of Udo Holzenthal, City Archivist of Willich)

The fire truck turned right at the end of this street onto Hochstrasse. (FCB)

The worst happened as they turned the corner. They immediately came under fire from the German vehicle up the street that was just sitting there waiting to fire at anything that moved on the main street. I heard the German gunfire and the nearly instantaneous explosion, saw the flashes and the flames and heard terrible screams. With all that had been going on since midafternoon, through the evening and most of the night, in the heat of the moment I said to myself, "Stupid! There's a war going on!" They were probably all older men, perhaps disabled veterans still able to function, or very young men, all wanting to do their duty. It was a total waste of life.

After the war I learned that a local baker and his son were on the fire truck, as well as another fireman and a fifteen-year-old boy. Schmithuysen Street in Schiefbahn is named after the father and son.

The German version of the efforts of the firemen is substantially different from what I witnessed. Local historian Ludwig Hügen again:

That same corner in 1986 where the fire truck had turned. The church, St. Hubertus, is two blocks to the right. (FCB)

It is still unclear how the four firefighters, who wore steel helmets and uniforms, were allowed through without incident. [Note that I had tried to stop them.—FCB] To get to the fire truck, the four men lifted the large gate at the school because the key to the lock was missing. Wilhelm Schmithuysen sat at the wheel with his son Herbert next to him, with Herr Brocker and fifteen-year-old Albert Rahm in the back.

With the alarm bells ringing, Schmithuysen drove from the schoolyard to Hochstrasse to turn to the church square and fight the fire at the Strucker house (the explosion of the ammunition on the half track probably started the fire). Before they got to the square, however, they saw that the Mertens' courtyard was also on fire. The crew laid out the hoses, but Bauer Mertens asked them not to try to extinguish the fire, as soldiers from both sides were fighting in and around the house. The firemen stopped, but young Herbert Schmithuysen was shot in the knee and fell to the ground. Hand grenades were thrown from the upper floor and from nearby Goossens' bakery, while machine gun fire ripped across the square. It was no longer possible to think.

The men carried Herbert into the kitchen, where they tied the leg off to stop the bleeding. His father ripped off his fireman's uniform and, even aware of the danger, decided to get Dr. Macke. He only made it to the front door, where a soldier wearing ammo belts shot and killed him. When Herbert Schmithuysen was able to be smuggled through to the hospital the next morning, it was already too late. Thus, two citizens of Schiefbahn, father and son, sacrificed their lives to protect their neighbors' property, fulfilling their duty as firefighters. It was an irony of fate that the doctor had been detained that night not in his practice, but by the Americans in a house next to the burning yard!

My recollections of the event are much different. I saw the fire truck round the corner, heard the German gunfire, and saw the explosion as the shell hit the fire truck. I witnessed the destroyed truck and bodies of the firemen on the Hochstrasse the next morning.

Whoever supplied this account likely made the judgment that it was too painful to relate that a German gun had fired at a civilian fire truck and killed four fellow Germans.

Ludwig Hügen continues:

Around 10:00 p.m., Bernhard Beschoten tried to get help at the hospital for his wife, who had been wounded. He didn't know what was happening outside on the streets or where the battle lines were. He walked across the road toward the hospital and wondered why there were so many German tanks and vehicles near the church. It was only after he was in the walkway to the hospital that he was stopped and addressed . . . in English.

He was taken to the American command post, which was located in the restaurant Aretz, today's Hoster household. When he explained he was looking for help for his wife, an army doctor immediately offered to accompany him to his wife. The doctor made it as far as the next street corner when he realized that the wounded woman was on the German side of the lines. Herr Beschoten was locked up in the hospital cellar and had to stay there until the next morning.

Herr Beschoten must have encountered parts of our company as we were controlling the area around the church at 10:00 p.m. I was not aware of this story until I read Herr Hügen's account, but so many things were happening simultaneously, and our piece of the battle was only one part of a wider conflict.

Add one more element of confusion: A platoon from Company C of our battalion with the new M24 Chaffee light tanks (slowly replacing the obsolete M5 Stuart) had come into town during the night and was pulling into the street directly across the plaza from us. They reversed in line with their engines against a wall, keeping their newly designed lightweight 75mm gun facing front, ready to fire.

Because of all the noise, we did not know the Chaffees were there. Ray Stewart in *Frances* saw what happened next:

We could hear tanks moving around, but because of all the noise, we couldn't make out whether they were Americans or Germans. The tank directly to our right saw something and fired. The shot hit what turned out to be a tank, and from that close range, that shot was not going to miss. We saw the crew bailing out as the tank began bursting into flames, and the bow gunner of the tank that had fired opened up with his .30 caliber machine gun on the fleeing crew. When things quieted down, I dismounted and went to the next tank over and asked whether they indeed had been the ones to fire on the tank just across the plaza. They had.

The next morning, a lieutenant from Company C came into our area and asked whether we had seen the action the night before. We answered yes and asked him whether anyone had been hurt. He told us that luckily there were no casualties, although the tank had been destroyed. The lieutenant had no idea that an F Company tank had fired the shot, and we did not tell him.

I got a radio report from Captain Johnson right after the Chaffee had been hit, alerting us as to what had happened. It was unnerving not to know where the shot had come from. Were the Germans that close and yet unseen? Later that night, one of my platoon's tank commanders found me. He was very upset because he realized he had ordered his tank to fire at the Chaffee, thinking it was a German tank, the Chaffee having a silhouette similar to the German Mark III medium tank. I tried to calm him down. I told him that these things happen, that he should forget about it and that I heard no one had been hurt. I never talked about this incident again to anyone, and no one to my knowledge ever reported the loss of the Chaffee as anything other than a result of enemy action.

After the action, we pieced together our information and realized that when we all had been introduced to the Chaffee during the new vehicle identification course given during our time at Teuven, this particular tank commander had not been with us. In the dark and with the tension wearing on us all, his presence at that training might not have made any difference.

01MAR1945 BATTALION DAILY REPORT

```
At 1800 enemy counterattack from the West with Armor and Infantry, strength unknown
but believed to consist of approximately five tanks of unknown type and a Company of
Infantry. At 1830, the counterattack was repulsed. C/66 [our light tank company]
lost one tank [the Chaffee] which was hit by enemy fire and burned; no personnel were
casualties. One Mark IV Tank, one SPAT [self-propelled anti-tank] gun was knocked
out by F/66AR.
Zeien Comdg
```

I am not sure whether the Mark IV we hit with the bazooka was the one that HQ counted in the daily report as the Mark IV that was knocked out by the company.

It was indeed a wild night, so wild that Lieutenant Trinen told me that Captain Johnson had said, "Brems is as crazy as we are!"

02MAR1945

We maintained our positions in Schiefbahn for the night, and by morning the Germans had moved out, probably to the north to find a gap between our leading elements and those of us following in support that would take them to the east. We moved out of our position from around the church with orders to head north to Willich. When we turned onto Hochstrasse, we saw the scattered parts of the fire truck still smoldering along with the bodies of the firemen, a sad and very unpleasant sight. I could only shake my head.

As we approached the outskirts of Schiefbahn, we also saw German prisoners of war being escorted by our infantry.

At our next battalion briefing, S-3 shared with us what they had learned from the prisoners. We had been up against elements of the German Panzer Lehr Division that had been cut off to our west by CCB's swift northern thrust. We all recalled that we had met elements of this division before and had beaten them then as well during the Battle of the Bulge.

Schiefbahn: German POWs coming up the road. That is the front end of our tank's 75mm gun along the lower left of the photo. Two Shermans sit farther up the road. (FCB)

S-3 went on to explain that, in their attempt to escape east to the Rhine, the Germans decided to counterattack through Schiefbahn. They overran the roadblock that our troops had established on the western outskirts of town and advanced onto town on Hochstrasse. This was the same street that ran in front of St. Hubertus Church, where my platoon had halted. It turns out that Hochstrasse was the most direct west-to-east route available to the Germans. They had to come to us.

We spotted a Mark IV tank abandoned in a field north of town. I thought that perhaps it was the one we hit with the bazooka rocket near the church and that the shot had been more effective than we thought. Or maybe the tank just ran out of fuel.

Either way, it looks like F Company had knocked out one Mark IV at Schiefbahn. Maybe two.

When we sent the above photo to Herr Holzenthal at the Stadt Willich Archiv, he published it in the paper and asked whether anyone recognized the spot where that Mark V Panther had been sitting. He got numerous replies that indicated the Panther had been sitting to the left of the road shown here. The selection of this spot was based on local memory, the shape of the skyline, the buildings along the curve in the road and Herr Holzenthal's personal survey of the buildings well beyond the new growth of trees on the left. (Courtesy of Udo Holzenthal, City Archivist of Willich)

Close-up of the previous photo of German prisoners. (FCB)

A 1947 photo showing a mother and two daughters sitting on a destroyed Stuart light tank, probably from CCA or CCB, which had been through the town before we got there. (Courtesy of Udo Holzenthal, City Archivist of Willich)

As we left Schiefbahn and entered Willich, we passed this knocked-out Mark V Panther tank. Being on the outskirts of Willich, it had to have been knocked out by one of the two combat commands that were in front of us, as the Panther was not noted in our battalion's daily report. (FCB)

A few days after the battle, the first sergeant called to me and said, "I want to tell you that one of your tank crews came up to me and told me they wanted to see the company commander. I asked them, 'For what reason?' [this type of question being a part of a first sergeant's job]. They told me they wanted to put you in for an award. I told them the CO had already started a citation."

I was proud of the fact that my commanding officer had put me in for an award, but I was even more proud of the fact that one of my crews had submitted my name for recognition. I did not know which crew had written up the action and submitted it to Battalion HQ. Mike Skovira was able to fill me in on that:

At the last 2n AD reunion, Lieutenant Brems was talking to Ray Stewart and me, both from his platoon, about Lieutenant Brems's Silver Star. Lieutenant Brems did not know that I was the one who had written to battalion about his heroic actions. My two sergeants, Harris and Evans, approved the report I wrote, and I submitted it to the company clerk, who then forwarded it to battalion. I was nineteen years old at the time.

When I visited Schiefbahn in 1986, I walked to the corner where the fire truck had made the turn. In the window of a store on that corner were several pieces of firefighters' equipment. It was Sunday, though, and the store was closed. I wonder whether the equipment in the window was a coincidence or a memorial.

For a German point of view on the fight at Schiefbahn, see *Elite Panzer Strike Force: Germany's Panzer Lehr Division in World War II* by Franz Kurowski. It was one hell of a night.

AWARD OF THE SILVER STAR MEDAL CITATION

First Lieutenant Frederick C. Brems, 01010943, 66th Armored Regiment, United States Army. For gallantry in action in Germany. On the night of 1 March 1945, an enemy counterattack overran the outposts of Schiefbahn and penetrated into the town. During the initial confusion, and despite heavy enemy artillery and small arms fire, Lieutenant Brems dismounted from his tank, contacted the enemy, and disposed his tanks in the best positions. To keep a true picture of the rapidly changing situation he set out on foot again and found a Mark V [sic] tank within fifty yards of his position. He organized a bazooka team and led it to attack, causing the Mark V to withdraw. Throughout the night, he repeatedly made reconnaissance trips through the area despite the artillery and with full knowledge of the fact that any movement invited enemy sniping fire. Lieutenant Brems' courage, devotion to duty, and professional skill were an inspiration to all. Entered Military service from Illinois.

I. D. White
Major General, U.S. Army
Commanding

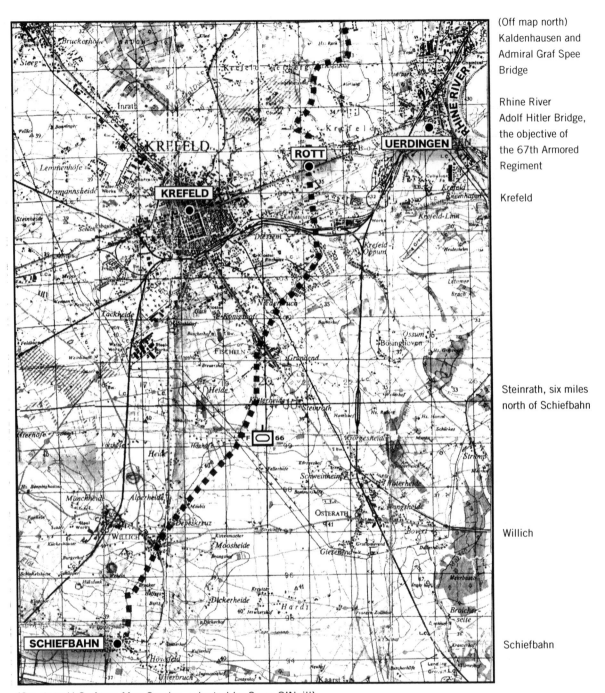

(Off map north)
Kaldenhausen and
Admiral Graf Spee
Bridge

Rhine River
Adolf Hitler Bridge,
the objective of
the 67th Armored
Regiment

Krefeld

Steinrath, six miles
north of Schiefbahn

Willich

Schiefbahn

(Courtesy U.S. Army Map Service; adapted by Gerry O'Neill)

7

Operation Grenade: Kaldenhausen

02MAR1945

We were reorganized and became Task Force Zeien with Lieutenant Colonel Henry Zeien commanding. From Schiefbahn, we moved northeast six miles to Steinrath, then north to a position three miles east of Krefeld.

03MAR1945

At 1300 we gathered seven miles west of Kaldenhausen, receiving orders at 1330 to attack and capture the Admiral Graf Spee Bridge, the sister bridge of the Adolf Hitler Bridge.

F Company was assigned to lead the attack. I realized early on that tank attacks should never proceed with tanks in line, despite the cheers of the onlookers at the charge I had led with M3 and M5 Stuarts at Camp Chaffee back in February 1943. Nonetheless, a charge in line is exactly what was ordered at Kaldenhausen. We were without a doubt desperate to get to the Admiral Graf Spee Bridge over the Rhine that led to Duisburg and the Ruhr before the retreating Germans blew it up. The charge looked to be a potentially costly gamble, but it also looked like a gamble that had to be taken.

We were essentially to charge six miles over open terrain to the Rhine to capture and secure the Admiral Graf Spee Bridge. The town of Rheinhausen anchored the west end of the bridge with Hochfeld on the east side.

The objective of the 3rd Battalion of the 67th Armored Regiment was the Adolf Hitler Bridge, eight miles to our south, which crossed the river at Mündelheim and led to Duisburg.

Capturing either bridge intact would be a real prize.

Admiral Graf Spee Bridge is due east.

Kaldenhausen

The dot is the location where my tank got hit.

F Company route (in dashed line), Rhine River

Adolf Hitler Bridge, objective of the 67th Armored Regiment

(Courtesy U.S. Army Map Service; adapted by Gerry O'Neill)

On 22 May 1936, the Admiral Graf Spee Bridge was inaugurated by Dr. Joseph Goebbels, chief propagandist of the Nazi Party. The Adolf Hitler Bridge was inaugurated just over two weeks later by Deputy Führer Reich Minister Rudolf Hess.

We were not destined to capture either bridge intact, as both were destroyed by the Germans on the night of 3 March 1945. The Adolf Hitler Bridge was rebuilt and is now the Krefeld-Uerdinger Bridge. The bridge between Hochfeld and Rheinhausen, the Admiral Graf Spee Bridge, was also rebuilt and is now the Bridge of Solidarity.

We knew that the bridge would be protected by several German 88mm dual-purpose guns, no doubt the German weapon most feared by tankers. Originally designed as an anti-aircraft

The Admiral Graf Spee Bridge and the Adolf Hitler Bridge, twin bridges crossing the Rhine at Duisburg. (Map from the front page of *The Stars and Stripes*, 1 December 1944 edition)

weapon, the 88 was discovered early on in the war to be a superb anti-tank gun—hence the "dual-purpose" adjective. These 88s would be part of the anti-aircraft defense of the bridge and would also be turned on us when we advanced. We did not realize that there would be a number of German panzers positioned supporting the 88s, but we figured the Germans knew we were coming.

At 1400, the entire company, all seventeen tanks, stepped out in line from a row of houses on the edge of Kaldenhausen, quickly accelerating to full speed as we entered the flat, open terrain. All tank commanders had their heads above the hatch ring to see what was out in front of us. Immediately on clearing the houses, we came under fire from several 88s.

The flat ground was crisscrossed with deep anti-tank ditches. Captain Johnson in the com-

Photo of an 88mm gun, set up here to be used as an anti-tank gun, being dug in behind an earthen embankment to protect the crew from small arms fire. (DAC)

mand tank backed into one early in the attack and got hung up, unable to move in any direction. Lieutenant Trinen's tank got hit soon after the attack began. He left that tank and ran to another tank in his platoon to command from there and continue the attack.

As we rushed forward, I spotted four 88s positioned on a built-up mound, but, to my surprise, they were not firing. The gunners may have gotten off a shot or two when we first appeared, but maybe the sight and sound of an entire company of tanks charging at them at full speed scared them off.

All of us were ready to fire with a shell in the gun's chamber as we moved, prepared to fire at any target that appeared. We were closing on the gun mound when my gunner shouted up to me that the shell casing of the high-explosive round we'd loaded into the gun had come loose from the projectile. The gun was jammed. Our main gun was now completely out of action until that very-possibly-live projectile was cleared from the gun, and that had to be done by pushing the rammer staff down the gun tube from outside the tank. We stopped the tank under some cover from the built-up mound, and I hopped out.

Small arms fire was zipping through the air and bouncing off the tank, but no anti-tank guns were zeroing in on us. I grabbed the rammer staff off the side of the tank, ran to the muzzle of the gun, which was lowered as far as the gunner could get it, and pushed the rammer into the barrel, hoping the round would not cook off when the rammer hit the round's tip.

I breathed with relief as the gunner yelled that the shell dropped harmlessly onto the turret's floor. I climbed back into the turret and got us moving forward again, able to fire our gun and take part in the battle.

We moved quickly across the open field, and as we swung diagonally to the right to cross a ditch, I spotted a tank to our front. The gunner traversed the turret and took it under fire, but our first shot hit what looked like a big pile of manure.

With that, we were hit by a blast of concussion right behind me to my left. An armor-piercing round had been fired from our left rear and hit the diesel fuel intake not more than four feet below and behind me. Time to get out.

I shouted to the crew, "Bail out!" and immediately I heard one of the crew ask, "What did he say? What did he say?"

I shouted even louder, "BAIL OUT!"

I climbed out and crouched on the rear deck so the gunner and loader could climb out the turret

Diesel fuel intake where the armor-piercing round hit. (U.S. Army Training Manual)

hatch. I was able to see the driver clamber out through his front hatch, and the bow gunner, who popped out like he was a jack-in-the-box, through his hatch.

Our ultimate objective, an intact Admiral Graf Spee Bridge, was off our map five miles to the east. F Company followed the blue line that I drew at the planning session the night before. Kaldenhausen, circled in blue, was our assembly area, but we started our "charge" to the east of the town.

At the time, I put a red mark on my map (shown on the map above as a mini explosion) to indicate the approximate area where our tank was hit. The tank that shot at us was probably in a patch of woods that was off to our left and rear, with the tank commander aiming his gun southeast and waiting for our tanks to move right into his sights.

Once everyone was out, I jumped off the back of the tank and took off in a sprint to the cover of a bushy area about fifty yards to our south. We all hit the ground as soon as we dove into the brush, and I took stock of our situation. No one was wounded. Our best move was to get out of the way we had come in.

We crawled for a bit before coming to an opening of about forty feet between our covered position and the next bit of cover. I told the crew that I would run across the space, and if no German had a machine gun trained on the opening, I would make it, and they were to follow immediately before someone did get a bead on that open stretch. I sprinted across the space, burst into the brush and found myself staring into the barrel of a .45 caliber pistol aimed directly at my head.

Thank goodness it was a veteran waiting behind that pistol, who took the time to see whom he was going to shoot before he actually fired. It was Lieutenant Critchfield, commander of the 3rd Platoon and my good friend, holding the .45. He lowered his pistol, and I dove into the cover right behind him. My crew saw that I made it across the opening, so they ran one at a time to the new cover.

Lieutenant Critchfield's platoon was front and center as we advanced. His tank was in the lead and had been knocked out early in the attack, and they used the same route we had to get out of the line of fire. I could see that Critch had received a wound around one of his eyes, for which he would be evacuated to Liège once he got to the aid station. His entire crew was with him, none of them wounded.

This was the fourth tank Critch had had knocked out from under him since Normandy. He received a Bronze Star and a Purple Heart for this action.

While I waited for my crew to join me, I reached inside my jacket and found I still had my old billows Kodak camera with me. I rolled over to face our tank and took this shot.

After the crew scrambled into the brush, we started to crawl and then run back to the 88-battery gun mound we had passed earlier in the attack.

We saw the entry to the bunker, ran inside and found Captain Johnson and a couple of men in a surprisingly large bunk area. There was even a mess hall and common room for the crews of the four 88s abandoned above us.

We knew we were out of the battle and done for the day. My crew, the commanding officer, the other men and I prepared to spend the night in the bunker, the safest place to be.

When we had entered the bunker, I spotted a knocked-out Sherman near the entrance with some equipment tied on the back deck. The firing had moved on to the east as our attack moved toward the bridge, so I figured it was safe to go out

(FCB)

and duck over to the tank to see what I could scrounge. I ended up finding a decent sleeping bag, which I promptly threw onto one of the lower bunks in the emplacement. From the bunk, I noticed a huge red banner with a large swastika on one wall. So, I got up and grabbed it, stuffing it into a bag.

Miracle of miracles, we could not believe that First Sergeant De Pratt came up with the company's distribution that night.

Within no more than ten minutes we had lost nine tanks, six of which had burned, including mine. Zieback's tank had taken a direct hit and burned, with the entire crew wounded.

Conner had been in that tank. When I made it to the rear, he was carried past me on a stretcher, his face blackened. I blurted out, "Conner! I didn't recognize you!" The corpsman gave me a very evil eye, and I immediately realized what I had said. Conner smiled weakly; I am not sure he recognized me or heard what I said. At least I like to think he did not hear me.

Trinen said that he saw the tank that hit me and that it had fired at me from the left rear, which made sense since the armor-piercing shell hit our left side. We all must have charged right by their supporting tanks.

I heard that one of our tank commanders had reported riding the momentum of the charge into the town of Rheinhausen before being stopped by the enemy, but still short of

Conner; photo taken after he had returned to the platoon. (U.S. Army Photo)

Ruins of the Adolf Hitler Bridge to the south of the Admiral Graf Spee Bridge, which was our objective, but they both probably looked very similar: destroyed. (U.S. Army Photo)

the bridge. It was hard to verify at the time, what with all the confusion, but we thought it entirely possible that one tank out of seventeen might make it.

In the end, that did not really matter. During the night we heard a tremendous explosion; the enemy had destroyed the bridge.

03MAR1945 BATTALION DAILY REPORT

The attack progressed fine to within one (1) mile of the objective . . . F/66 AR received Tank and Anti Tank fire from the objective and on the North and South flank. F/66 AR lost six (6) Tanks (burned) . . . and three (3) knocked out, but recovered. The attack was stopped at 1830 due to darkness; security was established for the night.

COMBAT EFFICIENCY: 60%

RESULTS OF OPERATIONS: Ten (10) A.A. (Ack Ack) dual purpose guns were knocked out. Estimated battalion of German A.A. weapons, over run. Mission not accomplished.

In the bigger scheme of things, von Rundstedt's divisions, doomed by Hitler to have to fight with the Rhine to their backs, were cut to pieces in the battle for the Rhineland. Two hundred ninety thousand Germans were taken prisoner.

The bunker we slept in that night was very likely the barracks for the entire artillery battalion, which would have consisted of three batteries of guns with four guns in each battery plus crews. In the haste to get out of the bunker, one of the men left his personal photos and postcards on the table next to my bunk. These documented some of this unit's life.

That night, Captain Johnson, sitting across from me in the bunker, asked, "Fred, you haven't been to Paris, have you? How would you like to go?"

What a question! And in such a setting! Of course I immediately answered, "Yes!"

The next morning, I pulled down the swastika wall banner and stuffed it into I don't know what, grabbed the photos and postcards that had been left behind, gathered my gear and took off.

I got back to the row of buildings that had been the jump-off line for our attack, and I looked for a way to get back to regimental headquarters. Someone pointed out an Opel sitting next to a house, and the key was in the ignition. I tried it, and the engine turned over, so I drove back to HQ, parked the car and just left it, with the keys still in it, for the next guy.

The photo was marked with the arrow and AV—perhaps the initials of the soldier below the arrow and perhaps the owner of the photos I found. Note that the 88s in this postcard were set up as anti-aircraft weapons. There are no embrasures built around the guns. (Author's Collection)

An 88mm multipurpose gun in a more permanent emplacement. (Author's Collection)

When I stepped into HQ and reported in, a staff member told me the regimental commanding officer wanted to see me. I'm unshaven and dirty, and my first thought was, why would the commanding officer want to see me?

I reported to him, and he asked me, "What happened to F Company, Lieutenant?"

I answered, "Sir, we just ran into a beehive."

He looked up at me, nodded his head and said, "I just want to make sure nobody screwed up."

I thought about this on the way to Paris. Perhaps we could have done more reconnaissance. Maybe we could have found a way to move through the woods or other existing cover, although there was not much cover to be had, rather than just charging across that open field.

But I concluded that time had been an issue. We had to get to the bridge before the Germans blew it. I think it was a calculated risk and would have been worth the risk if we'd captured the bridge. I guess we had to give it a try, but I also think the Germans had this all figured out, and that bridge was going to be blown up well before we ever got to it.

It also dawned on me that perhaps the reason Captain Johnson offered me a pass to Paris was to get an officer back to report to the colonel about the attack. Whatever the reason, the timing sure seemed strange to me.

(Author's Collection)

I came to the conclusion that the photos were this fellow's since he is in most of them. (Author's Collection)

I was given a clean uniform and a chance to wash up, and then off to Paris I went.

The same man is second from left in the photo. In the second photo, he is at the near end of the first row, with the big smile. (Author's Collection)

I did not know it at the time, but I would receive a Bronze Star for the action at Kaldenhausen. And so did Critch! Here is his citation:

First Lieutenant Donald A. Critchfield, 01012988, 66th Armored regiment, United States Army, for heroic achievement in connection with military operations against the enemy on 3 March 1945 in Germany. Given the mission of capturing the town of Kaldenhausen and securing the vital roads leading to the Adolf Hitler Bridge [note: actually the Admiral Graf Spee Bridge], Company "F", 66th Armored regiment, moved toward the objective on 3 March. The enemy had a prepared a strong point about the town and opened fire with 88mm and tank guns. After a brief encounter it was determined that only four tanks were available to continue the attack. Lt. Critchfield, disregarding personal safety and demonstrating a high degree of aggressiveness and eagerness to close with the enemy, moved his tank forward and urged the other crews to follow. As his tank approached the enemy it was hit and set afire, but he and his crew escaped and sought cover. Although painfully wounded, Lt. Critchfield led the crew in a dash over open ground into friendly lines and was evacuated only after the other crew members had been cared for. Lt. Critchfield's conduct throughout this action was in accord with the highest of military standards. Entered Military Service from Pennsylvania.

I myself would have awarded Don a Medal of Honor for having the presence of mind to determine whose head was sticking out of the bushes before firing his .45.

8

Off to Paris!

MAR1945

We were over three hundred miles from Paris. Not close, but I was not going to say no to a three-day pass. I hooked up with what I guess could be called a convoy, although it was not much of one, just an open truck and a jeep. I cannot remember why they were headed to Paris, but I was glad for the ride.

Along the way, we passed many abandoned and destroyed vehicles, stopping to check out this German Jagdpanther ("hunting panther") Sd.Kfx.173. It appeared to have been moving toward a railroad crossing on the main road and accidentally ran into this ditch, breaking off its gun in the process.

What an unbroken barrel on this monster looked like. (Wikimedia Commons)

On the left, Lieutenant Arthur with warrant officer Mr. Derdin on the right. The barrel snapped off, the hatch is left open, and this Jagdpanther is scrap metal. (FCB)

The engine produced 690 horsepower in order to push the Jagdpanther's forty-five-and-a-half-ton mass. (FCB)

The railroad crossing is visible to the front of the Jagdpanther. (FCB)

Our "convoy" rests on the way from Kaldenhausen to Paris; we are twenty-two kilometers from Rethel on N46 (now E46). (FCB)

The sign reads:
TO CAMP
OKLAHOMA CITY
CHICAGO
WASHINGTON
DETROIT
TAKE N46

We took a leisurely trip through the French countryside. Our companion jeep in our convoy follows behind us with a motorcycle going the other direction. (FCB)

We crossed the military bridge over the Seine going south into Mantes-la-Jolie, a suburb of Paris and the location of the first Allied bridgehead across the Seine, established on 9 August 1944 by General Patton's Third Army. We were going in the opposite direction this day.

Crossing the bridge south into Mantes-la-Jolie. Notice the end of the cathedral to the right rear of the photo. (FCB)

Passing through Collégiale Notre-Dame de Mantes-la-Jolie on the way to Paris. The sign at the Y in the road points to Nantes. (FCB)

The windshield of the jeep accompanying us can be seen to the left of the photo, taken from back of the truck. A local woman in widow's clothes was walking along the road. (FCB)

Letter Home

Yup, I am in Paris on a three day pass! Couldn't believe it when I was given a pass to Paris. We were right on the front line, so it could not have come at a better time. I am going to the officers sales store today—then on a city tour. Guess who I met? Col. Maulsby, then Major Meyer and Captain Meriwether. Meriwether told me that Millie Woodward has been writing to him quite frequently since she received the bad news about Hank. No good. I had some photos taken and will send them right off. I am staying at a hotel that the Red Cross converted into a club for officers. I had a swell double bed, sheets and all. They did everything to make the stay pleasant for officers including providing suggestions on where to go and brochures with the details on entertainment, sight-seeing and tours.

I wandered into the lobby of the Ritz Hotel and began speaking with an elderly and very refined woman. We spoke for about fifteen minutes before I checked in at the reception desk. The clerk asked me, "Do you know who you were just talking with?" I said no, and he told me, "That is Madame Marie-Louise Ritz, owner and manager of the hotel."

While that started to sink in, I got this tremendous slap on my back! I turned expecting someone other than the person who greeted me. It was General Harmon! He immediately said in his gravelly voice, "Always good to see one of my boys."

I was walking down the Champs-Élysées and bumped into some of the enlisted men of my old 14th AD, and they said to me, "Hey, Lieutenant Brems, we heard you was killed."

I had heard that Lieutenant Heist, one of my platoon leaders when I had the company of the 14th Armored Division, had been killed, a mortar shell landing directly in his open turret. He was the tank commander who had flipped his tank upside down into the river during training. The men had confused me with Lieutenant Heist.

At the Arc de Triomphe, the burial place for the French unknown soldier from World War I. I was not part of any group, but someone must have gathered us all up for this group photo. I am standing at the far right. (FCB)

I took this photo because of the little girl who was so intrigued with the hole where the eternal flame usually would be. (FCB)

The patch on this soldier's left arm indicates that at least one soldier from the 75th Infantry Division was visiting the Arc de Triomphe, probably on leave from the Netherlands, where the division had just been attached to the XVI Corps of the Ninth Army on 1 March 1945. The 75th entered Germany on 10 March 1945. (FCB)

A shot down the Avenue des Champs-Élysées. There were GIs everywhere. (FCB)

Same place but earlier time and certainly different uniforms. A bunch of Adolf's boys stand around the eternal flame. Not sure where I got this photo. I am guessing that it was one of the personal photos I found in the bunker at Kaldenhausen, but I could not find a familiar face. I wonder what they were thinking as they considered the significance of this memorial. (Author's Collection)

The National Academy of Music. Helen was a musician, so I took this photo for her. (FCB)

Notre Dame. (FCB)

The Trocadéro. (FCB)

The Eiffel Tower. (FCB)

I spent my first evening at the famous Folies Bergère, which featured an excellent vaudeville show with jugglers, acrobats, a really good chorus line and a fine orchestra.

On my second night, an officer in the Signal Corps and I decided to catch a show at a club called Tabarin, named after a famous street clown of the 1600s. We were sitting in the mezzanine at a front table, and I saw a gorgeous young woman on the main floor. I told my companion that I was going to dance with her, so I dashed down and asked her to dance. We danced for a bit, and she asked me, "You want come with me after dance?" Reason took over, and I am not sure of my exact words, but no way!

I went back to my table, ready for the start of the show, and, lo and behold, when the show started, the same woman came out in the middle front of the dancers wearing nothing but a spear! Well, it showed I had taste.

The *Stars and Stripes* constantly ran charts of the increasing incidence of sex-related diseases, providing a big incentive not to mess around. But more important, the entire time I was in the military, I prayed to God to get me back to my Helen. I knew that if I did not believe in my part of the bargain and stepped over that line, in the next battle I'd be killed. Captain Fawks even came to me once relating that some in the company thought I was a homosexual since I did not fool around. What? Far from it. I straightened that out right away.

While making my way back from the dance floor, I passed General Harmon. Twice now in one day. I recall him saying, "Don't watch the old man too close. I'm here to have fun tonight!" I understood that to be an order and never looked back.

This is the original program from that night. (Author's Collection)

Everyone goes to Paris! (FCB)

168

Letter Home

The pass ends tomorrow, and we have an 18 hour train ride and truck ride ahead of us. Grr . . . but it has been worth it. I sent you two packages, one containing a large Nazi flag that I picked up in that German bunker near Kaldenhausen and the other a German bayonet.

I saw a lot in Paris!

A jeep was able to pick me up where the truck dropped me off. I decided to take advantage of the transportation and scour my burned-out tank, which was still on the field, to see whether there was anything salvageable. My charred musette bag was on the outside of the tank; my two shell fragments from my time in I Company were lost somewhere in the debris along with the rest of my things. I climbed up to look in the turret but saw there was nothing worth saving.

While having my photo taken by the tank, a truckload of infantry rolled by and hooted and hollered at me, "Oh pretty boy," and stuff like that. Since I was in full dress uniform, they probably thought I was a rear echelon officer up to get my photo taken by a burned-out tank. I just smiled. Not much else I could do.

I walked around the tank and noticed that the left track was broken. I figured that the tank that hit us had put another round into the tank right

With the tank that fired at us on the far side of the tank, the crew dove out to the side I am on toward the cover of bushes. Notice all the hatches are still open and the gun still aimed at the pile of manure we had hit just before we got hit from the left rear. It was a direct hit on the left diesel fuel intake. I am still in my dress uniform that I had worn in Paris. The jeep and a passenger are behind the tank, with another passenger sitting on a log to the right. The driver took the photo. (FCB)

(FCB)

< The fuel intake where the first shot hit us was located here. I was looking out through the open turret when we got hit, the open wing of my hatch visible on the top of the turret.

< The broken track

169

after we bailed out but before the tank burst into flames. That commander was going to make sure we were not going to move forward any more.

We'd been told that Company F had moved out of the front lines and headed south, so after seeing our tank we drove south to find my platoon.

Many things had happened while I was in Paris. On the day I left, Company F had been detached from Task Force Zeien and attached to Task Force Caruthers. Both task forces then moved from the Kaldenhausen area to establish an outpost line of resistance along a canal to the north, capturing three German soldiers in Kaldenhausen along the way. That night, hourly patrols were sent out, and both task forces took light enemy artillery fire, suffering no casualties.

The next day, Company F was released from Task Force Caruthers and returned to 1st Battalion, 66th AR. During the day, the 95th Infantry Division relieved us, passing through our position as it moved to the north and northeast. We were then ordered to move to an assembly area near Steinhausen, twenty miles to the south, for a much-needed rest and refit.

We found our unit pulled into the assembly area where it had begun a first echelon maintenance of vehicles and weapons. We would spend until 26 March in Steinhausen.

I caught up with the company in the late afternoon, just in time to get to Mass and take Communion. As soon as I got to the company area, Lieutenant Trinen started pulling my leg right away. "Hey, Lieutenant! Your tank didn't burn!" I told him he was crazy since I had just seen it in the field.

Trinen was crazier than the rest of us. One time while the company was under fire, I was in my tank on the left flank when I spotted who I thought might be Trinen running across the open field to our front, and he was being followed by exploding shells. I was not sure it was Trinen, so I radioed the company and asked, "Is that one-six out there ['one' being first platoon, 'six' being the commander]? I sure hope he makes it!"

The response: "Yes, it is one-six!"

He made it across the field, but it was close all the way.

Letter Home

I am now back with the company, in a nice warm house, but the electric system is kaput, so I am writing by the light of a dim candle. All is quiet. A big pendulum clock is ticking. One man breathes heavily over there on a couch asleep . . . so very quiet.

You bet that trip to Paris was super. I saluted the Perpetual Flame at the Arc de Triomphe, and chills ran up my spine; I watched as every soldier who approached the flame saluted. I haven't read into it, but I like to think of it as a tribute to . . . , it's hard to put into words . . . but it must burn as a symbol of something which we all want and don't seem to be able to get or even adequately define because we certainly go about getting to that goal the hard way. I know it's a symbol for a lot of good men who have left us because of that something—but I'm not making sense. But some so-and-so always has to come around and mess things up, to wit: Hitler and his bunch of hoodlums. I know what I want. It's all very nicely consolidated

(FCB)

at 2210 North Lamon. Hitler and his hoodlums—how true that is. The only thing is that it's an understatement. It's late. Time 0005.

I learned on my return that during our attack on the Graf Spee Bridge, T/5 Lester C. Eaker of our company had penetrated to the outskirts of Duisburg at the western end of the bridge before his tank got hit and set on fire. He got the farthest of any of the company and received a Bronze Star (one of six he received during his active service) for his actions in the attack.

Probably because of Company F's losses at Kaldenhausen, the combat efficiency of our battalion was determined to be at 75 percent from 4 March until 7 March. By the time we moved out, it was at 90 percent, probably the highest one could realistically expect.

From the 2nd AD's viewpoint, the Rhineland Campaign, or Operation Grenade, was an overall success. The Rhine River had been reached, and enemy units had been cut off from the Rhine by the division's rapid advance.

More German units were isolated when the bridges over the Rhine were destroyed. In our division's front alone, the enemy suffered 900 killed, and we captured 2,500 prisoners. We also took out 37 tanks and destroyed or captured 225 guns, counting the 88s we had captured at Kaldenhausen. We had captured 150 German towns over an area of 140 square miles. The 2nd AD paid a price, however, losing 90 killed, 286 wounded or injured and 38 missing. The tanks we lost? They could be replaced.

At the time, though, some criticism was leveled at high command that the objective of the operation should have been to move more quickly to capture intact bridges and establish bridgeheads across the Rhine with appropriate support allocated for that. We certainly had tried to do that, but it is speculation to say that more resources could have gotten us over the bridges instead of having to stop, as some stated it, on the "wrong" side of the river. To my mind, those bridges were going to be blown up whenever we got to them.

There was one major and welcome exception that took place to our south, however.

Lieutenant Colonel Henry Zeien. He had been a master sergeant before the war and a first lieutenant in the 66th AR's Machine Gun Company at Fort Benning back in 1941. He said about being promoted, "They sure are making it difficult for me not to salute second lieutenants first." He was a good man. This photo was taken after the war at the officers' quarters in Preusslitz in occupied Germany. (FCB)

07–08MAR1945

Sixty-three miles to the south and east of our assembly area at Steinhausen, the Ludendorff Bridge, spanning the Rhine at Remagen, was captured compliments of the rapid advance of the 9th AD of the First

Army. The bridge had been badly damaged by German explosives, but combat engineers were able to repair enough of the bridge to allow troops and vehicles to cross to the east side of the Rhine to secure the bridge's defense.

Engineers immediately constructed a steel tread-way bridge, a heavy-duty pontoon bridge and a Bailey bridge, which allowed a substantial bridgehead to be established. The Ludendorff Bridge finally collapsed on 17 March 1945, killing twenty-eight engineers and injuring sixty-three. But because of the bridge-building efforts and sacrifices of the combat engineers, the bridge's collapse did not slow our buildup of forces on the east bank of the Rhine.

A photo of the ruins of the Ludendorff Bridge at Remagen that collapsed on 17 March 1945, ten days after our forces had captured it. By the time it collapsed, three bridges were constructed by U.S. Army Engineers for just such an eventuality; two of them are visible here. The view is to the north, and U.S. forces moved from the left (or west) of the photo and crossed the Rhine to the right (or east). (U.S. Army Photo)

The 2nd AD's next objective: get our tanks across the Rhine and drive deep into Germany.

9

The Central European Campaign:
Encircling the Ruhr River Basin

07–08MAR1945

The capture of the Ludendorff Bridge spanning the Rhine at Remagen provided General Dwight D. Eisenhower, the Supreme Commander of the Allied Expeditionary Force, with one bridgehead on the eastern shore of the Rhine and a jumping-off point for the next advance into the heart of Germany. We were going to need more than just the one bridgehead. The 2nd AD, seventy miles to the north of Remagen, prepared to do its part to make and exploit its own bridgehead. Our assigned role was to punch across the Rhine, circle to the north of the Ruhr River basin, meet up eighty miles east of the Rhine with the 3rd AD, which was coming up from the south, and cut off the entire Ruhr area's industrial production from the rest of Germany. A tall order, and it was going to take three weeks for all Allied forces to prepare and coordinate for this final wide-front advance.

07MAR1945

It was a relief to all of us that Steinhausen was well off the front lines. No patrolling was required, and there was no incoming German artillery. The weather was overcast with rain, but if that was all we had to complain about, so what? Our combat efficiency jumped to 80 percent, probably just because we were all able to get some sleep. During that first day, we received instructions in interior guard duty relating to rear-area security, practiced tank gunnery, did maintenance of vehicles and weapons, and, we enjoyed this, the "rehabilitation of troops."

Sometime during this period, our tank losses were made good, but Lieutenant Don "Critch" Critchfield, commanding officer of the 3rd Platoon and my buddy, did better than the rest of us. He was ordered to pick up five new M26 Pershing tanks. While we got Shermans, Critch was getting brand new Pershings! He gathered skeleton crews to drive the tanks and went by truck to the rear to pick them up.

11MAR1945

We got more sleep. Our combat efficiency hit 85 percent. It was still rainy and overcast, but for a nice change there was no training; nothing but athletic games and recreation all day. The day's battalion report affirms that the "training schedule [was] complied with."

All other days were filled. An inspector from headquarters oversaw tank crew drills. Classes on identification of enemy and friendly armored vehicles and airplanes reminded us of what had happened to that M26 Chaffee light tank back in Schiefbahn. We washed our tanks, practiced first aid for gas casualties, fired our tanks' guns, reviewed several of our previous operations and studied platoon tactics and problems. Inspections paid specific attention to "maintenance of physical condition." We got Sundays off to attend church services. Our combat efficiency inched toward 90 percent.

13MAR1945 LETTER HOME

Standing right before me are two Coca Cola bottles!!! Both belong to me, and, as a miser with a hoard of gold, I eye them greedily. A cool refreshing nectar from another world. A real treat to thirsty tankers, two precious bottles to each man. Never did I believe that I could be so affected, so deeply stirred by a five-cent Coke. Right now, I wouldn't trade one small sip for ten greenbacks. A favor, can you send me a jar of Noxema? It's a great shaving aid. Toss it in with some tuna and stuff. Yum, that's good.

Took a couple of pictures standing by my burned up tank at Kaldenhausen. If they turn out, I will send them to you. The condition of the tank will surprise you. I still have the camera, and it is in good shape. Spent much time scouting around in Paris for film to add to my supply, but no luck.

Saw a detective movie this afternoon, "Falcon Out West." Not too bad, but I don't know why they can't send better pictures out here. Only rarely do any really first-rate films arrive.

Yes, we were in this last move to the Rhine [Operation Grenade]. It was a fast piece of work. I took a few photos, which, if they turn out, should be interesting. I spoke with a man from the public relations office today. Might be a news story. Will let you know if I get any further details.

14MAR1945 LETTER HOME

There was a breath of spring in the air today. And I lucked out when I walked into a real treat tonight. I had a little business with the Captain and went into the house where he is staying. "How'd you like a couple of fried eggs—fresh ones!" At first, I did not believe him, but it was TRUE! He produced two eggs, a skillet, some butter, bread and a fire. They were delicious. Don't know where he procured them, but I am not worrying about that.

18MAR1945 LETTER HOME

Another Sunday. Went to mass at 1600. Father said mass in a little stone church near here. I made use of the DK20 you sent, and Lt. McClung and I developed five rolls of film. Then last night we printed some. Our methods are crude, but the negatives came out very well, although the prints are rough. I'll enclose three of them.

Don't feel badly that your letters are taking so long to get to me. Maybe you should send a V-mail at least once a week; then, if airmail is delayed, we can have a V-mail visit anyway. I still prefer airmail, as V-mail is not very private, but this is an emergency. We've had the delays in mail delivery explained several times. There is so much mail that airmail doesn't even go by air but by boats and trains and trucks. Soon that huge stack from you should arrive.

19MAR1945 Letter Home

Today I saw and heard, in person, Andre Kostelan-etz and Lily Pons! Kostelanetz didn't have his regu-lar orchestra, but an excellent one had been organized using soldier musicians. They were good! I sat in the second row center and lost myself completely in the music. When Lily Pons sang Estrellita, I just couldn't keep the tears out of my eyes.

(U.S. Army Photo)

The program included a Victor Herbert medley, Ave Maria, Begin the Beguine, Rhapsody in Blue, The Warsaw Concerto (played by Theodore Paxton, who had accompanied Nelson Eddy), Holiday for Strings, Stardust, Dixie, Summertime and more. I could have sat there for hours. Truly a super program.

So many fine things in the world, and how it is abused. I've gone through many of these shelled, bombed towns. It's an eerie feeling. Once they were homes, now just ruins. Perhaps the greatest effect is at night, when the lone walls stand out; holes which were once windows stare at you and reveal nothing but a void; rubble piled high in the street; shadowy mountains, and you have to wonder what those piles hide. Burned, charred, blown to bits—can't possibly be repaired. Enuf.

21MAR1945

The captain who was our battalion's S-3 in charge of battalion operations suddenly left the battalion. In a real surprise to me, I was assigned to take his place. I guessed that the decision was based on what was in my personnel file, which HQ had in hand, that indicated each of the numerous training courses I had taken and had also taught. They also had to be aware that I knew many of the officers and men in two of the companies that made up our battalion, I and F Companies, having served as an officer in both. I was no longer commanding "my" 2nd Platoon of F Company but was now responsible for every aspect of the entire 1st Battalion's training when we were off the front lines. In addition, I was in charge of operations planning when the battalion moved to the front, which meant having to anticipate the combat situations the battalion might encounter and design plans and procedures for handling them. I also would have to communicate and explain those plans to all the units and staff officers involved in the action. The S-3 was likewise responsible for the battalion daily reports, something Sergeant Alvis Z. Owen had been doing very ably since 14 December and was going to continue compiling until our last daily report on 8 May. Important for other reasons, my address for mail from home also changed.

Sometime after I joined S-3, Critch and his crews returned to our assembly area with his five brand-new T26E3 tanks, soon to be called the M26 Pershing. On the trip back to Steinhausen on the autobahn, Critch and his crews had thrown out items in the new tanks that they determined they did not need. At the same time, they tried to clean off as much of the tanks' protective Cosmoline as they could. When the platoon arrived, we pitched in to finish removing the Cosmoline; it took quite a while, but we had the time and certainly the enthusiasm.

Once we had them all ready to go, Critch and I each grabbed a crew from Critch's platoon, drove two tanks out to a quarry and fired the 90mm gun. WAHOO! *That* certainly was going to level the playing field. Critch was sticking way out of the turret the first time he fired the 90mm. The muzzle blast blew his helmet off and threw his binoculars around the back of his neck. His comment was "It's too late, but we finally get a gun."

Since his Sherman *Fearless Fosdick* had burned at Kaldenhausen, Critch decided to change the name on his new tank to *Fancy Pants*, a name he had used before that showed a creative beginning of the name with an adjective so he had more options for "F" names.

Don took the photo and asked me to jump in it. I wondered whether naming the tank *Fancy Pants* was Critch's way of poking fun at me now that I was with S-3 and not in a tank. I learned that he gave this name to previous tanks, but I bet that it was a poke at all rear-echelon folks. This photo was probably taken at Steinhausen.

"My M26 General Pershing Heavy Tank *Fancy Pants* with the 90mm gun. It is seen here with the gun facing the rear and cradled in the support for travel. There were only five Pershings in the entire 2nd Armored Division. We finally get a gun! This was to be my last tank. It was lost at Magdeburg." 3rd Platoon, Fox Company, 66th AR, 2nd AD. (DAC)

One of Critch's Pershings coming through the streets of Steinhausen. (FCB)

My only concern with the Pershing, besides not having more of them, was that there were too many belts driving too many parts. My thinking was that those belts could break pretty easily. That being said, the 90mm gun was a great improvement.

24MAR1945

The officers of our battalion played a game of softball with the officers of 2nd Battalion, and we beat them 16–4. Good exercise; it was very good weather for that sort of thing. I also got to take a ride on a motorcycle today; I hadn't forgotten how to handle one. I had to talk to one of the company commanding officers, and there was no other transportation. It was fun.

26MAR1945 LETTER HOME

Cleaned up my paratroop boots today. They really needed it. Still lots of scratch marks and cuts, but serviceable. Spent about an hour on them. Got the saddle soap in Paris at the PX.

27MAR1945

The 1st Battalion of the 66th AR was split up, with I Company attached to the 377th Infantry Regiment and F Company attached to the Maintenance Company. One has to think that F Company was designated to the Maintenance Company due to the losses we'd sustained at Kaldenhausen. Being the new S-3, I would now travel with the 1st Battalion HQ. By the end of the day, the battalion was ready to move out.

At our tactical level, we were not aware of the size of the operation in which we were involved. Strategically, the Allied front stretched 450 miles from the mouth of the Rhine at the North Sea south to the Swiss border. Ninety divisions, including twenty-five armored and five airborne divisions, had been brought up to full strength in preparation to cross the Rhine and make the push to finish the war.

Our part in this massive effort was to encircle the industrial area that stretched along the Ruhr River from Duisburg on the Rhine one hundred miles east to Hamm, Germany. While one corps of the Ninth Army occupied an eleven-mile stretch of the Rhine south of Wesel to block any German counterattacks west, the 2nd AD was to lead the other corps of the Ninth Army over the Rhine in a drive that would go as fast as possible nearly one hundred miles due east. Our objective was to link up with the 3rd AD of the First Army circling up from the south near the city of Paderborn. This maneuver would sever the Ruhr industrial area from the rest of Germany, taking out of production the largest concentration of German industrial capacity left to Nazi Germany.

The push was to be led by our three battalions of the 66th AR.

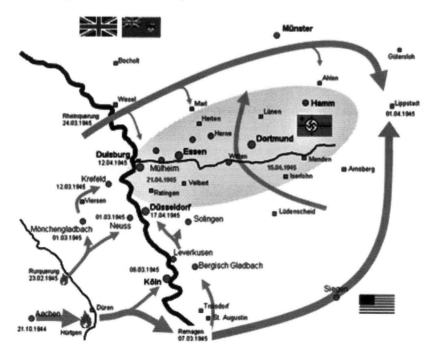

2nd AD to the north of the Ruhr. When the 2nd and 3rd Battalions turned south toward Lippstadt, our 1st Battalion went to the northeast toward Oerlinghausen (not shown on the map).
The Ruhr Industrial Area is lightly shaded.

3rd AD swinging up from the south of the Ruhr and then turning north. The 2nd AD and the 3rd AD met up just west of Paderborn at Lippstadt.

(Map by Kernec, CC BY-SA 3.0, https://commons.wikimedia.org/w/index.php?curid=5648151)

Lt. General William H. Simpson, CO of the 9th Army, . . . began by moving elements of the XIX Corps' 2nd Armored Division, commanded by General I.D. White, into the XVI Corps bridgehead on 28 March with orders to cross the Lippe east of Wesel, thereby avoiding that city's traffic jams. After passing north of the Lippe on 29 March, the 2nd Armored Division broke out late that night from the forward position that the XVIII Airborne Corps had established around Haltern Am See, 12 mi northeast of Dorsten. On the 30th and 31st, the 2nd Armored made an uninterrupted 40 mi drive east to Beckum, cutting two of the Ruhr's three remaining rail lines and severing the autobahn to Berlin. As the rest of the XIX Corps flowed into the wake of this spectacular drive, the First Army was completing its equally remarkable thrust around the southern and eastern edges of the Ruhr. (Edward N. Bedessem, Central Europe *[1996])*

27–28MAR1945

Much of our movement throughout this campaign took place at night to maintain the element of surprise. The Allies controlled the skies, so we were not doing this to avoid the German Luftwaffe, which was virtually nonexistent by this time, but this was a tactic General "Pee Wee" Collier had used with success during the Bulge.

Just before midnight on 27 March, the battalion moved north out of Steinhausen, through Schiefbahn, which we remembered well, to Willich, to the east of Krefeld and then to the west of our battlefield at Kaldenhausen. When we entered Rheinberg, we turned east for an early morning crossing of the pontoon bridge that Company E, 17th Armored Engineer Battalion, had thrown across the Rhine. This feat was done in the record time of under seven hours while under enemy fire from the far shore. We closed in on our assembly area east of the Rhine at 0830 on 28 March, having traveled nearly forty-five miles in just over eight hours.

Troops crossed to the east side of the Rhine on improvised ferries in order to build up a defensive bridgehead there to protect the engineers who were assembling pontoon bridges and make sure German troops could not interfere with the crossing itself. (U.S. Army Signal Corps)

The sky to the east was starting to brighten when the battalion crossed the Rhine at dawn. Our HQ truck followed the Sherman tank in front of us. It was loaded with gear on the back deck. The commanding officer is looking out the turret, with half of the hatch cover swinging out to his right. (FCB)

Our division was one of the largest armored formations in the Allied army. Its tanks, self-propelled guns, armored cars, half-tracks, trucks and looted German vehicles (including bulldozers) made a column seventy-two miles long. It took the column nearly twelve hours to pass a given spot. The 66th AR was leading this long column, putting us ahead of the heavy traffic.

Crossing the Rhine. (U.S. Army Signal Corps)

28MAR1945

At 2200, the 1st Platoon of Company A, 802nd Tank Destroyer Battalion, was attached to our battalion, adding much-appreciated fire support in all of our operations. A half hour later, the battalion moved out and crossed the Lippe Canal and the Lippe River, reaching our next assembly area at 2400.

29MAR1945

The morning was overcast as the 1st Battalion moved forward with orders to follow and support the 2nd and 3rd Battalions. At our first stop, battalion HQ sent out two forward outposts, each manned by a section of tank destroyers from the 802nd and one squad of infantry from Company K, 377th Infantry Regiment. The reconnaissance platoon, having pushed farther to our front, captured fourteen prisoners.

30MAR1945

The 2nd and 3rd Battalions led off an attack at 0600 to seize the crossings of the Dortmund-Elms canal. The 1st Battalion continued to follow in reserve to the rear of the 2nd and 3rd. We passed through Ottmarsbocholt and took over the defenses of Drensteinfurt, where twenty Germans were taken prisoner, one German soldier was killed and one motorcycle was captured. Up to this point, German resistance had been light.

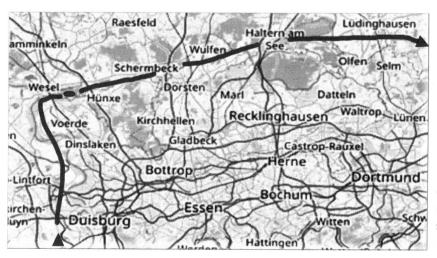

The 2nd AD moved north toward Wesel, crossed the Rhine just south of the city to avoid possible traffic congestion, turned north over the Dortmund-Elms canal and the Lippe River, and headed east, leading the Ninth Army's drive along the northern flank of the Ruhr River basin. The Ruhr flows east from Dortmund and west to Duisburg, where it empties into the Rhine. (Base map © OpenStreetMap, see https://www.openstreetmap.org/copyright)

The HQ truck that I rode in at the start of the operation would have looked very similar to this truck. We carried the battalion's radio equipment, indicated here by the antennae, plus we were hauling what was nicknamed a Ben-Hur trailer, named after its major manufacturer, the Ben-Hur Mfg. Co. The trailer was capable of carrying a one-ton load. (U.S. Army Photo)

The terrain on the east side of the Rhine was very flat, perfect for steady and swift tank maneuvers.

Our battalion was in among the houses of another town when we spotted a German column coming down a road that was only two hundred yards to our right front. Our tanks fired at them, but we were assisted by P-47s that dove on the column, each Thunderbolt dropping its three five-hundred-pound bombs and firing its rockets.

Whether we called in the air support or they were already on patrol over us, I do not know. I can

My vista for taking any photos out the back of the truck was blocked a bit by the Ben-Hur trailer. (U.S. Army Photo)

This is a shot I took from the back of the radio truck. The antenna, visible in the upper right of the photo, is tied down to the Ben-Hur trailer to avoid overhanging branches. The photo is looking west toward the Rhine. (FCB)

We passed several knocked-out armored vehicles. The one in the center of the photo is a Sherman, probably from the 2nd Battalion or 3rd Battalion, which were leading our advance. The vehicle to the left is difficult to recognize, but it has large bogey wheels and no visible turret, meaning it could be a Jagdpanther. Two rectangular shapes on the distant horizon might also be knocked-out vehicles. (FCB)

The P-47s were long gone by the time I got out my camera, but the smoke from the devastated German column and burning buildings was still in the air. (FCB)

A P-47 Thunderbolt had a maximum load of four rockets, three five-hundred-pound bombs and ammunition for its eight .50 caliber machine guns. (U.S. Air Force Photo)

still feel the tremendous impact of one of those five-hundred-pounders dropping on a building next to the German column two football fields from us. We had nothing to worry about from them after that.

We came across an abandoned Panther tank. Someone had written *SHOOT YOUR FADED* on the gun, which made no sense to any of us, but there it was. It did mean that some GI had been there before we got to it. There was no sign of it having been hit, so we put some fuel in it, and we all took a ride. The fact that it had run out of fuel told us a lot about the condition of the enemy.

Our curiosity knew no bounds. I did not know everyone in HQ well yet, but you can tell from the clean uniforms that these men are "rear echelon." I guess I looked that way, too. "Fancy Pants" all of us. (FCB)

31MAR1945

The 2nd Battalion advanced to the town of Ahlen, expecting a major encounter. Aerial reconnaissance had shown a dozen tanks plus a large force of infantry defending the town.

The story got back to us that a middle-aged German military doctor convinced the German troops to withdraw to fight another day, got the civilians to clear the streets and unfurl white sheets out their windows, went west to meet the incoming 2nd Battalion commanding officer and turned over the town without a fight. Seeing that perhaps the will to fight was not very strong in this sector, a communications officer put through a phone call to the German officer in the next large town, Beckum, with the news that the 2nd AD would be on the outskirts of his town by midnight. The added threat that Beckum would be leveled by the 2nd AD's tanks and artillery convinced the German commanding officer to surrender. The 2nd Battalion was in Beckum by midnight.

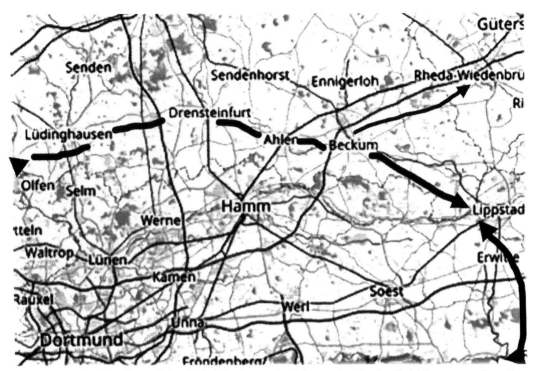

The 2nd and 3rd Battalions of the 66th AR advanced quickly east while the 3rd AD came up from the south. The two units met at Lippstadt, completing the encirclement of the Ruhr industrial region. The city of Hamm essentially marks the geographic eastern terminus of the Ruhr basin. On 1 April, our 1st Battalion neared Beckum and moved from a supporting position behind the two lead battalions to take the lead on a movement to the northeast in the direction of Rheda-Wiedenbrück and Gütersloh. (Base map © OpenStreetMap, see https://www.openstreetmap.org/copyright)

Our 1st Battalion shadowed the two lead battalions throughout the day, steadily moving east. While we advanced, we threw out roadblocks to protect the regiment's flanks, pulled them in and then moved forward again, establishing more roadblocks. At 1300 we relieved all roadblocks and at 1445 stopped operations for the day ten miles north of Lippstadt. We were only one hundred miles from the Elbe River.

In three days we had gone seventy miles from the pontoon bridge that had taken us across the Rhine.

01APR1945

The 3rd Battalion joined the 2nd Battalion in Beckum the next morning and moved southeast to Lippstadt, where early in the afternoon they met up with units from the 3rd AD coming from the south. While the 2nd and 3rd Battalions headed toward Lippstadt, our 1st Battalion broke away from the Ruhr basin and moved northeast toward Rheda-Wiedenbrück and the North German Plain.

When the 2nd AD and the 3rd AD met at Lippstadt, they sealed off the Ruhr industrial complex along with German Field Marshal Walter Model's Army Group B, made up of the 5th Panzer Army and 15th Army. These armies consisted of seven corps made up of nineteen divisions with their support troops and headquarters, a total of three hundred seventeen thousand troops. The fight to clear the Ruhr pocket

General Maurice Rose in Normandy, France, in 1944. (U.S. National Archives and Records Administration)

Field Marshal Walter Model. (Wikimedia Commons)

would end on 18 April with eighteen U.S. divisions from both the Ninth Army and the First Army taking part in the fighting. Over three hundred thousand German troops were taken prisoner along with twenty-four generals. The Germans did not give up easily. The Americans suffered two thousand men killed or missing in action and eight thousand wounded.

General Maurice Rose, commanding officer of the 3rd AD, was killed during the 3rd's sweep north to Lippstadt. He became the eleventh American general killed in action during the war.

Field Marshal Walter Model, commanding officer of German

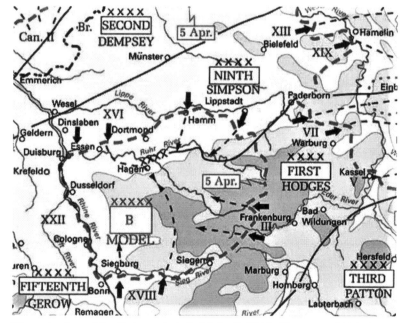

The reduction of the Ruhr pocket, 1–18 April 1945. (Courtesy of U.S. Army Map Service)

Army Group B, which was trapped in the Ruhr pocket, believed that a German field marshal should not surrender; he committed suicide on the afternoon of 21 April, nine days before his Führer killed himself.

10

The Central European Campaign:
The Run to Magdeburg and the Elbe

Within the Battalion HQ Company, I worked with Captain Alvis Z. Owen, who headed the battalion's S-3 group and signed off on the S-3 report on each day's actions. My task was to conduct reconnaissance and gather information about the day's actions both for the S-3 report and to plan the next day's operations. During our move to the Elbe, S-3 staff were so engaged both by day and into the late night that I wrote no letters home and took no photos.

03APR1945

We were now designated Task Force Zeien. Making up the combined arms force were the 1st Battalion, 66th AR (minus F Company), and C Company, 66th AR (minus 1st Platoon), as well as A Company, 119th IR, and A Company, 823rd Tank Destroyer Battalion.

While units of both the First and the Ninth Armies began the tough process of reducing the Ruhr pocket behind us, we moved out to the northeast. At 0530, I Company and infantry of

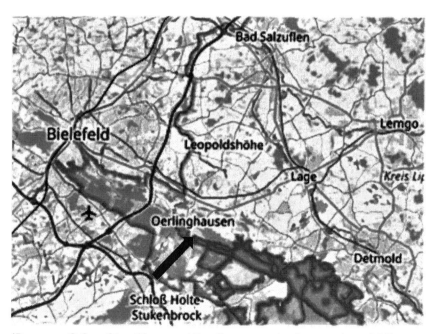

(Base map © OpenStreetMap, see https://www.openstreetmap.org/copyright)

the 119th IR attacked the town of Oerlinghausen, which was located thirty miles northeast of Lippstadt in the Teutoburg Forest.

The wooded heights of the Teutoburg Forest provided excellent positions for defense. Aerial reconnaissance revealed German army barracks and training sites spread throughout the area. The chances that we would be able to advance quickly through towns that had no desire to fight were over.

After the attack we learned the town of Oerlinghausen had been occupied by a small force of Volkssturm ("people's storm") militia units, including two "ear" battalions made up of men who had lost some or all of their hearing. Alongside the Volkssturm militia were a number of very aggressive young recruits of the Hitlerjugend (Hitler Youth) from an SS training battalion led by experienced infantrymen who were officer candidates in the school in the area.

The original plan for the attack on Oerlinghausen was to circle the town to the west, but the wooded, sloping terrain proved too difficult for tanks. The decision was made on the spot to change course and attack due north, directly into the middle of the town.

Postcard of Oerlinghausen showing the wooded and mountainous terrain. (Author's Collection)

Volkssturm with Panzerfausts, which were the predominant weapons of these troops. This anti-tank weapon was easy to manufacture and simple to point and shoot in combat. The only drawback was that the man firing the weapon had to be fairly close to the enemy vehicle to use it effectively. (Photo courtesy of https://warfarehistorynetwork.com/)

In the little town and the pass beyond it, the two forces engaged in a furious hand-to-hand battle. The young SS recruits, most of whom had only been in the Wehrmacht a couple of months, fought bravely and boldly. Their arms were limited—rifles, machine guns and Panzerfausts. But they made good use of them, including knocking out one of their own Tiger tanks by mistake; whereupon the unfortunate culprit was shot by his own enraged comrades. By darkness the Germans had gone over to the counterattack. (Leo Kessler, The Battle of the Ruhr Pocket)

The counterattack was stopped, and the town was cleared by 2200. I Company was hit hard, with one Sherman disabled by a shot from a Panzerfaust, and three tank commanders and the company commander wounded, all immediately evacuated. Twenty German prisoners were turned over to the infantry, while it was estimated that forty enemy were killed.

Starting here and throughout this operation, we ran into groups of the Hitler Youth. I had always thought of them as similar to the Boy Scouts we had in the States, but I was wrong. These boys were fanatics, and they died hard. They had known nothing but the hateful realities Hitler had spewed for their entire lives and knew no other way to serve except to fight as hard as they could, come what may.

That night, the battalion settled in and around Oerlinghausen with Task Force B in the vicinity of the interestingly named Objective "Brem." All vehicles were refueled and resupplied with ammunition.

04APR1945

I was involved in planning what we considered a textbook attack on Müssen, four miles east of Oerlinghausen. We prepared the town by hitting it with a heavy smoke barrage and pushing the tanks through the smoke, with guns loaded and ready for action. As our tanks emerged into the clear air, an elderly lady was standing in the open staring at them. She looked at our tanks quizzically for a moment or two and then told us the Germans were long gone. The battalion daily report read a little differently.

04APR1945 Battalion Daily Report

```
At 0730 the 1st Battalion I/66th AR with A Company/119th IR riding on their tanks,
the light tanks of C Company/66th AR with C Company/119th IR riding on their tanks,
one platoon from the 823rd Tank Destroyer Battalion and the Assault Gun and Mor-
tar Platoon of I/66th AR moved from Oerlinghausen to line of departure and, took
up battle formation for an attack East on MUSSEN, Germany. The attack jumped off at
0800, and the mission was accomplished by 1000. Twenty POWs taken in MUSSEN. No
resistance met.
```

The battalion gathered outside of Müssen at 1000, and by 1300 we were en route to Lemgo. At midnight, we pulled into our assembly area in Aerzen. Our fuel trucks always managed to find us to fill us up in preparation for the next day's move. Our combat efficiency was rated at 80 percent. We had gone thirty miles this day and were now sixty miles from the eastern end of the Ruhr pocket.

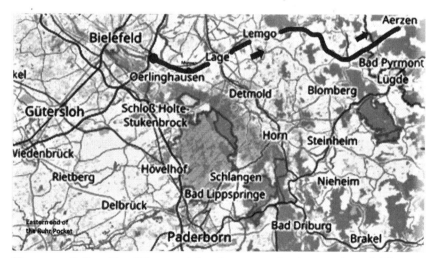

(Base map © OpenStreetMap, see https://www.openstreetmap.org/copyright)

05APR1945

Visibility was poor with clouds and rain as the task force moved out of Aerzen four miles east to Ohr, a town on the Weser River. Our objective was to turn southeast from Ohr and seize and destroy the bridges over the Weser at both Emmern and Kirchhausen. The terrain along the banks of the Weser was

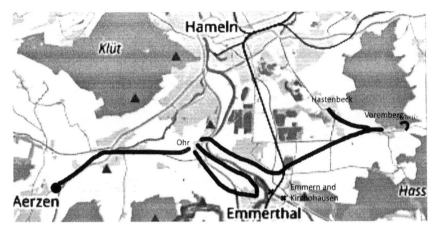

(Base map © OpenStreetMap, see https://www.openstreetmap.org/copyright)

flat, allowing I Company/66th AR with infantry on board to attack with two platoons of tanks abreast and one in support. One section of tank destroyers was on each flank of the advancing platoons, with the light tanks of C Company on the right flank and the assault gun platoon following in the rear. The mortar platoon was deployed to fire on the objective. By 1045 we had accomplished our mission, destroying both bridges. We met with no resistance.

That afternoon, we moved the three miles back north to Ohr, crossed the Weser and attacked southeast along the river to clear our flank and rear. The attack turned east to Voremberg, where high ground farther east was outposted by a platoon of Shermans and a platoon of infantry. The rest of the force moved back to secure the town of Hastenbeck and spend the night. During the course of the day, one light tank of C Company/66th AR was lost to a mine in Ohr, and six POWs were taken in Voremberg.

06APR1945

The weather continued to be cloudy with rain. We were able to slow down a bit, staying in Hastenbeck until 1300. We moved a short distance north to Afferde, which we all noted was a suburb of Hameln of Pied Piper fame, and then east to Bessingen, six miles outside of Hameln. We outposted the town and remained there for the night.

For the entire month of April thus far, for the line on our S-3 daily report that asked for the location of adjacent and supporting troops, we could only fill in "Not applicable." We were moving so fast that we could only suppose we had friendlies to our flanks, but we did not know for sure, and certainly we did not know what units those friendlies might be.

07APR1945

The late start the day before proved to be a fluke. We got up early, moved out at 0630 and marched eighteen miles northeast to Schulenberg, closing in on the assembly area at 1000. At noon, a platoon of light tanks moved two miles east and then northeast across the Leine River to Barnten, meeting no resistance, although they did receive 88 fire from the north and northeast, showing that the enemy still had some bite.

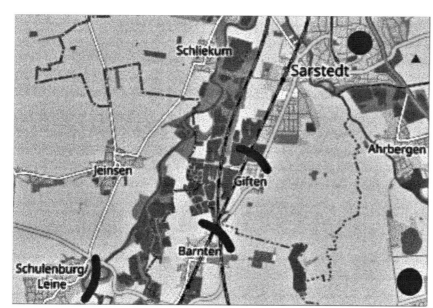

Task Force A's position in Sarstedt.

Platoon of Shermans and a platoon of infantry at Giften.

Platoon of light tanks at Barnten.

Giesen, just off the map to the right, where Task Force B was positioned.

(Base map © OpenStreetMap, see https://www.openstreetmap.org/copyright)

At 1330, a platoon of Shermans and a platoon of infantry passed through our troops in Barnten and moved another two miles north into Giften; this unit came under artillery fire but otherwise met no resistance.

The remaining elements of Task Force Zeien remained in Schulenberg and were on alert status as a mobile reserve for Task Force A, which was located to our northeast. Outposts were established on all roads leading from the town.

We were billeted in a house in Schulenberg for a couple of days while the battalion moved northeast to Barnten and Giften. Doc O'Neill and I were on the second floor, with the CP (command post) downstairs. Living in the house was an old woman in her nineties. She was blind and her daughter was taking care of her. Normally we moved all civilians out of the houses we occupied for security reasons, but we allowed them to stay . . . both being elderly and very weak.

In the upstairs living room was a glassed-in case with shelves covered with small art objects. Four glass figurines of ballet dancers caught my eye immediately. I was admiring the statuettes when the daughter passed, and I remarked something like "Sehr schön" ("Very nice"), pointing to the dolls.

Without hesitation, she asked whether I would like to have them. I could not resist the offer and said yes. She then said, "Alles sowieso kaput" ("It's all over anyway"). I wrapped them as carefully as I could and took them with me. Unfortunately, I did not have a chance to send them home until August, and they took some hits along the way, but nothing that was irreparable.

(FCB)

The Messerschmitt Me 262 was the world's first operational jet-powered fighter aircraft. Although design work started before World War II, production delays kept the aircraft from seeing action until mid-1944. The Me 262 was faster and more heavily armed than any Allied fighter, including the British jet-powered Gloster Meteor that was introduced nine months after the Me 262. The jet served as a light bomber, fighter, and reconnaissance aircraft, plus there was an experimental night fighter version in the works. A total of 1,430 Me 262s were built, although only two hundred were ever operational at one time. Because of fuel consumption, they could remain airborne only between sixty and ninety minutes. Pilots claimed a total of 542 Allied aircraft shot down. (Wikimedia Commons)

We had some German air activity while in Schulenberg, something that had not happened very often lately. I was up on one of our Shermans when I heard a plane going over. I could tell it was not one of ours, as it was making a sound I had not heard before. As soon as I spotted it, I fired the .50 caliber machine gun that was mounted on the tank's turret, but the plane was gone before the gun even started chattering—a waste of bullets. I'd never seen anything that fast in the air before. Turned out it was an Me 262 fighter jet.

We had considered one house for our CP and actually stayed in it for a couple of hours, but then HQ personnel found the house occupied by the elderly women, which was larger and more suitable for the CP. We moved there and set up our equipment. Not long after arriving at the new site, the house we had been in just a short while before took a direct hit by a German bomb, completely destroying the house and killing the German civilians inside. Our CP could very easily have been in that house.

Doc also was blown through a door by a second bomb that struck a building nearby, but he wasn't hurt at all . . . just bruised and covered with a bit with plaster.

Captain "Doc" O'Neill (FCB)

The house where we set up our CP in Schulenberg. One of our men is repairing the hole in the roof, probably with the help of another inside. The vehicle parked by the building appears to be Doc O'Neill's M3 half-track ambulance. About fifteen thousand standard M3s were produced during the war. In addition, more than thirty-eight thousand variant units including ambulances were manufactured. (FCB)

Another view of the house we used as our CP. One of our motorcycle messengers is with his Harley-Davidson bike cleaning part of the motor, while Sergeant Evans, our half-track driver, makes like one of Bill Mauldin's cartoons from behind the tree. We were all dirty and unshaven. I am almost positive that I left my dog tags hanging on the bedpost at this house after taking a helmet bath. (FCB)

We had not seen or heard any large German bombers in a while, and they would have dropped loads with multiple bombs. Since the Me 262A-2a Sturmvogel (Storm Bird) could carry two 550-pound bombs, we figured it likely a Me 262 had dropped both its bombs on the town. It might even have been the one I shot at.

08APR1945

The weather was clear today with scattered clouds and good visibility. For the first time since 3 April we noted adjacent and supporting troops on our S-3 report. Task Force A was six miles to our northeast in Sarstedt, and Task Force B was six miles across open fields directly to our east in Giesen. I was not aware which 66th AR elements composed those two task forces, but my old company, Company F, with Lieutenant Critchfield and his platoon of Pershing tanks and Lieutenant Trinen, was in one of them.

We remained in Schulenberg on one-hour alert until 1730, when we were ordered to move ten miles east through the Klein Forest just north of Giesen, cross the Hildesheim Canal and take the town of Harsum. HQ already knew that the bridge over the canal was blown, so elements of the 17th Engineers with bridge-building equipment were attached to our task force. A platoon of our Shermans provided covering fire as our infantry crossed the canal in M2 assault boats provided by the engineers and established a bridgehead on the eastern bank of the canal.

U.S. Engineers using an M2 assault boat in Europe. (U.S. Army Photo)

The main balance of the infantry from A Company/119th IR followed those lead troops and pushed on to capture the town of Harsum, while the tanks of the 3rd Platoon remained at the crossing site to cover the bridge-building operations. The rest of the task force remained in the Klein Forest for the night.

At 2100, F Company/66th AR reverted to 1st Battalion control with C Company/66th AR returned to our command the next morning at 0600. Nearly the entire 1st Battalion was under united command again with Critch and Trinen back in the fold, but this situation would not last long enough for me to even talk to them.

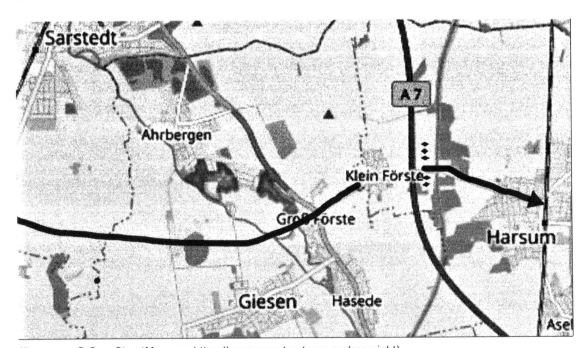

(Base map © OpenStreetMap, see https://www.openstreetmap.org/copyright)

09APR1945

We woke up in Klein Forest to scattered clouds with good visibility. By 1230, the 1st Battalion and its attachments were assembled back at Schulenberg and remained for the night. That evening, our next day's objectives were set, and at 2300 HQ got busy. Based on those objectives, the decision was made to assemble our units into three task forces: Task Force Zeien was assigned three platoons of tanks, a company of infantry, both a mortar platoon and an assault gun platoon, one platoon of tank destroyers and my element, the HQ Company of the 1st Battalion/66th AR. F Company/66th AR joined Task Force Owen, along with a company of infantry and one platoon of towed 57mm anti-tank guns. Task Force Herlong consisted of a company of light tanks, a company of infantry, a mortar platoon and a machine gun platoon, one platoon of towed 57mm anti-tank guns and the HQ Company of the 1st Battalion/119th IR. Each task force was prepared for any contingency.

The U.S. M1 57mm anti-tank gun was modeled very closely on the British six-pounder anti-tank gun. Two six-pounders were imported from England for study, and the gun's design was modified to U.S. manufacturing practices and standards in order to produce the weapon for Great Britain under Lend-Lease. Production began in May 1941, and approximately sixteen thousand were made through 1945, although none made it to the U.S. troops until the end of the North Africa campaign in early 1943. The gun was light, easy to maneuver on the battlefield, could fire fifteen rounds per minute and fired both armor-piercing ammunition and a high-explosive shell, although limited production of HE rounds relegated the gun by necessity to an anti-tank weapon. The 57mm armor-piercing shell was able to penetrate two inches of armor at one hundred yards, but it was ineffective against larger German tanks. A Panzer IV's frontal armor, for example, was 3.1 inches thick. One drawback was that the gun had a horrendous recoil, unlike other U.S. artillery that had built-in recoil mechanisms, making it less popular with the troops. Still, the weapon had a long life, being used in the Korean War and seeing its last action during the 1971 war between India and Pakistan.

Our officers and men were getting good at our craft. Each of us had acquired enough combat experience by this time to recognize what force levels and types of units needed to be teamed in order to ensure that the next day's objectives were achieved. The ability to reorganize and combine units fluidly and rapidly into task forces keyed to reaching those objectives was one of the strengths of our organization. We were now an extremely efficient fighting machine, moving long distances every day with the flexibility to take on whatever the enemy had in mind.

10APR1945

The day was clear with good visibility, perfect conditions for the day's operations. At 0900 all three task forces headed south out of Schulenberg with Task Force Zeien in the lead. By 1300 we had moved thirty miles and our lead elements attacked the town of Reppner, where they were met by Panzerfausts and artillery fire. Within an hour, the objective was taken, along with forty prisoners.

Task Force Owen moved in to Reppner to defend the town, while Task Force Zeien moved southeast to the next objective, Lebenstedt. By 1500 Task Force Zeien was attacking Lebenstedt, where it encountered stiff resistance from Panzerfausts and artillery fire, knocking out a full battery of five 88s mounted on

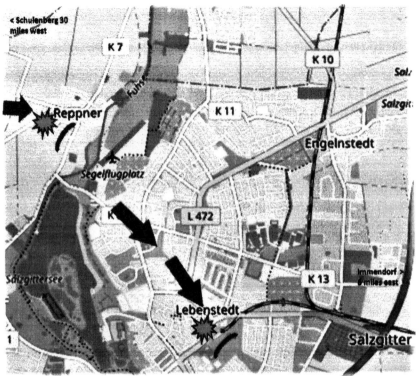

Immendorf, six miles east, was to be our next objective.

The gray and white dashed line marks the railroad. Our task force ran into the railcar-mounted 88s at the rail yard on the spur, turning to the left.

(Base map © OpenStreetMap, see https://www.openstreetmap.org/copyright)

railroad cars in the rail yard near the center of the town, destroying five wheeled vehicles and taking 150 prisoners. At 2000, Task Force Owen reinforced Task Force Zeien. The town was secured for the night, our units having taken no casualties and traveling an estimated thirty-five miles that day.

Among its many uses, the 88mm gun was mounted on railway cars and used in an anti-aircraft role. In some cases, full railway batteries were positioned in the all-important railroad yards to guard against Allied bombers. This is what we ran into in Lebenstedt. (Photo courtesy of https://www .defensemedianetwork.com/)

11APR1945

Our battalion was moving so fast that the line on our daily report asking the location of our front lines continued to read, "Not applicable." We had another clear day with fair visibility. We moved out of Lebenstedt at 0600 heading south and east, with the objective of circling a large factory complex and cutting its main roads to its east. We could see the smokestacks as we moved east.

The layout of the roads and the terrain stopped our advance at 0900 just to the west and within sight of the complex.

We had no choice but to gather into an assembly area and await orders. At 1600, we moved out, but instead of circling the factories as originally planned, we passed through them.

Visible on the horizon are the factories that were our objective for the day. (FCB)

We were lucky, as only two days before our advance on the factory, a brutal battle had taken place there when Task Force B ran into a defensive belt of dual-purpose 88s defending the factory. An effective flank attack and artillery barrage silenced the 88s, with sixty-seven of the guns destroyed or captured. It had to have been hot work.

F Company with attached infantry led the way into the now much quieter factory and captured three hundred POWs and destroyed four 88s. More and more, the POWs we captured were non-German workers. We had to treat them all as POWs, however, as German soldiers might be concealing themselves as laborers.

Our HQ Company followed F Company across the open fields toward the factories and entered the complex, which turned out to be a huge steelworks. In one building, we saw long steel tubes stacked around the room, strikingly bright in appearance and probably stainless steel. We assumed these were for making gun barrels, their length suggesting they had been destined to become 88s. The sixty-seven 88s that had been captured or destroyed by Task Force B might very well have been cast and assembled here.

It indicated to all of us that Germany had been capable to the very end of manufacturing the necessary weapons of war.

We soon learned that we'd entered the "Reichswerke Hermann Göring." We found out later that it was part of an industrial conglomerate in which Göring had had a majority stake since 1938. This large

Hermann Göring visiting one of his factories. (Wikimedia Commons)

An aerial view of part of the Reichswerke Hermann Göring factory that we entered, located between Salzgitter and Immendorf. This photo was taken by the "Trolley Mission," a U.S. Army Air Force flight mission carried out in May 1945. It was also known as the "Low Level Tour," the "Low Level Mission" or the "Cook's Tour." Aerial photos were taken with the express purpose of showing German cities at "zero hour" just as World War II ended. (Photo courtesy of U.S. Army Air Force Trolley Mission)

mining factory with its sixteen blast furnaces and two coke plants was a regular target of the Royal Air Force and U.S. Army Air Force. We saw numerous bunkers within the complex that were no doubt frequently used as bomb shelters.

The conglomerate was dismantled by the Allies in 1945 and rebuilt with seven blast furnaces in 1949. One of the original blast furnaces from 1945, number 6, is still standing.

We got word that elements of the 66th AR had reached the banks of the Elbe, sixty miles ahead of us.

12APR1945

The weather closed in on us with an overcast sky, and visibility was only fair, but considering how light resistance had been lately, the poorer visibility did not concern us. At 0400, Task Force Zeien moved from the Immendorf area eight miles east to Wolfenbüttel, where we captured 150 POWs. We took over the defense of the town, while F Company stayed behind in Immendorf to guard the steel mill complex and control the civilian population.

We also learned that President Roosevelt had passed away.

Letter Home

The President's passing came as quite a surprise, even though it was known his health was bad. He had a rugged time of it.

13APR1945

We were ordered to stay in Wolfenbüttel, with the mission of guarding supply dumps and hospitals while controlling the civilian population, which now included liberated slave laborers who had been held in the three concentration camps in Salzgitter. The camps were established by the SS to provide slave labor for the Hermann Göring Reichswerke. The prisoners were overjoyed to be liberated, and our job was to prevent them from looting and rioting. Hard to blame them, though. F Company remained back in Immendorf. For once, we did not go anywhere. That night, our units were again divided to form three combined-arms task forces: Zeien, Owen and Herlong.

14APR1945

A big day for the battalion; we were ordered to move fifty-two miles to circle east of the major city of Magdeburg, move ten miles south of the city and force a crossing of the Elbe River in the vicinity of Schönebeck. The only German forces west of the Elbe River were in Magdeburg. At 0400, Task Force Zeien took the lead, followed by Task Forces Owen and Herlong. At 0900, the column received orders to halt, coil off the road and await orders. At 1100, we received orders to move into the towns of Wellen and Ochtmersleben, which was accomplished by 1200. Our objective changed as units of Combat Command B driving from the south were now slated to attempt the crossing of the Elbe. Our new orders, received at 1730, now had us moving southwest to set up a main line of resistance three miles east of Magdeburg. We moved into an assembly area at Hohendodeleben while a reconnaissance unit scouted our new positions east of the town. We moved into those positions at 2000. Tanks moved into positions prepared by bulldozers, and infantry, mortars and assault guns provided support. Fields of fire facing east at Magdeburg were laid out.

Our light tanks of C Company outposted Hohendodeleben to our rear and served as a mobile reserve.

Initial positions west of Ottersleben on Hill 125.

Black line of train tracks running east–west–north of Sudenburg marked the 30th ID/2nd AD boundary.

Central Magdeburg

Elbe River (Courtesy U.S. Army Map Service)

Our southern flank tied in with the 3rd Battalion/119th IR of the 30th "Old Hickory" Division, our northern flank with the 2nd Battalion/41st Armored Infantry Regiment.

15APR1945

All roads out of Magdeburg west of the Elbe were blocked. CCB had succeeded in securing a bridgehead across the Elbe on the morning of 31 April in an attempt to cut Magdeburg off from the east, but due to enemy pressure the bridgehead had to be abandoned on 14 April. The Germans could still retreat east over the bridges of the town, but our control of the air made retreat over the bridges very difficult.

At 1700, F Company/66th AR (minus one platoon) and A Company/119th IR moved toward Magdeburg to shorten their lines and concentrate their fire.

15APR1945 Letter Home

At last an opportunity for another written "visit." We have been quite busy and very much on the go, but no doubt you know that from the newspapers. We've really covered some ground seeing Germany. The thing that has struck me most forcefully is the sight of the thousands of slave laborers. Russians, Poles, Czechs, French, Hungarians, prisoners of war, all displaced persons. Taken from their homes to work for the Germans. I saw a prison where political prisoners as well as criminals had been kept. The men looked more like corpses than living persons. I saw a guillotine room where 21 men had been executed in one day. The Nazis had removed the guillotine itself, but the base supports for the blade's frame were still there. Plus, there was a stack of crude coffins along the wall. It is as though you had stepped into a movie which portrays the filthy horrors of the middle ages—unbelievable.

I realize that we have been moving very rapidly, and we have been getting some bags of mail, but still none of mine has arrived. I can't understand it. Sending off some more copies of "Stars and Stripes" today with a photo taken of the group that took the tour of Paris standing in front of the Arc de Triomphe.

My new position is really all right. To my surprise, I am still here in battalion headquarters. Our battalion commander, Major Zeien, under whom I am directly working, is tops. Incidentally, there's a possibility that his picture may appear in "Life" magazine—had one of their photographers with us one day. I didn't believe this job would last. Never can tell, but right now I'm here.

16APR1945

Staff from the 30th ID negotiated with the staff of the German troops holding the city and the mayor in an effort to get them to surrender. The Germans were advised that the city was surrounded and that surrender was a logical option. It was made clear that the only alternative to surrender would be that the city would be bombed and attacked. At 1200, the mayor communicated the refusal to surrender, whether because he was a Nazi Party member or "urged" by an SS officer.

After the refusal, our division commander, General I. D. White, called on the air force to bomb Magdeburg, but the air force was not able to mount the attack. Instead, General White called on his divisional artillery to shell the town and the autobahn bridge over the Elbe in preparation for the coming attack, while his troops remained in position.

17APR1945

At 0100, I Company/66th AR was detached and moved to the right to join 2nd Battalion/41st AIR. At 0200, orders were received for the 30th ID and the 2nd AD to attack the city. The 30th ID was to attack from the north of the city, while the 2nd AD attacked from the west and southwest. Elements of the 119th IR of the 30th "Old Hickory" Division would provide our infantry support and were on our flank. We'd worked closely with the 30th ID before and were glad they were on our flank.

A ground haze made our visibility poor and obscured the targets on the ground, delaying the airstrikes until it cleared, but the bombing run was still on. Contradictory orders to some units caused confusion as troops were ordered to both seek shelter during the bombing and move forward to their departure lines. We backed up to get out of the bombers' way.

At 0900, our force was divided into two attack groups. The north force was made up of the 1st and 2nd Platoons of F Company/66th AR with Captain Henry Johnson back and in command, tank destroyers, mortars, a company of infantry and my HQ element. Lieutenant Critchfield's 3rd Platoon of Pershings from F Company/66th AR (including *Fancy Pants*), tank destroyers, a platoon of light tanks and a company of infantry constituted the south force. Two platoons of light tanks were to follow the two attack groups a kilometer to the rear, patrolling and blocking roads that led into the flanks.

The city of Magdeburg burning from the shelling and bombardment that preceded the American attack. (U.S. Army Photo)

We all moved west off the main line of resistance, away from Magdeburg, to distance ourselves from the aerial bombardment—the north force to Hohendodeleben, the south force to Schleibnitz. The bombers roared over us starting at 1145, with the massive bombardment continuing until 1515.

At 1445, we stepped off our attack. Both attack groups moved east using the main highway entering Magdeburg from the southwest as the axis of advance, with north force north of the highway and south force to the south. The infantry climbed on the tanks to ride as far as they could go before enemy fire would force them to dismount.

At 1530, both groups entered the outskirts of Magdeburg and immediately met stiff resistance from Panzerfausts, mortars and small arms fire, all the infantry jumping to the ground while the tanks

Tanks from the 2nd AD and infantry from the 30th ID on the outskirts of Magdeburg. (U.S. Army Photo)

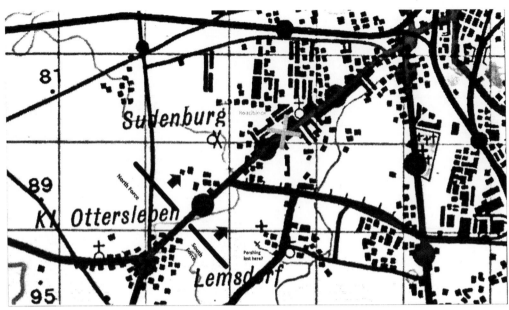

Gray cross marks roadblock.

Critch loses a Pershing.

(Author's Collection)   [Start line.]

opened up. The infantry was able to advance, albeit slowly, as each house had to be cleared. Our tanks followed in close support, ready to use their firepower when called upon.

The advance hit a brick wall, literally, at 1630. The advance came to a standstill when it ran into a strongly defended roadblock. Paving blocks stretched from the houses on each side of the street to a gap in the middle of the street, with a streetcar pulled across the gap to complete the roadblock. Heavy fire of Panzerfausts, mortars and small arms protected the roadblock, forcing our infantry to stay in cover.

A tank dozer moved immediately to the front to push the blocks out of the way, but two enemy shots hit the arm that lifts the blade. No one was injured, but enough damage was done to the dozer that it had to withdraw. An alternative plan was devised; the light tanks of C Company were directed to come forward, swing around the left of the main axis of advance and come in behind the roadblock, but they ran into another roadblock and were unable to proceed. B and C Companies/119th IR consolidated their position in front of that roadblock and sealed our left flank from any German attacks from the north.

A Company/119th IR, in heavy and close fighting, finally cleared the roadblock at 1930. The roadblock was broken down so the tanks could follow, but as the force advanced, there was little lessening of the heavy enemy fire.

The Germans had constructed numerous roadblocks throughout the city, and in practice, few of those roadblocks were taken frontally. Attacks from the flanks and rear were required to take them out, and the roads had to be cleared to move the supporting firepower of the tanks forward. This was primarily an infantryman's fight, with the tanks having a supporting role. When the infantry spotted a definite target, they would call on a tank to come forward and take it out. A major role of the tanks was to the rear, securing areas that the infantry had already cleared by guarding intersections against German attempts to attack the advance from the flanks or from behind.

The defenders had to rely on Panzerfausts, rifles and anti-tank guns, with a few mortars to their rear lobbing high-explosive rounds in support. The Germans did not use artillery when defending the streets, except for several multipurpose 88mm anti-aircraft artillery. There were reports of rounds from 88s ricocheting through the streets. Artillery only came into play when our advancing troops got closer to the Elbe, with guns positioned on the east bank of the river firing on us.

Lieutenant Don Critchfield (center, without helmet) and the crew from *Fancy Pants*. (DAC)

By 2016, the sun was setting, and soon the fighting in Magdeburg was taking place completely in the dark. The main road entering Magdeburg from the southwest continued to serve as our axis of advance, with the south force moving across flat terrain crossed by streams that formed occasional ponds. As Lieutenant Critchfield pushed his platoon of Pershings forward, Critch's driver, unable to see in the dark, drove *Fancy Pants* directly into one of those ponds. Everyone got out of the tank safely, with Critch taking over another Pershing as the command tank, but *Fancy Pants* was not going to see any more action for a while.

At 2100, phase line 9 was reached and both forces held up, consolidating their positions and establishing eight roadblocks and posting tanks, tank destroyers and anti-tank guns at each roadblock, with troops from the 119th IR in support. Mortars were set up back from the line in a position to provide fire support, zeroed in on each of the roadblocks. All attacks ended at 2200.

We got word back at battalion HQ that Captain Johnson, F Company commanding officer, had been killed. I was assigned to move up and identify his body. As I approached where I thought his body was reported to be, I encountered a crowd of quiet civilians. I asked them, "Where is the American officer?" in German, but no one responded. They were afraid, no doubt, that they would be blamed for his death.

I pulled out my .45 and, waving it in the air, asked again in a louder voice. At this several of them pointed to a building nearby. I entered the building and went down into the basement. The captain had been carried there and was still wearing his flight jacket, which I knew he had been very proud of. The jacket had been ripped open, the buttons ripped off and sulfa poured into the wound, no doubt by a medic who had tried to help him, but it was no use.

Afterward, I found out that Captain Johnson had pulled his tank between two buildings for protection as he guided F Company forward. At some point the lieutenant in the infantry unit supporting F Company moved forward to clear the enemy troops out of the buildings ahead. The lieutenant had not advanced far into the street when he got wounded.

He fell directly to the front of Captain Johnson's tank. Captain Johnson saw him, got out of his tank, and tried to move the lieutenant into cover. The captain had to have been spotted by a Panzerfaust team, which the Germans used primarily as an anti-tank weapon but also employed in an antipersonnel role.

The Germans fired, the shot hitting near the two officers, blasting fragments into the air and killing Captain Johnson. The infantry lieutenant survived and had the highest praise for Captain Johnson as an efficient combat officer, expressing his deepest sorrow that he had been killed.

I had heard that Captain Johnson's father, a colonel, had visited the unit earlier in the year and spoke to Sergeant De Pratt, saying, "You take care of my boy for me, Sergeant." The first sergeants were all well respected. They were buffers between the troops and the commanding officers, acting like mother hens.

We all mourned the loss of Captain Johnson, even more so as it happened less than twenty-four hours before the fighting ended for our battalion. I knew him well, having served under him at Schiefbahn and Kaldenhausen, and he had written up my Silver Star recommendation. Captain Johnson had been planning to get married in Paris after the war. He had arranged for his bride's wedding dress to be made from a parachute. A good man.

At the end of the day, we had killed forty of the enemy and taken one hundred POWs. Our losses: one medium tank with a 75mm gun knocked out by a Panzerfaust, five enlisted men of F Company wounded, and F Company Commander Captain Henry Johnson killed in action. The medium tank was reclaimed. Apparently word of the loss of *Fancy Pants* did not get to S-3 in time to be included in the daily report. In fact, I did not even know that Critch's tank was out of the action until the next day. I was glad to hear there had been no injuries. Our combat efficiency was at 80 percent.

18APR1945

The weather was holding clear with fair visibility. At 0600, attacks were resumed on the city using the same axis of advance as the previous day. The light tanks of C Company and the infantry of the 119th IR remained in their position to the north of the advance to stop any German movement from that sector. Opposition to our advance had lessened, with only some Panzerfaust and sniper fire from houses.

As we closed on the river, the enemy demolished the bridges to the east bank of the Elbe. It is not clear how many German troops were able to escape the city before the bridges were blown, but many of the enemy were cut off from the east bank and isolated in the city. It is possible that many did not want to escape but favored capture by the Americans rather than continue in a losing battle.

On 18 April, this Sherman from our division, heavily sandbagged for protection against Panzerfaust fire, advanced through Magdeburg. The casual poses of the tankers indicate that the fighting was over. (U.S. Army Photo)

At 1000, forward elements reached another objective and were ordered to push on to the railroad east of that objective. At 1100, the railroad line was reached and the position consolidated, with orders to hold until further notice.

The 3rd Platoon of C Company/66th AR patrolled in the rear of the forward elements on each flank.

By 1245, the capture of Magdeburg was complete.

At 1500, our tanks moved a short distance south into an assembly area in Hopfengarten, closing in at 1540. Patrols were sent out immediately, each patrol consisting of two jeeps with three men in each. Patrolling was kept up through the night.

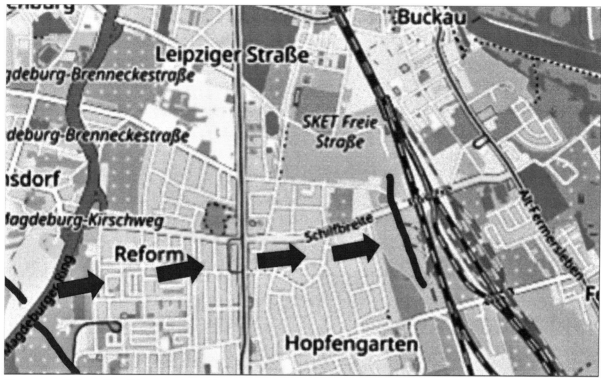

(Base map © OpenStreetMap, see https://www.openstreetmap.org/copyright)

Pershing tanks of the 2nd AD rolling into Magdeburg.
To my knowledge, Don Critchfield's platoon was the only
platoon in the 2nd AD with Pershings, so this is more
than likely his 3rd Platoon, F Company/66th AR. (U.S.
Army Photo)

Our mission was successfully accomplished.
We had taken all of our objectives, two hundred
POWs were taken and an estimated twenty enemy
were killed. Our losses for the day were one enlisted
man in F Company wounded. In total, twenty-
six hundred prisoners had been taken and large
amounts of supplies captured. Magdeburg had
been completely reduced through the combined
efforts of the 2nd AD and the 30th ID.

11

The Occupation of Germany Begins

In 1944, the Allies knew that they were going to win the war. With that expected outcome in mind, the United States, Great Britain, France and the Soviet Union met and worked out an agreement to divide Germany into four occupation zones. Berlin was to be divided into four zones as well, one for each occupying power.

One result of this agreement was that General Eisenhower ordered U.S. forces to stop advancing east once they reached the Elbe River, which was located in what would become the Russian zone. Very likely another factor in his decision to stop at the Elbe was that the Western Allies were not in a position to force their way into Berlin. The Russians had two and a half million troops approaching Berlin from the east, while the United States had only twenty-five divisions, which were covering an immense front and still heavily engaged with the Germans.

When the U.S. Ninth Army reached the Elbe, Lieutenant General William H. Simpson, its commander, asked permission to continue the drive east to capture the German capital, but Eisenhower gave the order to hold on the Elbe.

Ike turned the British Second Army north to the Baltic Sea, and the U.S. First Army southeast toward what was conjectured to be a heavily fortified redoubt in Bavaria that could be the possible site of the Nazis' final stand.

By mid-April, the 2nd AD had units across the Elbe and was primed to get to Berlin. We were told that our units were to withdraw from those bridgeheads and cross back to the west of the Elbe. The Russians were to be "allowed to liberate" Berlin. We were not very happy about this news. Giving up real estate we'd captured was not in the 2nd AD's book of operations, although returning to the west bank of the Elbe probably saved the lives of many American soldiers. In July, when we occupied the American sector of Berlin, the locals told us they were hoping that we, the Americans, would take Berlin. They feared how the Russians would treat them.

Although the war was still on, the Elbe River decision meant that we had little fighting to do. The occupation of Germany actually began now, two weeks before the official end of the war. The 1st Battalion/66th AR was ordered to return to the Immendorf area, where we had just been a long week before.

19APR1945

Message from Headquarters, 2nd Armored Division, Office of the Division Commander:

We are now across the Elbe. No defensive positions, behind which the enemy could reform to halt the Allied advance, remain. For him the war is finally and irrevocably lost, and our victory has been made possible by your blood and sweat. No unit has written a brighter chapter in the history of this war. It remains only to add the final page to that chapter. I know you will make it as brilliant as the rest—a fitting climax to two and a half long years of campaign.
—Major General I. D. White

At 0300, a light tank and a jeep with an officer in charge patrolled routes that we would use to the west to return to the Immendorf area. The patrol returned at 0800.

The local two-jeep patrols continued throughout the night and day, with nothing to report.

At 1600, guards were posted in the railroad yards, where large amounts of captured German supplies were located, and at a nearby tank factory. Our morale was high. At the end of the day, our combat efficiency was 90 percent and our mission accomplished.

Critch and I took a short walk from our assembly area in Hopfengarten and took photos of each other. That had been a nice house behind us. A great deal of work was going to have to be done to put Germany back together.

(FCB)

(DAC)

20APR1945

With clear weather and good visibility, we moved west out of Magdeburg at 1130, eventually dividing our force to occupy and patrol three towns that were located just south of Immendorf, where the Reichswerks were located: Lobmachtersen, Vienenburg and Ringelheim. All units closed into their new areas at 1800. Our HQ Company billeted in Lobmachtersen for the night. Patrols were sent out continuously in each town, looking for any installations that needed guarding, enforcing the blackout and maintaining order. The rest of the division

Here is one of the camps we passed on the way to Immendorf. I am not sure whether this was a POW camp or one set up for the liberated forced laborers. (FCB)

went to Braunschweig (Brunswick), seven miles to our north. We moved over seventy miles this day.

As we drove from Magdeburg to Immendorf, we passed German POWs moving along the side of the road or halted and waiting to continue the march west.

Our driver, Sergeant Fisher, standing with the camp in the background. (FCB)

One of our HQ jeeps pulling a trailer while driving by the camp. (FCB)

21APR1945

OUR FRONT LINES: Not Applicable.

At 0700 we were alerted for immediate movement to Wolfenbüttel, ten miles to our north. At 0900, the 1st Battalion/66th AR (- F Company) moved north to Wolfenbüttel, effecting all reliefs by 1230. We took over the mission of guarding supply dumps, factories, railroad yards and providing security within the town, running continuous patrols throughout the night. F Company stayed behind to garrison Lobmachtersen, Ringelheim and Vienenburg with a tank platoon positioned in each town. Two POWs were taken in Vienenburg. We only traveled an estimated twelve miles today.

(Base map © OpenStreetMap, see https://www.open streetmap.org/copyright)

Entering Wolfenbüttel; taken from our jeep. (FCB)

21APR1945 Letter Home

I'm in a very high-ceilinged room with electric lights, easy chairs and running water in this very big house. Unaccustomed luxuries. Besides that, I have before me a hot cup of coffee. I filled the jug at suppertime at the company kitchen. Time is 2135.

Made a deal with a fellow the other day, with the result that I now have a very fine camera, a Rolleiflex. Uses 120-size film; that size film is readily available. Chaplain Bolin has some, so I'm all set to take lots of pictures. 620 size, the size your little folding camera uses, is very hard to find here. I am still in Battalion headquarters. I enjoy the work very much and have a good Sergeant Major and corporal clerk. Both know their jobs and are hard workers. Reminds me of my old job while in training before I went to OCS.

V-mail is the only thing coming through to me. I just received a Christmas card from Al Nichols—a Christmas card just arriving? I am enclosing six negatives. I sent the prints from them before and hope they arrived. That air mattress and Boy Scout sleeping bag you sent me are serving me well. I have sheets inside of it now. Feels good. Heard mass the other day. Mass tomorrow, too, at 11:00. S'good.

I quote from your v-mail: "Such good news coming over the radio; wonder if you too are in this great push?" Rest assured that when any pushing is done, the 2nd Armored is always in on it. We certainly were, as you probably know from the papers.

(FCB)

Second Letter Home of April 21?

Coming at you again via the tzpewriter . . . and before we go anz further let me explain the letter "z" which will crop up where it should not crop up. The tzpewriter which I am using is German, and the kezboard is exactlz the same as ours with one exception: the "y" is where the "z" should be and vice versa. I'll correct for that from here on.

I hear old bed-check Charlie overhead, or, as he is also known, "washing machine Charlie" because of the sound of the plane's engine that is deliberately set to misfire. Just heard the plane fly over, but all is quiet again.

It was a shock to hear about Eddie Wear's death at Iwo Jima. As you know, Eddie was a close childhood friend. Mrs. Wear has had it rough. That's how most of the men feel. It isn't themselves so much. It's always the question, "How will it go back home?" I've seen seriously wounded men pulled out of a tank and in almost all cases they have asked, "Is the rest of the crew ok?"

22APR1945

The 1st Battalion/66th AR remained in the positions that we'd occupied the day before, our mission unchanged. Patrols in Wolfenbüttel continued throughout this period. Fifteen POWs gave themselves up to F Company in Vienenburg.

23APR1945

All 1st Battalion/66th AR (- F Company) guards on installations and roadblocks were relieved by the 14th Field Artillery. The battalion assembled in reserve in Wolfenbüttel and was put on two-hour alert status for possible movement to any sector of the 2nd AD area. Patrols continued in town with the ongoing mission of maintaining order.

24APR1945

No movements took place while we spent the day maintaining our vehicles and weapons. Our combat efficiency was rated at 90 percent, and the day's mission accomplished.

Letter Home

My Rolleiflex is working very well. Took some pictures yesterday. Gotta get them developed next. Movies today at 1300, 1500 and 1900. Hope it's a good picture. Don't know what time I'll go, but I'm going.

My hand luggage took a beating this trip, wet and dusty. My blouse was all wrinkled, and the left sleeve was covered with mildew. I hung it out; been out for three days now, and the way it has straightened out amazes me. I was even able to brush the mildew out of it, and it doesn't even show. We usually store our luggage on the company supply truck, but this time they loaded it into a trailer that was hooked behind the truck. Mud, dust and water were thrown into the trailer from the truck wheels, but it's all straightened out now.

25APR1945

We stayed on two-hour alert status and spent the day maintaining vehicles and weapons and restowing our gear into the trucks and tanks. Easy day. Mission accomplished!

26APR1945

At 1000, the 3rd Platoon of B Company/702nd Tank Destroyer Battalion was detached from our battalion. At 1300, the engineer platoon placed barbed wire around the important installations of an airfield east of Braunschweig to discourage people from looting. We spent the day once again maintaining our vehicles and weapons and got some time to clean and organize our personal equipment as well.

27APR1945

The engineers were given the mission of checking out the installations at the airfield, where they had laid the wire the day before, for booby traps and demolitions. However, they were unable to complete the mission, even though the daily report states, "Mission Accomplished."

01MAY1945

Critch and I were awarded our Silver Stars today for our actions at Schiefbahn back on 1 March 1945. The awards were presented by Major General Isaac D. White, commanding officer of the 2nd AD, the event taking place in Bernburg, contrary to what is on the back of the official photo, which states that the ceremony happened in Wolfenbüttel. Critch and I traveled seventy miles by jeep to Bernburg.

Critch is the "yours truly," and I am to his right. The jacket I am wearing makes me think the weather was cold. (DAC)

The caption on the back of the official photo of the event reads:

ETO HQ 45 44702-13 1 MAY
CREDIT . . . US ARMY SIGNAL CORP
PHOTOG—PVT. DANIEL C. REKOSKE . . . 168
LT. FREDERICK G. BREMS 2210 NO. LAMON AVE.,
CHICAGO, ILL., MEMBER OF THE ARMORED 66TH
REGIMENT, RIGHT, RECEIVES SILVER STAR MEDAL
FROM MAJ. GEN. ISAAC D. WHITE, COMMANDING
GENERAL, 2ND ARMORED DIVISION, 9TH U.S. ARMY,
AT CEREMONY AT WOLFENBUTTEL, GERMANY. (B)
66TH AIR, 2ND ARM DIV, NUSA, WOLFENBUTTEL, GERMANY

Some errors, but we have seen those before. AIR stands for Armored Infantry Regiment, which the 66th was not, and the ceremony did not take place at Wolfenbüttel. But it is a great photo. Seeing the photo, I am sure that this is the look I had on my face whenever I took communion.

The ceremony took place in the center of town. As we walked away from the area, several local women came up to us, looked at the medals and said such things as "Ach das [or dat] ist schön!" which translates to "Oh, that is lovely!" or something like that. Ye gads, do you realize why we got these medals? Usually for killing Germans! Oh boy!

28APR1945

Our task forces continued to be broken up, reducing the combined-arms task forces to their component parts. At 1900, the engineer platoon was detached. The process of detaching units would continue, and soon the 66th AR would be back together and under one command for the first time in a long time.

Shortly before hostilities ended, the Germans sent projectiles loaded with propaganda leaflets stating:

(U.S. Army Photo)

American Soldier!
After the Swastika then the Rising Sun
and then, American Soldier,
the Hammer and Sickle!

I sent one of these leaflets home in the mail, but it never made it. I am thinking the censors did not allow it. I heard similar words from captured German soldiers: "When are you going to give us rifles, so we can go fight the Russkies with you?"

29APR1945 LETTER HOME

All things considered, this has been a very nice Sunday. Quiet, like the type we enjoy. Breakfast at 0700, Mass at 0930, went to communion. Remember, no fasting is necessary. On the way back to headquarters, I stopped at our kitchen, where an American Red Cross Clubmobile we had arranged was set up. I had four hot doughnuts and a big cup of coffee. Got my camera and took some pictures of the Clubmobile. Then I took a little walk to a picturesque little spot where a creek flows swiftly past a line of buildings built right along the edge of the stream. Came back, read a murder mystery and then ate lunch . . . pork chops.

The big event of the day. I thoroughly scrubbed out the bathtub and filled it up. I soaked in the hot water while reading another murder mystery (first reading in some time, found some Ellery Queen mysteries). After all the soaking, I scrubbed and really rubbed. I now claim to be the most sanitary person in the European Theater of Operations. That sort of bushed me, so I crawled onto my sack and napped. Next came supper, shredded (canned) chicken.

There was no limit on the doughnuts; they kept on coming and they were hot. (FCB)

Read another murder mystery and answered a few phone calls. Have to sit on a court martial tomorrow. Read another murder mystery. Everything is ok dandy.

30APR1945

The order of the day is to take care of personal hygiene. I was way ahead of everyone with my bath yesterday. Word traveled fast that Adolf Hitler had committed suicide. Definitely mission accomplished.

During April 1945, the 66th AR took 7,420 prisoners and destroyed or captured 352 artillery pieces, 723 vehicles, 24 tanks, 44 aircraft, 11 entire trains and 14 locomotives.

01MAY1945

At 1800, orders were received to take one platoon of medium tanks, the intelligence and reconnaissance platoon, and the mortar platoon to Ahlum, three miles east of Wolfenbüttel, to stop a riot. By the time our units arrived in Ahlum, the riot had stopped. We learned from the civilian police that the two Russians and the Pole who were involved had fled north two miles to Salzdahlum. The force was sent back to Wolfenbüttel, but the two Russians and the Pole plus the civilian police were picked up and put into the POW cage at 2100.

02–03MAY1945

The 1st Battalion/66th AR remained in Wolfenbüttel. More maintenance. Not much happening.

04MAY1945

At 0730, the Armored Infantry Company was detached from our battalion. The battalion—minus F Company, which was still patrolling the three cities to the south, and C Company, which remained at Osterlinde to our west—moved from Wolfenbüttel six miles west to Watenstedt, near Salzgitter. We delivered our vehicles to the maintenance battalion to be checked and repainted.

05MAY1945

Maintenance and painting of our vehicles continued.

Letter Home

Brrr, this can't be May. So cold. Hope it warms up soon. News has certainly been great. The Allies have taken Denmark now. Saw a USO show. Don Rice was the emcee. Quite a comedian. It was a show strictly for the 2nd AD, and as a result a lot of his jokes were directed at us. He was clever. One of our radio operators is from Evanston, and he receives many Chicago papers through the mail, so I get to catch up on some local news.

06MAY1945

Sunday. No work required.

07MAY1945

It was a fairly routine day, as our vehicles continued to be checked and painted, until 0241, when the German High Command, in the person of General Alfred Jodl, signed the unconditional surrender document that formally ended the war in Europe. The agreement was signed at Reims in northeastern France. At 1940, the British Ministry of Information announced the signing of the surrender and declared Tuesday, 8 May, as Victory in Europe (VE) Day.

08MAY1945 (VE DAY)

F Company rejoined the battalion and immediately went to maintenance to be checked and repainted. At 0900, we began the move to abandoned German barracks just north of Lebenstedt. At 1000, I Company returned to battalion control. The 66th AR was finally back under one command.

I told one of the members of the maintenance battalion that the war was over. His response: "Say, that's good news," and he returned to his tire. (FCB)

09MAY1945

At 1300 the HQ Company moved to Lebenstedt, closing in at 1430. Someone decided that, with the end of the war, daily reports were no longer required. The 9 May 1945 report was to be our last. The "Result of Operations" line read, "Maintenance of vehicles and repainting in progress."

Of all days, the final two words of the final report should have emphatically emphasized "Mission Accomplished." But no, we just closed out with checking and repainting.

10MAY1945

Lebenstedt, Germany. We all arrived at Lebenstedt and moved into fairly comfortable German Army barracks that they had just recently evacuated. We spent time getting ourselves cleaned up and getting the dirt off the vehicles, repainting and remarking the insignia. We held a Saturday morning inspection as well. It had been a while. We were getting back to normal army.

We parked vehicles all around the barracks. (FCB)

Critchfield snaps another photo; always with the camera going, but I should talk. (FCB)

Our tanks parked to the rear of the barracks. Note the laundry line! (DAC)

Uniform regulations were enforced now. We were required to keep our collars buttoned, and that didn't help anything but discipline. Actually it was a pleasure having only very little things to

Covering up our newly cleaned and painted vehicles so we would not have to clean them again. (FCB)

HQ Company of the 1st Battalion/66th Armored Regiment in Lebenstedt. (FCB)

worry about. It was great to be able to open a door and let the light streak out; no shades were needed on windows anymore. We no longer had to censor mail either—although we had pretty well let up on that a while back.

I had sent a lot of my photos home, and now I had time to take a lot more. One of our guys in the battalion was responsible for developing all my film. He messed up only once when he put the film in the wrong bath—lost all of those. My best recollection is that there were a lot of photos of tanks in trees in that batch. But whatever they were, they are lost forever. No loss compared to Robert Capa's lost D-Day shots, for sure, but a loss nonetheless.

11MAY1945

We held our HQ Company retreat today. You could see the relief on everyone's faces. It had been a long war . . . but it was over.

Me on my bunk; taken by Critch with my camera. (FCB)

Lieutenant Morris sits for his portrait. (FCB)

Sergeant Weinert leaning on an M4A3E8 Sherman—the Easy Eight—with its 76mm gun. That's *Frances* in the background. (FCB)

Company F Saturday inspection with (left to right) Cignetto, Manning and Wynn. On the tank, Sergeant Weinert, Lieutenant Goodnight and Captain Fawks with his back to the camera. Note the name on the tank—*Five Fools*. (FCB)

Saturday inspection. (FCB)

Sergeant Harris and Captain Fawks. (FCB)

Above: Lieutenant Critchfield, Captain Fawks and Sergeant Harris. (FCB)

Right: Sergeant Fisher next to one of our Pershings. (FCB)

Bottom right: Schnapps the Mascot with *Frances* behind—notice "2 Δ – 66 Δ" on the glacis of the tank, indicating 2nd Armored Division—66th Armored Regiment. (FCB)

15MAY1945 LETTER HOME

Right now v-mail is about the only thing coming through. I surely hope you are receiving my airmail. I went to see the movie "Gildersleeve's Ghost," but left before it had run three minutes. It was very hot in the theater and so crowded that it was difficult to hear from where I was sitting—way back—most of the rear rows did leave. It might have been a good picture; we're getting some good ones now. "Objective Burma" is on tonight. I'm going early enough to get close up. Weather is cool, too. They only have a 16mm projector, and for a full-sized theater, the projector is too small.

Major Owen, our executive officer, is quite a fan when it comes to hunting. Yesterday, he asked me if I wanted to go deer hunting with him. I did. Golly it was great to get out and roam through these woods. Beautiful forests. We bagged one little buck and had him for dinner today. Very tasty. Hermann Goering apparently used to hunt in that same woods. He had a hunt-house built on the side of a hill. Pine trees; took my helmet off (only wear the helmet liner now) and got needles down my back, in my hair (still got some left—hair I mean). Let me look in my pockets; bet there are still some there . . . pause . . . omeomy . . . plenty of 'em.

Shifted rooms. The other room faced the street, and tanks had chewed up a lot of ground which has dried now and is really dusty. Woke up the other morning in a cloud of dust blown in by the wind. I have a much better view from this side. I can see a long row of small mountains and grassy fields; much better.

Lt. Trinen just dropped in. He's going home. He's been over for a long time, since the days of Africa. He's a rugged little character. What a fighter! We've seen a lot of it side-by-side, and I should also say platoon by platoon. I gave him our home phone number and told him to call if he gets the opportunity.

I wish I could say I was doing the same. There is nothing much I can say except that I am just holding tight. There are so many that have been over for a good stretch. Our day shall come. It's time for chow.

16MAY1945 LETTER HOME

Saw the movie about Roger Toughy and his gang last night. The theater was crowded and very hot. After the movie, I went swimming. Just a dip as the water is very cold. All around this area are large concrete pools, static pools, and I believe they were designed to be used in fighting fires in case the regular system failed. Our engineers pumped all the old water out; we got a few German PWs to clean the rocks and pull the trash out, and then we filled it with clean water. It's all right.

17MAY1945 LETTER HOME

Had a big decision to make yesterday, and I pray that I made the right choice. At first reading I know this opportunity sounds very good, and you may think me foolish to have turned it down, but I shall attempt to show both sides of the picture.

I was asked if I would care to serve as Aide to Major General Ernest Harmon. You may remember he formerly commanded the 2nd AD. The job would mean a promotion to Captain in three months time . . . for certain. A Major General has both a Major and a Captain as aides. I gave it some very serious thought but turned it down. I hope I can adequately express my reasons. I realize that, as the General's Aide, I would no doubt meet many interesting people and people in high places, and I would probably have made many good contacts.

On the other hand, the job I now have is very interesting, and it also calls for a promotion. The request for my promotion has already gone in . . . twice . . . and unfortunately it is just sitting. There is an overage of captains, similar to what I ran into during training in the States. Captains get wounded, go to hospital and in their absence someone is promoted, and, when they come back from hospital, there is an overage. I am now about the ranking Lieutenant in this outfit. I think that after all this time I've been plenty patient and have a gripe coming. I fully realize that they want to promote me and just can't, and I should be satisfied with that, but I still would be very happy to see this straightened out. I like the work I am doing, and I surely do like this outfit. The 2nd is my outfit. After all, I have seen some rugged days with it. In addition, I know the men here, and they are real. As time goes on, they go on.

The General's Aide job would mean I would definitely spend another year, perhaps more or perhaps less, in the European Theater of Operations. It would, on the other hand, keep me from going to the Pacific . . . maybe. If I stay here, many things can happen. I might stay as part of the occupation forces, I might go to the South Pacific directly or there via the US, or I might just stay where I am and some day be rotated home.

My points aren't high. I have 73: 47 for service, 11 for overseas service, five for the Silver Star, 10 for two campaign stars, a possible five more, as I have been recommended for a Bronze Star (but it may not go through). Under the present system, you must have 85 points to be considered for a leave or discharge, and then being an officer casts a little different light on it. At any rate, I know I will be around for a while. It is as it should be. Those who have been overseas longer are given the first chance to go home, if they are not essential. I believe the system to be as fair as possible.

If I were to become the Aide to General Harmon, my duties would be, well, sort of as a valet. Keep little things from bothering the General. An administrative job. In other words, a high-class lackey; in army words, a "dog-robber." It would mean a good deal of traveling and seeing things, but I have had enough of that. Perhaps he would be easy to work for, and I feel certain I could handle the job, but I thought that part of the position over very carefully. I believe that that was the biggest reason for turning it down. My time or life would definitely not be mine. (Lord knows it is limited enough as it is.) "Jump" and I would have to jump. No sir, not for me.

Perhaps all this would be set off by the "high position" and the contacts and the publicity it would bring. Who knows? The job would pay about three hundred dollars more over and above what the Captain's pay would give me, but that extra allowance would go for fancy uniforms, laundry and pressing, tailor work.

But even now I am glad that I rejected it. The future will tell whether or not I made a mistake.

Dad, you have always had your own business. You know what I mean. I sent you a story about "Gravel Voice" from Newsweek, "Gravel Voice" being General Harmon. The men of this outfit respect him as a great commander. I actually went to Father McPartland and asked what he thought about the offer. He felt much the same as I have expressed.

Actually, it boils down to this: I want to do the thing that will bring us together again as soon as possible. Perhaps that is a selfish attitude, but I feel as though I have done my fighting, although the Japanese are still to be dealt with.

Glad I have let all of this out of my system. All's well. The Lord has been very good to me; my blessings are many. He has certainly watched over me for the last months. I am feeling okay.

Let me know what you think about this. It's over with now, but I would like your reaction.

I wrote this on "liberated" German Army stationery. It's dusk now, and a beautiful evening it is.

18MAY1945 Letter Home

The more I think about that offer that I turned down, the more satisfied I am that my choice was the wiser. I heard today that General Harmon is doing all he possibly can do to get to the South Pacific.

19MAY1945

We returned in jeeps and trucks to Wolfenbüttel to take part in a dismounted parade of the entire division. Since I was part of HQ, I was unassigned and able to wander around and take photos. The complete division comprises approximately ten thousand troops. During the war, the 2nd AD suffered 20,659 killed, wounded, captured or missing. We had two times the number of casualties than we carried as our full complement.

Major General I. D. White, commanding officer of the 2nd AD, arrives for the parade. General White was the man who pinned the Silver Star on me at Bernburg. (FCB)

The division parade begins. (FCB)

Passing in review. (FCB)

"Okay, we'll salute . . . sort of . . . but we are ready to go home." (FCB)

Colonel Bruce Stokes, commanding officer of the 66th AR. (FCB)

I was walking down a street in Wolfenbüttel after the review when a shabbily dressed fellow came up to me and began gesturing, holding both hands coiled in front of his eyes, putting his arms at his side and then waving his hands up in the air. I could not figure it out at first, but then I began to think perhaps he was trying to tell me something about binoculars. I was right. I figured out later that he was waving his arms up to indicate an explosion and to tell me that the binoculars were for artillery spotters.

He motioned for me to follow him; he led me to a building and a long flight of stairs that went down into a very dark room. I motioned for him to lead, and I unsnapped the button on my holster, grabbing the grip of my .45 so I could pull it out rapidly if I needed to.

We went down the stairs and entered a well-lit room that had many long tables. It turned out that my guide was a Frenchman taken from home and sent into forced labor by the Germans. He worked in this small but very elaborate prison factory with other slave laborers, assembling binoculars for

After the review, Major General I. D. White smiling as Brigadier General "Pee Wee" Collier, the general who "visited" me in Dochamps, approaches him. Note the officer coming down the stairs slapping his gloves into his left hand, showing his satisfaction in a job well done. (FCB)

the German Army. He led me past some shelves that looked like they served as bunks. He lifted a board from a bunk and grabbed a small, golf-ball-sized potato entirely covered in dirt. He popped it into his mouth and proceeded to chew it with what seemed to be actual relish. He then looked at me, read my reaction and just sort of shrugged his shoulders.

My guide showed me more false bottoms on the shelves. Apparently the prisoners would slip binoculars into these compartments, perhaps to keep them from German use. He opened one of these false covers, and there were eleven pairs of binoculars inside. He gave me all of them. I found them to be lighter than ours and easier to carry.

Draped in binoculars, I walked out of the basement and told him to wait as I went to get some

I gave all but one of the binoculars away. They were not made of quality glass, but they would have served their purpose. Along the side of the eyepiece and embossed on a plate it read: Dienstglas 6×30 261620 ddx. (FCB)

things for him. I am not sure what all I gave him, but I am sure there was a carton of cigarettes, probably some chocolates, maybe a K-ration and whatever else I could gather.

Wolfenbüttel was a fairly good-sized city. Civilians were ordered to turn in all their weapons, and they really did. Of course, I am sure they knew that in the local police stations or some city office all these weapons were registered and could easily have been traced.

Collecting weapons in Wolfenbüttel and selecting a few souvenirs. Sergeant Robbins is holding a rifle. (FCB)

Photo taken on my return to Lebenstedt after taking photographs at the division parade. We certainly got all dressed up for the occasion. (FCB)

I am sure we had no intention of doing that; in fact, I truthfully do not believe it was a necessary order to have all these weapons turned in. Perhaps it was done more for psychological reasons than as a precaution to prevent any use against American soldiers.

Beautiful sets of Browning shotguns and rifles were turned in, as well as all kinds of handguns, rifles, shotguns, swords and bayonets. I was able to get a 16 gauge shotgun and a 7mm rifle, plus a .25 caliber automatic pistol that I was able to send home in my footlocker. Good weapons, but I missed out on some really prized pieces.

I saw stacks of perfectly good weapons run over and crushed by our tanks.

22MAY1945

The Ministry of National Defense of Belgium released a decree by Prince Charles, Regent of the Kingdom of Belgium, awarding the 1940 Belgian Fourragère to the 2nd AD for being the first American troops to enter Belgium on 2 September 1944, marking the beginning of the liberation of Belgium, and for our actions during the German offensive in the Ardennes in December 1944. Those of us who were attached to the 2nd AD for the occasions for which the citations were awarded were entitled to wear the Fourragère as a permanent part of our uniform.

I was assigned to temporary duty with the 41st Armored Infantry Regiment five miles to the north of Lebenstedt in Lengede, Germany. HQ sent me there to round out my experience and pick up some more points. The company I was assigned to was the one that we worked with during the Bulge. I felt at home. A motorcyclist from battalion brought me my mail, and in the evenings, I was able to grab a jeep to go back to battalion HQ. I was with the 41st for fifteen days.

Prince Charles was named regent by the Belgian Parliament soon after the country was liberated, as a cloud of suspicion hung over his older brother, King Leopold III, for perhaps surrendering too quickly to the Germans and possible collaboration. Charles was regent from 1944 until 1950, when his brother was allowed to return to power. (Wikimedia Commons)

25MAY1945 LETTER HOME

Saw a movie tonight in Agfacolor. It was a German musical with dialogue and songs all in German. It was good. I really enjoyed it. The translated title was "The Wife of Your Dreams." The star of the movie was very versatile, being able to sing, to toe dance, tap, and ballet and do dances similar to our fast dances. Scenery was excellent as were the costumes. Frankly, I enjoyed it more than any of the stuff Hollywood has sent over lately. Perhaps because it was a musical and in color.

I was still in Lengede with the 41st AIR. The battalion continued in Lebenstedt, staying busy conducting extensive training and indoctrination for newly received reinforcements and refresher training for the remainder of the men. I reached eighty-three points and waited to see whether the Bronze Star would come through, giving me more than the required eighty-five points to go home. It was not clear whether points mattered for officers, but I wanted the points anyway.

26MAY1945

Today's *Stars and Stripes* featured a letter in the Mail Call column from my good friend from high school, Ed Hoy.

27MAY1945 LETTER HOME

Saw another movie tonight: "Christmas in Connecticut." I really enjoyed it, maybe because they first showed a Donald Duck cartoon.

30MAY1945 LETTER HOME

Regiment conducted a Memorial Day ceremony today. Chaplain Luke Bolin made the address. It was a well thought out talk, and I asked him for a copy of it. Fr. McPartland then led us in prayer. The National Anthem was played, the guns from five tanks fired a volley, taps were sounded, and the regiment passed in review. Even the locals lined a nearby road as spectators. Memorial Day mass tonight at 2100.

Here I am after the war in my major's dress uniform with the Belgian Fourragère over my left shoulder. (FCB)

Father McPartland taking a break in Lebenstedt. (FCB)

Left: Chaplain Luke Bolin at the division parade in Wolfenbüttel. I still have the copy of the Memorial Day address that he delivered. (FCB)

One of the men just invited me to have a snack. French fried potatoes, one fried egg, green onions, bread, coffee and beer. A real snack. Those fries hit the spot. This 41st AIR is the eating-est bunch. I sent a package with the Silver Star first class. Let me know when it arrives.

During my time with the 41st, I was able to complete a two-day course on educational advancement. The Army Information and Education Program offered several courses I thought I would like to take. I came across a folder the program provided on the pulp and paper industry, which was pertinent to what I was planning to do when I got back home. I thought my best opportunity was to return to Marquette Paper Corporation in Chicago.

03JUN1945 LETTER HOME

I returned to the Battalion CP tonight to write you a letter. Hmmmm, new ribbon in the typewriter. This is the same typewriter which gave all the trouble with the "y's" and "z's," but that has been corrected. I can't see much through the window; the light in here is too bright. There is a displaced persons camp out there on the other side of the railroad tracks. I can hear some of the men singing. Not sure, but I believe it's Russian. Sounds good. The voices blend nicely.

This country, when first we came here, was mean. Everything seemed sinister. I know it was because we were fighting. Now it is rather nice. Yesterday it warmed up enough to use the swimming pool. It was refreshing, and it felt so good to swim again. Pork chops and venison with some wild boar for dinner tonight. And one of the men "found" some potatoes, so we had French fries.

One of the men leaned out of a window yesterday and called, "Lieutenant, could this be you?" and then tossed a New York paper to me. I am enclosing the article. The tanker featured in the article was not me but Lt. Trinen, who was quoted as saying that he was fired upon by a man who must have been 80 years old. We asked Trin if he got the fellow. He answered, "I don't know, but we knocked the building down around him."

I've heard this story of a gunner in one of our battalion's tanks. The tank commander saw a German soldier run into a building about 1400 yards away. The building had a door in the center and a room on either side of the entrance hall. The CO told the gunner what was happening and indicated the house.

Thinking that there might be more enemy soldiers in the place, he asked, "Can you hit the house?"

The gunner asked, "Which way did he turn when he went in the building, Sir?"

"I'm sure he went to the right," was the somewhat skeptical answer (according to the gunner).

The gunner fired one high explosive round 1400 yards right through the window of the room on the right side of the house.

We really have some tankers in this outfit.

01JUN1945

We remained in the vicinity of Lebenstedt, conducting intensive training and indoctrination for newly received reinforcements and refresher training for the veterans. Nontraining hours were filled with recreation and athletics, plus we took courses from the Information and Education Program.

Recreation and athletics included competitions between companies in baseball, volleyball, football and other team sports with the goal of eventually selecting division champions in each sport. Of note: "Calisthenics and other forms of athletics conducted 'by the number' will be avoided." Cross-country hikes, road marches and cross-country runs, daily fifteen minutes of close-order drill and one ceremonial parade for each battalion with the band playing rounded out the physical activities.

Short courses in the wearing of uniforms, saluting and military courtesy, day and night patrolling, map reading, use of codes, clear and concise writing, and recognition of British, Russian and French insignia of rank were also held.

We knew we were back in the army when each company and battalion had to submit training schedules in quadruplicate to the division's S-3.

We were very aware that the thinking was going beyond the occupation of Berlin when we started orientation for all troops in the America's Interest in the Pacific and Pacific Areas—Peoples and Countries course. Another course was held on the Japanese soldier, his equipment and the current war situation. The very real possibility that the war might not be over for us yet hung over all of our heads.

05JUN1945 LETTER HOME

The entire army in the ETO will celebrate tomorrow, a holiday, a day of rest. It is D+365 . . . one year since D-Day. At this time last year, I was aboard a ship heading for Scotland. Did I ever dream I would spend a year of my life as this one?

Got another court-martial tomorrow. It won't take long. Only one case.

08JUN1945

Brigadier General John H. Collier assumed command of the division with Major General I. D. White departing for the United States.

11JUN1945

This was a good day on several fronts. We were issued two bottles of Coca-Cola, and I put one under a faucet to cool it off. The six rolls of film I had submitted to be developed came back, and I divided them into small batches to mail home to avoid any major losses if they went astray. Even if the prints didn't all make it home, I still had the negatives with me. I thought about making a large photo album when I got home, explaining each photo to my folks and Helen as I put it in the book. Also, I learned that there was a chance that I might be able to go home in December. With things so up in the air, though, I did not get my hopes up very high at all.

12JUN1945

Softball game after supper tonight between the officers of our battalion and the officers of the 2nd Battalion, a provisional battalion. We were ahead 8 to 1 in the fourth inning when it started to rain. Too bad we could not finish the game.

We received an addition to our 2nd AD patch: a strip of cloth with the motto "Hell on Wheels" in gold letters. We sewed them on right under the triangular patch, and it looked good.

16JUN1945–30JUN1945

Operations and Training S-3, Headquarters, 1st Battalion, 66th AR, 2nd AD.

17JUN1945 LETTER HOME

I will receive the Bronze Star, so I now have 88 points. I really don't believe that these points are going to mean much in the case of officers. If we're considered essential, that's it . . . period.

My footlocker arrived from England. The green shirt we bought in Fort Smith, Ark was still in it.

Last night, Lt. Hunnings and I went to an organ recital given at a beautiful Lutheran church established in 1604. The organ, with over 3000 pipes, was made in 1621 and "modernized" in 1877. The last number was heavy on the bass and loud, and I liked it the best.

Received our rations today: Milk Duds, Old Nick candy bars, gum, can of orange juice, can of peanuts, three cigars which I gave to Major Owen, 14 packs of cigarettes which I shall give or trade away, two chocolate bars and a package of pipe tobacco.

Went to the dentist last Friday. He found two cavities and filled one before he was called away. He practically crawled into my mouth admiring the superb gold inlay job that Doc Smith had put in. Every dentist I've gone to in the army does the same thing. Doc Joe Smith . . . without a doubt, an excellent dentist.

We received notice stating that a shipload of mail from here to the U.S. had run into trouble. One hold full of mail had flooded. Hope none of my mail was in there.

17JUN1945

The 2nd AD was alerted for a possible move to Halle in the Soviet Occupation Zone in preparation to our entrance to Berlin. We were to be honored by being the first U.S. Army Division to enter and occupy Berlin, albeit in a token occupation. Billeting parties were placed on seventy-two-hour alert status.

18JUN1945

We held a division parade today, during which the Belgian Fourragère 1940 was officially awarded to the division and the 66th AR for its part in the liberation of Belgium. Billeting parties departed Lebenstedt for the Halle area to prepare for the arrival of the division. Our battalion's next stop would be Preusslitz, Germany, in the Soviet sector.

12

A Day Trip to Braunschweig

In early June, while we were still at Lebenstedt, Critch, Ed Fawks and I grabbed two jeeps and a driver for a sightseeing tour fifteen miles to the north of Lebenstedt around Braunschweig (Brunswick). I found out long after the war that Rolleiflex cameras were produced in Braunschweig before and well after the war. In a way, my camera was visiting and documenting great changes in its place of origin. An interesting and at the same time touching thought.

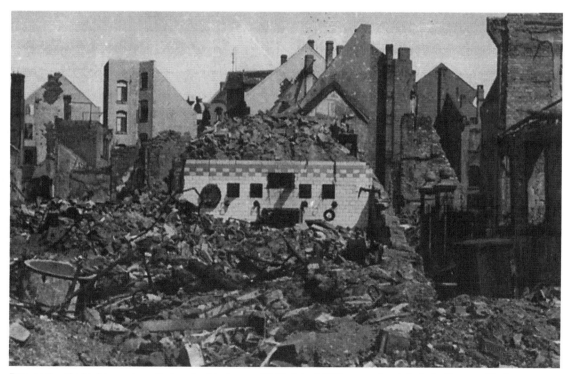

Braunschweig had been heavily bombed between 1941 into 1945 approximately forty times, with four thousand to five thousand civilians perishing in the attacks. Both Critch and I took pictures of this building in Braunschweig, which we think was a bakery, as there was an oven inside. We took the photo because we had no idea how the building could still be standing. (FCB)

We passed the Braunschweiger Schloss (Brunswick Palace). The memorial in front of the palace was initially erected in memory of the victims of the bombing raid on 15 October 1944, the most devastating of the forty raids. (FCB)

10JUN1945 LETTER HOME

This afternoon Capt. Fawks, Lt. Critchfield and I hopped into a "peep" and went roving over the countryside. Beautiful day! We were out hunting with our cameras. I used up three rolls of film. During our roving, we came upon the Von Cramm family's summer place, Castle Oelber. Took some pictures of it. A beautiful peacock was wandering around the place, couldn't get a picture of it, however, as the dern critter flew up into a tree and just stuck there. Winding staircases, crossed lances on the walls, deer and elk horns, and perched on a huge chimney was a stork's nest. Gottfried von Cramm is the Cramm who plays tennis.

After the war, we found out that Gottfried von Cramm was a German amateur tennis champion who won the French Open twice. He was nicknamed by some "The Baron of Wimbledon." He ranked number two in the world in 1934 and 1936 and number one in the world in 1937. The Nazis tried to exploit his Aryan appearance and skill as a

That is our jeep in the photo. The peacock was up that pine tree directly behind the jeep. There was a clay tennis court on the grounds, the same court surface used at the French Open. (FCB)

Left: The guard at the front door of the von Cramm castle. The best estimate is that construction of the castle began in 1296. (FCB)

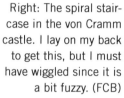

Right: The spiral staircase in the von Cramm castle. I lay on my back to get this, but I must have wiggled since it is a bit fuzzy. (FCB)

symbol of Aryan supremacy, but he refused to identify with Nazism. He was persecuted as a homosexual by the German government and jailed briefly in 1938.

In 1940, von Cramm was conscripted and sent to the eastern front as a private, despite being a noble, with the Hermann Göring Division. Von Cramm became a company commander and actually earned an Iron Cross. He was flown home in 1942 due to frostbite, and because of his conviction in 1938, he was dismissed from the army.

Von Cramm continued to play tennis after the war, including playing Davis Cup tennis until he retired after the 1953 season. He still holds the record for most wins by any German Davis Cup team member. Our reconnaissance battalion used the castle for its command post.

We were told about an airstrip in some woods northeast of Braunschweig. We were directed to a dirt road, which we found and followed to see whether we could find the airfield to have a look around. Not far outside of the city, we spotted what we at first thought was a firebreak, but it proved to be the airstrip we were looking for. Wrecked planes were backed into the woods and scattered throughout the area on either side of the wide strip.

Ed Fawks looking down the dirt and grass airstrip. Remains of a plane are parked at the edge of the woods. (FCB)

There were no runways beyond the dirt roads that we saw, no power lines, no railroad tracks, not even any paved roads running into the area. There was nothing to indicate that this was an active airfield, and its presence and use had us scratching our heads. Who destroyed the planes? We were unable to solve any mysteries of this airfield at that time.

We followed the dirt roads around the area and came across a number of airplanes in various conditions. One of the most impressive planes we found was a Heinkel 177 Greif (Griffin) Bomber, which had been developed with two huge engines and

The wrecks were back in and surrounded by grown trees. We had no idea what we were seeing. The size of the trees around the planes on all sides suggested that the planes had been sitting there a while. (FCB)

Above and left: Critch and I climbed into the bomber through the open bomb bay doors and worked our way up to the nose of the plane. The plane actually looked to be in pretty good shape, although it was certainly not airworthy. (FCB)

Critch climbed on top, and I got into the nose. "Top of the world, Ma." Ed took the photo with my camera. (FCB)

A fairly intact Messerschmitt Bf 109 fighter plane. I got right down into the cockpit, and Ed took this photo with my camera. Notice the strands of camouflage netting. (FCB)

props. Engines this size had never before been attempted, but, after much testing, the He 177 was able to carry the same payload the same distance as our four-engine bombers. It saw little service on the western front, so seeing this plane here was an unusual sight. It had been moved into a protected area between two revetments.

We did not see too much damage to the airframes of the planes, but the windows were blown out, not in. The absence of bomb craters surrounding the wrecks made us think the planes were not damaged from the outside by Allied aircraft but had been sabotaged with explosives planted inside the planes. Whatever caused the damage, the flying days of these planes were over.

We drove right up to an Arado Ar 234 German reconnaissance jet bomber. This was the world's first operational jet bomber, but it was employed primarily on reconnaissance missions. Allies found it nearly impossible to intercept the Arado the few times it was used as a bomber. Introduced in September 1944, only 214 were produced. The last German Luft-waffe aircraft that flew over England was an Arado in April 1945. The Arado certainly had been sabo-taged, with numerous bullet holes concentrated on the jet engine. Two empty Jerry cans were nearby as well, the gas used to set fire to the plane.

To find out more about this airfield, in July 2021, my son contacted the administration of the City of Braunschweig. His email was forwarded to the Stadtarchiv Braunschweig (Municipal Archives of Braunschweig). Archivist Thorben Gützlaff responded to the inquiry with the follow-ing information:

Our driver, Ed and Critch by the nose of what appears to be an Me 109. (FCB)

> With regard to your question about the aircraft and the airfield, we suspect that these constructions are related to the "Deutsche Forschungsanstalt für Luftfahrt" or Aeronautical Research Institute, also known between 1938 and 1945 as "Luftfahrt-forschungsanstalt Hermann Göring" or Hermann Göring Aviation Research Institute. It was a secret facility for airframe, aero-engine and aircraft weapons testing during the war. The institute was located north-west of the city in Braunschweig-Völkenrode and was mostly hidden inside a forest.

The secret facility, launched in 1935, covered one thousand acres of forest. It grew to over sixty buildings that were spread throughout the site, with none of the buildings being taller than the trees that provided cover from aerial reconnaissance. For the same reason, none of the buildings had chim-neys, with all of the power needs of the buildings supplied underground from the nearby City of Braunschweig, including electricity and steam heat.

This aircraft was so thoroughly destroyed that we were unable to identify it. (FCB)

Construction of the site's first wind tunnel began in November 1936; eventually, the Institute of Aero-dynamics had five wind tunnels. No planes took off from this site, which would have given its presence away, and all testing took place indoors. There were no runways or taxiways, just the dirt roads along which the planes were moved to the various test and design centers. The buildings were well hidden from us as well, as we saw none while we were there. Perhaps we did not want to venture far into the forest, as we did not know how secure the area was.

Research was carried out at the institute on a number of different aircraft, including the Arado Ar 234, the Me 109, and the He 177. The airplanes that we saw surrounded by old and new-growth trees must have been early models that were parked in the woods and forgotten as the engineers moved ahead with design modifications suggested by the various tests they put the models through.

We were at the site in early June, but it turned out this airfield was of interest to more than casual tourists. A team of British scientists led by Sir Alfred Hubert Roy Fedden, an engineer who was involved in the design of the Bristol Engine Company's piston aircraft engines, was sent by the British Ministry of Aircraft Production to numerous

A Messerschmitt Bf 109 fighter being put into a wind tunnel at the Hermann Göring Aviation Research Institute at Braunschweig-Völkenrode, Germany, in 1940. (Photo courtesy of tormentor45555 at flickr.com)

sites in Germany to examine German aeronautical expertise and research. Among the sites visited was Braunschweig-Völkenrode, the same one we had visited. One source has these visits taking place 12–23 June, although Herr Gützlaff's notes state that the visit to Braunschweig-Völkenrode was on 9–10 May, making it before our visit.

That night we caught a movie, *Murder, My Sweet.* It was the first movie to feature the character of private detective Philip Marlowe. Good picture. We were now getting more recent releases and better-quality movies.

Left to right: Captain Fawks, me and Lieutenant Critchfield after our picture-taking tour. We are standing in front of the command post of Captain Fawks's F Company, situated in Lebenstedt. Our driver took the photo with my camera. (FCB)

13

The Move to Preusslitz

20JUN1945

At 0659, the leading elements of the division moved out of Lebenstedt and marched eighty-three miles to the vicinity of Trebnitz, with most of the regiment closing by 1600. The 1st Battalion settled in Preusslitz, ninety-seven miles southeast of Berlin and in the Soviet sector. Our first three days in Preusslitz were allotted to housekeeping activities and maintenance of vehicles and weapons, after which training was resumed.

23JUN1945 LETTER HOME

We are now in Preusslitz, a small, picturesque farming town 85 miles southwest of Lebenstedt and in the Russian Sector. It is very close to Bernburg, where Critch and I received our Silver Stars. There are lots of flies, as the town has a power sewage system that is not working. My quarters are top-notch, with windows on three-sides, potted plants and a cherry tree right at the window. I found two photos today, one of which identifies that yellow-handled short sword I sent you; a German naval officer is wearing one just like it. A very interesting lighting system here— must be alternating current, because it is continually alternating between on and off.

There is a Lutheran church with a swell chiming clock in front of the house. The minister is now in one of our PW camps, which seems unusual. He may have been mixed up with the Nazi party.

I played 11 games of table tennis today. Played with Captain "Doc" O'Neill, our medical officer, Critch, and then Corporal Quigley, our radio operator.

The weather has been perfect, bringing out all kinds of flowers and ripening fruit and vegetables. I've eaten a lot of big, juicy, fresh strawberries.

We have it. It's definite. Our next stop is Berlin. Parades, ceremonies, inspections will abound. The 2nd AD will be representing the U.S. Army. They could not have picked a better outfit.

About a month ago, we filled out a questionnaire. One question was: "Do you desire to remain in the service for the duration of the present emergency (meaning until the defeat of Japan, I am sure)?" My answer was no, and I feel that is the right answer for me. I feel, like the English put it, "You've 'ad it, chum, you've 'ad it." Incidentally, my promotion request has gone in for the sixth time now.

A few weeks ago, I gave a note to a Lieutenant from the 8th AD and asked him to please deliver it to Steve Kelly in the division Army Post Office. The result was a letter from Steve. It surely was great hearing from him. He's in Czechoslovakia and is a Buck Sgt. now. I'll send the letter to you. He's a swell fellow.

Officers' quarters in Preusslitz were set up in the estate of a duke and duchess. (FCB)

The entrance to the estate. (FCB)

One view of the extensive gardens surrounding the main house of the estate. (FCB)

My very comfortable quarters with a great view of the greenery. (FCB)

Left to right: Major Owen, Colonel Parker, Lieutenant Hemmings and Doc O'Neill relaxing with a game of billiards. (FCB)

Doc O'Neill and Colonel Parker in a quiet moment. The constant strain of decision-making has left the colonel's face. (FCB)

We were told that Göring had a hunting lodge in the nearby Harz Mountains, so we took a day trip organized by Major Owen, the avid hunter in our group, to see whether we could locate it. We saw no evidence that Göring had a lodge there, but the hunting was very good.

On the road into the forests of the Harz Mountains. (FCB)

The hunt was very successful. Note the "2△ 66△" HQ markings on the trailer. (FCB)

We bagged four large bucks; left to right: Major Owen, Mr. Derdin and Major Barron. (FCB)

None of this seemed new or unusual to the children in the area. We assumed they had encountered many deer hunters. We could not help but notice how thin they were. (FCB)

(FCB)

(FCB)

The eldest boy in the family was responsible for the pet fawn. (FCB)

We feasted on venison that night in the dining room at the officers' quarters. (FCB)

Soon after we arrived in Preusslitz, a Russian column passed through on the main thoroughfare. The older men had seen a lot, and they carried it in their hardened faces, while the younger soldiers showed their relief that the war was over. I took the following photos and will let them stand by themselves without comment.

(FCB)

(FCB)

(FCB)

While we were standing behind a fence watching them pass, Russian soldiers would come over to the fence and hold out American scrip while pointing at our watches. I did not like the idea, but I learned (or was told) that the scrip was no good for them in Russia—and they were offering $400 for a watch. That was the cost of half a car back home. I thought about it a little more and finally persuaded myself to do it.

24JUN1945

We received the first of three letters of instruction from 2nd AD HQ outlining our mission as an occupational force in Berlin. The letters included the administrative details of the regiment's move to our sector of responsibility in Berlin. Plans for the move included laying out and reconnoitering the routes to Berlin for each battalion and company, establishing control points along the route, and organizing the billeting parties that would precede the division.

25JUN1945

Critch and I received the Bronze Star for our actions at Kaldenhausen. I was very proud of mine, as it had the "V for Valor" on the ribbon. We stood at attention in front of one of Critch's Pershings.

Colonel Hillyard, 66th AR commanding officer, pinned the Bronze Star on each of us. (U.S. Army Photo)

Critch receiving his Bronze Star. (U.S. Army Corps)

Major Warren reads the general orders awarding the Bronze Stars. (U.S. Army Photo)

On the west side of Preusslitz, we came across the site of what had been a slave labor camp. An elderly man told me that the first Americans who came through the town were careful and polite in their dealings with the civilians, until one day a large mass grave was discovered a short distance outside the town. The GIs' attitude immediately changed. All male occupants sixteen years and older were required to exhume the bodies by hand, carry the remains through the streets of the town, return to the site of the camp and dig individual graves for each body. They then put lime in each hole, completing the proper burial of each victim. The same man told me that the only reason he could do it was because the mayor of the town was kneeling right next to him on his hands and knees—digging. They all, of course, claimed no knowledge of the goings-on at the "camp." I was accompanied by Corporal Caddey to the site.

I found out after the war that Leau (formerly Ploemnitz) was a sub-camp of the Buchenwald concentration camp and had begun operations in March 1944 primarily as a forced labor camp as opposed to an extermination camp. Most of the Buchenwald sub-camps were assigned to specific manufacturing processes. Prisoners from Leau were forced to work for Solvay, a chemical company the Nazis had nationalized in the 1930s, and the Junkers airplane factory, located in the city of Dessau twenty-three miles to the east. Many of the prisoners died while working at these sites. In February 1945, a women's camp was added with 150 Jewish inmates from Hungary. The Soviets exhumed and reburied many of the victims at the Soviet memorial at Bernburg, the city where we had received our Silver Stars.

I was unaware of the grim look on my face when Corporal Caddey used my camera to take this photo. I do remember that what I was seeing reaffirmed my conviction that the war to defeat the Nazis had to be fought. The reasons were all around us. (FCB)

Corporal Caddey here and in the photo to the right. (FCB)

Corpses exhumed from a mass grave at Work Camp Ploemnitz-Leau. The bodies were then reburied in the cemetery that we visited, seen in the previous photos. (Photo from the United States Holocaust Memorial Museum, courtesy of National Archives and Records Administration, College Park, Maryland)

30JUN1945

Our final letter of instruction was received. It instructed us to depart for Berlin on 3 July, with the billeting parties leaving on 1 July. A part of the four pages of instructions below illustrates typical U.S. Army attention to detail:

Uniform and Equipment:
(1) Uniform: Field with helmet liner. Neckties and scarves will not be worn and top shirt button will be unbuttoned.
(2) Vehicular windshield up with tops down unless otherwise ordered in event of inclement weather.
(3) Vehicle guidons will be displayed.
(4) Vehicular weapons aligned and centered; gun covers off; tank .50 cal AA guns rest diagonally across the gun mantle; all hatches open; tank commander waist deep in the turret. Half track commanders standing on seat, .50 cal MG (machine gun) manned.

We'd be taking the autobahn . . . at the roaring prescribed speed of eighteen miles per hour. We also learned that the sector we would be taking over had yet to be demined.

From 1 June to 30 June, the medals that the members of the 66th AR had earned slowly caught up to us. Most of these medals, if not all, had been earned before the end of the war.

Distinguished Service Cross	5
2nd Oak Leaf Cluster to the Silver Star Medal	1
Oak Leaf Cluster to the Silver Star Medal	2
Silver Star Medal	32
2nd Oak Leaf Cluster to the Bronze Star Medal	1
Oak Leaf Cluster to the Bronze Star Medal	2
Bronze Star Medal	72
Purple Heart Medal	7

14

The 2nd Armored Division Occupies Berlin

01JUL1945 LETTER HOME

Sunday night, and I am up late—11:15 p.m. Actually, we don't get to bed much earlier any night.

We are definitely going to Berlin. We shall really be on show there, representing the entire U.S. Army.

I now have, officially, #83 points. When the division is officially notified that it is eligible for the Central European Campaign Star, I will get five more, making 88. The critical score for officers in the theater is 85. However, there is a big IF—an officer can very easily be classified essential, meaning even with 85 points, an officer declared essential will not be going home. Still, it is probably better to get one's points.

I am taking a beating regarding my short haircut—they're all having a lot of fun out of it. "What—did'ya lose a bet?" "Get too close to the threshing machine?" But I'm comfortable, and I believe it will be well worth it in the long run; much easier to take care of.

I have sent a number of things home: the money order for $50 from Marquette, two bayonets, the silver star and bronze star and some pictures. I hope they all reach you.

I was still with S-3, Operation and Training, Headquarters Company, 1st Battalion, 66th AR, 2nd AD, and would be until 19 August 1945.

03JUL1945

As per the extensive letters of instruction, the entire division moved 184 miles in seventeen hours along the autobahn from Preusslitz and made our entry march into Berlin. We were the first major unit of the U.S. Army to occupy the American zone.

On the autobahn to Berlin. Notice the tanks in column halted in the far lane. (FCB)

As we crossed the new bridge, the destruction of the autobahn bridge came into full view. (FCB)

Fixing a broken track. Always a pain, but there were lots of folks around to help. (FCB)

Stopping for a K-ration lunch break. Caddey is on the right. (FCB)

As we got closer to Berlin, the road cut through heavy forests. (FCB)

Local traffic was virtually nonexistent, but here is a car going in the opposite direction on the autobahn. (FCB)

Note the two motorcycles. We had scheduled stops, so I had plenty of time to take photos. (FCB)

Also going in the other direction was this truck carrying Russian troops and pulling a Russian gun. The truck appears to be a Studebaker US6, made in the United States and sent to the Soviet Union in the Lend-Lease program. The gun appears to be a Russian ZiS-3. It featured a low frontal armor plate, which in this photo appears to be folded up to provide road clearance. (FCB)

Over two hundred thousand of these Studebaker trucks were made. Stalin actually sent a letter to the head of Studebaker thanking him for making a truck that perfectly fit the Soviet Army's needs. (FCB)

A close-up of the ZiS-3 gun. (FCB)

04JUL1945

The 2nd AD entered the American sector of Berlin on Independence Day; the symbolism was not lost on any of us.

09JUL1945 LETTER HOME

We're here. We made it. We are finally sitting in Berlin. No doubt by the time you receive this, you will have read about it in the papers. As yet, I've seen very little of the city, as this job of mine is confining. Last night I went to a GI show, and it's the only time I've left our area.

For the first few days in Berlin, we had a half-track parked in front of the house with our driver on call. As we got more settled in, we used jeeps instead.

I have a little room to myself in house number 52 Monopol Strasse.

We have the house-frau and her children, a boy of 9 and girl of 16, doing our laundry and policing the house. Companies even have men hired to do KP duty. We do no menial labor. We have enough to do with our military duties.

(FCB)

(FCB)

(FCB)

(FCB)

Two children and two cows outside Monopol Strasse house. (FCB)

11JUL1945 LETTER HOME

Still in Berlin, and it appears that it is going to be the scene of some historic doings, but I believe I will miss most of it. It's off to school again for me. I leave on the 16th and go to Paris until about the end of the month. It's an S-2 school, Intelligence again. Seems like I am always getting tied up with S-2. Well, I like that work. I hope to really be able to see Paris now. The school is located about 10 miles outside the city.

I now have the entire 88 points. I am trying to decide on the right course of action. A slight delay in coming home might pay off in the future. Right now, the 2nd AD is scheduled to go to the states by next December. Those who stay with the division will be in a good position, which is only fair. Anyone who decides not to stay with the division who has the points could be transferred to an outfit that is being disbanded and sent home or maybe sent to a replacement pool; believe me, I had that once and do not want it again. If I decide not to stay with the division, I could be discharged and sent home. Thinking it over, I believe it would be best to get out now if it were possible. There are too many ifs right now.

My application for promotion has gone in again, and I know it has gone beyond division; army has it now. If I decide not to stay with the division, my promotion might be stopped. From all I have been told by the Colonel, my chances of getting the promotion look good.

12JUL1945 LETTER HOME

I am now writing by candlelight; the electricity has failed. A lot has happened since my letter earlier today. I just received word that I am leaving for Paris tomorrow instead of the 16th. I am getting a jeep for the trip. That will be a long ride in a 1/4 ton, but it should be interesting. I went to headquarters to get my orders for school, but they weren't ready, so I shall have to go up again in the morning. It's a ten-day course.

In late January 1938, Adolf Hitler had assigned Albert Speer to build the New Reich Chancellery to replace Bismarck's Old Chancellery, which Hitler deemed unsuitable as the headquarters of a Greater German Reich. The chancellery was Hitler's official residence, with grand representational halls and rooms on the ground floor. Hitler's living area was on the upper floor. Behind the building was a large garden area and the underground *Führerbunker*, where Hitler committed suicide at the end of April 1945.

After I finished packing for the trip to France, Sergeant Caddey and I took a jeep tour of Berlin with Private Brunner as our driver. The Reich Chancellery, the building where Hitler made his "last stand," and its balcony from which he launched many a tirade, including his "Thousand-Year Reich" speech, was easy to find and a very popular tourist spot.

Private Brunner and Sergeant Caddey with *Jane* the Jeep. (FCB)

One of the main entrances to the Reich Chancellery that led directly to a grand hall on the first floor. Notice the bullet marks. A Russian soldier walks toward me on the sidewalk, and I think the man wearing a beret coming down the steps to the right is a British soldier. (FCB)

Reich Chancellery plinth. (FCB)

Above left: A grand hall on the first floor of the Reich Chancellery. I was able to pick up some official stationery while in the building and used it for letters home. (FCB)

Center: Another grand room, with debris from the ceiling covering the floor. It was in one of these large rooms where I was approached by a very young Russian soldier wearing a very dirty tunic. In his hand was a German Iron Cross with the swastika. I showed him a package of gum, and a swap was made. I still have it. (FCB)

Right: The doorway at the end of the hall shown above. (FCB)

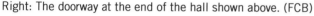

Left: This life-size bust of Hitler was in the chancellery. It had a .45 caliber hole in the cheek. I could have taken it, but what would I have done with it—use it as a target? Notice that the head is broken off the base. (FCB)

Right: Sergeant Caddey in the open square within the Reich Chancellery. (FCB)

The damage from bullets around this one part of the square was extensive. That and the positioning of the armored car and wooden wagon blocking that corner window indicate that this might have been the site of one of several final struggles to hold the Russians back. (FCB)

We stopped in front of the Hotel Kaiserhof, located next to the Reich Chancellery, where on 30 January 1933 Joseph Goebbels, Ernst Röhm and other Nazi officials awaited word that Hitler had been sworn in as chancellor. They did not know he had been appointed until he returned to the Kaiserhof to inform them that the deed was done. (FCB)

Berlin was horribly torn up, the devastation defying description. We continued our short tour and stopped many times to take photos of the shattered remains of the city. Photos only begin to convey the pain and suffering we saw and felt throughout the city.

Private Brunner and Sergeant Caddey. (FCB)

An 88mm multipurpose gun. (FCB)

It was evident that one of the first things the surviving citizens did to try to get life back to some kind of normal was to clear rubble to make paths through the streets. (FCB)

Abandoned and destroyed military equipment was on every street, and scars from thousands and thousands of bullets marked all the walls. (FCB)

Serviceable bricks were neatly stacked on the sidewalks for use in rebuilding. (FCB)

Every street we passed looked like this at first glance. (FCB)

But the details of what was down each street differed greatly. The rubble in the street in the above photo partially hid two destroyed cars, an artillery piece (possibly a 15cm sIG 33, *schweres Infanterie Geschütz 33*, or "heavy infantry gun") and a rare instance of an only partially cleared walking path. (FCB)

A familiar scene throughout Berlin; it looked like everything they owned might be in that cart. Our attention was constantly drawn to the number of bullet impacts we saw. (FCB)

The community stacking bricks for the rebuilding to come. (DAC)

Critch standing in front of a pile of bricks. (DAC)

A black market. Pickings were probably slim and expensive. (FCB)

At what price peace? (FCB)

Three children at play. (FCB)

A Russian soldier with a bust of Hitler. It appears to be the same one I took the photo of in the Reich Chancellery. The base is broken off, with the line of the break following a similar line on both busts. And that just might be a bullet hole next to the nostril. A small world. (Photo © SZ Photo/Bridgeman Images)

12JUL1945 LETTER HOME

We got back to our quarters just before chow, and an envelope had come down from regiment. Among the documents in the envelope were the papers that had been submitted for my promotion. Our division commander, General Collins, had approved it, but 7th Army returned it unapproved along with two promotion requests to major and two others to captain . . . all unapproved. 7th Army said this: "Not favorably considered at the present time." This is the sixth or seventh time, and I am not sure how much I should read into the choice of the words "present time." I make no further comment.

13JUL1945

At 1100, we got into our jeep for the 781-mile journey through Germany, Holland, Belgium and France for the Military Intelligence School course to take place in Dreux, France, west of Paris.

(FCB)

15

Back to France for Class

12JUL1945

Travel order No. 398. I was ordered to depart Berlin on 13 July for Dreux, France, forty-eight miles from Paris, to attend the Military Intelligence School at the St. Georges Hotel with a return to Berlin in sixteen days. There were six of us from the 2nd AD: Captain Jackson from CCB with a sergeant and driver; Technical Sergeant Grose, our regimental S-2; our driver Private First Class Vollstedt; and me. We drew six days of field (K) rations from the mess for the trip.

Our route to Paris took us on and off the autobahn and through some familiar territory. We went around Magdeburg and Braunschweig, and we crossed the Rhine at Duisburg. The only difference was this time we were going west.

We gassed our two jeeps up at U.S. Army service stations set up in gas stations previously run by Germans. We also stopped for gas near Hannover, getting filled up at a British dump. (FCB)

The six of us gassed ourselves up at this casino-guesthouse near Hannover with some good German beer. (FCB)

Except for cyclists and an occasional truck, we had the road to ourselves, but not all the gas stations were operating.

We took the autobahn in much of Germany and were always bypassing towns, but once we hit the Ruhr area, the autobahn was so badly torn up that we could only use local roads the rest of the way.

We spent the night in Wiedenbrück in a beautiful home. The owner of the house had had a part interest in a plywood concern. His wife was now running the business. The husband had been arrested by the Nazis after his partner, a member of the Nazi Party, turned him in for listening to an English broadcast. We heard it from two sources that the partner did this to get control of the factory. The husband was condemned to death and was taken to prison in Magdeburg, dying on 12 April, the same day President Roosevelt died. On that same day our forces were only a day away from his prison in Magdeburg, so it is probable that the Germans killed him when it seemed likely that we would take the town and release the prisoner.

That night, I spoke with an eighty-three-year-old man who was living in the house. He seemed to be a good old fellow, very well dressed and with excellent English. He said, "I'm an old man and have no reason to lie to you. We never realized or knew of the horrors of Buchenwald, Dachau or any of the other camps. We had seen men taken away but never thought that these places were what they have been found to be." These statements of innocence by civilians were pretty hard to swallow for the average GI.

At Duisburg, we crossed the Rhine on a pontoon bridge maintained by the British. A few miles north of this bridge, the Admiral Graf Spee Bridge—the objective of our tank attacks at Kaldenhausen—and its partner bridge, the Adolf Hitler Bridge, lay in huge fragments in the Rhine.

The exit "ramp" to Hannover veers off to the right here. (FCB)

I stood on a bridge over the autobahn about thirty miles outside of Hannover. The burned-out gas station seen in the above photo is to the left of the photo here, with the turnoff to Hannover to the right. I'd crossed this same intersection during our trip to Braunschweig. (FCB)

Two cyclists and a local truck are out in front of us here. Notice the wire-cutter bar attached to the front of the jeep on the left of the photo. (FCB)

We ran into heavy traffic in the towns, but that gave us time to see the sights and watch people.

(FCB)

The bridge was one lane, so we had to wait a while to cross over. The Brits provided a pedestrian lane . . . if you were in a hurry. (FCB)

Not sure whether this fellow in the cart being pulled by the truck was angry with us or the traffic. (FCB)

We wondered who this was behind us. He was definitely not with our group, and he was out of uniform as well. It is a U.S. military vehicle, though. We ended up deciding that it was none of our business. (FCB)

(FCB)

Destruction and rebuilding. (FCB)

Two boys hiding in the girders on the right side of the ruined bridge. Looks like they'd been swimming. (FCB)

We passed supply depots in France that held proof we had prepared for a long haul. Here we found enormous piles of tires and inner tubes. (FCB)

We gassed up and ate a meal at the local mess in Brussels—now *that* is a beautiful city. All we could carry for the trip were K-rations, so whenever possible, we supplemented our meals.

While still in Germany, we stopped at a farmhouse and had the farmer fry up some eggs for us—delicious. Some military police put us up for the night in a small French town they were guarding and fed us tomato juice, corn flakes, fresh eggs, bacon, bread, butter, coffee and plums for breakfast. We rarely (if ever) saw these kinds of meals at the front. Really a treat.

We passed a field full of gliders. There just in case, but we hoped no one would need these anymore. (FCB)

At our destination—the St. Georges Hotel, Dreux, France. The hotel owner joined us for the photo. (FCB)

Five of my classmates with the instructor (fourth from left). Unfortunately, I did not note names. I noted with curiosity that one of our classmates was Chinese, a Captain Ling. (FCB)

17JUL1945 LETTER HOME

This is the first chance I've had to write since we left Berlin. I am sitting in the writing room of Vanderbilt's French Estate. The division is still there, and I see by Stars and Stripes that the President inspected elements of the outfit. I've been missing out on a good lot of historic events. But I have no regrets; this trip has been well worth it. The Autobahn is a marvelous road with not one road crossing it; roads either go under or over it.

(FCB)

School has gone on for two days now, a rather good course. We will have to save telling what it is about until a later date. We have an athletic period every day as a regular part of the school. We played volleyball yesterday with swimming today. A very nice swimming pool. The Vanderbilts certainly went all out when they had this place built.

All goes well. I'm feeling very good.

The course turned out to be about the 2nd AD's possible deployment to the South Pacific. We discussed Japanese tactics, our possible role as a strategic reserve and the invasion of Japan. It ended up that the 2nd AD did not have to go to Japan. We were all very glad about that, although many of us had thoughts we might be going to war with Russia soon.

Thank you for the bridge, 2nd Battalion, 1303 Engineers, of Patton's Third Army.

On the way back into the American zone, we recrossed the Rhine River on the "highest, widest, longest fixed military bridge in the world," dedicated to Patton's Third Army. The bridge led into Mainz-Wiesbaden, Germany. (FCB)

Christ Church (Christuskirche) in Mainz, across the Rhine and to the left in the photo, was badly damaged in 1945, the roof of the dome collapsing. (FCB)

Reconstruction of Christ Church started in 1952 and was completed in 1954. (FCB)

16

Back to Berlin

31JUL1945

Back in Berlin after 2,643 miles in a jeep! Although we put on some of the miles driving around school and seeing some sights, it was still a long, long ride. Jeeps are not that comfortable.

Letter Home

The course was an orientation on Pacific warfare. God grant it will be the nearest I get to that theater. My final grade was a 95—it was an easy course. Good instructors, many of whom had fought the Japanese. Very glad that you received the mailing with the Silver Star. You should receive the Bronze Star shortly.

That was Sgt. William R. Harris who called you. He was formerly my platoon sergeant and then became the company's First Sergeant. Surely was swell of him to call. He's a great fellow.

We are still scheduled to hit the States in December. Fingers crossed. All is well. Good night.

On my return I was appointed commanding officer of the Regimental HQ Company, 66th AR—the so-called Head and Head Company—which was a big move up from battalion to regiment.

I certainly missed a lot while I was in France. Probably the biggest event I missed was the division review held for President Truman, Prime Minister Winston Churchill and Field Marshal Montgomery on 16 July along a stretch of the autobahn running through the Grunewald Forest in the southeast corner of Berlin.

On 18 July, a review was held for General George C. Marshall, General Henry "Hap" Arnold,

Dress rehearsal for review of 2nd AD by the visiting dignitaries. (DAC)

Admiral Ernest King and Field Marshal Sir Alan Brooke, Chief of Staff of the British Army.

On 20 July General George S. Patton and Secretary of War Henry Stimson reviewed the division (it was noticed by all that Patton sported the patch of the 2nd AD, and some reported that he wiped his eyes a couple times).

I probably would not have been able to get their autographs on my short snorter, but I did have some regrets that I missed the reviews.

The Big Three—Soviet leader Joseph Stalin, British Prime Minister Winston Churchill (replaced on July 26 by Prime Minister Clement Attlee) and U.S. President Harry Truman—met in Potsdam, Germany, from 17 July to 2 August 1945 to hammer out postwar terms of agreement. President Truman took a day off from the meetings for the twenty-mile ride to Berlin to review the 2nd AD and see some of the city.

President Harry S. Truman, with his hat over his heart, reviews the 2nd AD. Sharing the front of the half-track with the president and wearing the helmet is General John H. "Pee Wee" Collier, commanding officer of the 2nd AD. (Wikimedia Commons)

My photos of the *Strasse* (street) where the parade took place were all taken well after the dignitaries had gone. The tanks were still lined up when I got there, but they were all now covered to protect them from the weather . . . and so they would not need to be cleaned up again. (FCB)

Left: The president took in some sites as well, including the ever-popular tourist spot of the Hitler balcony at the Reich Chancellery. (U.S. Army Photo)

Close-up of the photo of F Company shows the company guidon with, from left to right in the row behind the guidon: Critch, Ed Fawks, Colonel Parker and Major Owen. (U.S. Army Photo in the Author's Collection)

2nd Platoon, Company F. Those in *italics* were with me when I led the platoon. Gentile was my driver, Jutras my gunner and Marino my bow gunner. Ray Stewart also missed the photo, as he was seconded to another unit in order to accumulate more points.

Top row: Kello, *Abshire*, *Brierly*, King, Crocker
Second row: *Korneder*, Goff, Racibosky, *Skovira*, Shafer
Third row: Freizland, Wyen, *Gentile*, *Jutras*, *Marino*, *Rose*
Fourth row: *Cignetto*, Weinert, Mathers, Unglesby, *Conner*
Bottom row: *Captain Fawks*, First Lt. Lightsey
(FCB)

Although technically I was no longer with F Company, I would have liked to have been in the photos taken of the company and the platoon. I liked that tankers still wore their service caps tilted to the left side of the head.

We were slated to stay in Berlin for a while, so we took frequent sightseeing trips throughout the city. One day we visited Tempelhof Airport (Flughafen Berlin-Tempelhof). The field was officially designated an airport on 8 Ocotber 1923 and underwent a massive reconstruction in the mid-1930s by the Nazi government. We used it for supply runs, but it also had numerous German aircraft in various stages of ruin parked both in the hangars and on the field. Tempelhof Airport served as the center of the Berlin Airlift of 1948–1949.

We also found several vehicles abandoned on the airfield.

Numerous windows showed smoke trails, evidence of fires probably set on purpose in rooms and offices of the main building of Tempelhof. (FCB)

One of our DC-3 aircraft, nicknamed "Old Crow," bringing in supplies. (FCB)

Major Owen and Colonel Powers in front of the main building at Tempelhof. Heavy smoke soot staining around windows was clearly visible. (FCB)

What's left of an Arado 234 jet lying in a destroyed hangar. (FCB)

I cannot resist sitting in a Messerschmitt Bf Me109. (DAC)

Engines sitting on racks beyond the plane in which I am sitting. (DAC)

A Focke-Wulf Fw 190, a single-seater fighter bomber. I think that is Critch taking the photo, but I do not remember the soldier standing on the wing. (FCB)

A row of Messerschmitt Bf 109s. The Me 109 first saw action as a fighter in Spain in 1937 during the Spanish Civil War and became the backbone of the Luftwaffe through the end of World War II. (FCB)

Critch jumped right on this Kettenkrad, a motorcycle/half-track that was mass-produced starting in 1939. Its main use was as a hauler. It had a towing capacity of up to a half ton of supplies in a small two-wheeled trailer. It could also tow a small artillery piece or carry large spools of communication cable or wire over rough terrain. Its use here at Tempelhof was probably to tow baggage and tools around the field. (FCB)

Next to the Kettenkrad (visible to the left) was a rare schwerer Wehrmachtschlepper (sWS) half-track designed as a tractor and a supply vehicle. The Wehrmacht's widely used Sd.Kfz half-track models, with their off-road mobility, speed and multiple uses, suffered frequent breakdowns, particularly on the eastern front. To counter this issue, in May 1942 Hitler demanded a simplified half-track vehicle. A tracked truck, the Wehrmachtschlepper, began production in late 1943. Concessions made to keep its mechanics simple resulted in slower speed, leaving it unable to keep up with quick-moving troops and armor. Relegated to shuttling infantry, the slower and less mobile half-track suffered heavy losses during the retreat along the eastern front, with troops soon losing trust in it. It devolved to a supply transport, although some had anti-aircraft guns mounted on them. Only 825 of these were produced, with this one ending up at Tempelhof. (FCB)

One rainy day, Ed Fawks and I decided to visit the Olympic Stadium (Olympiastadion), the site where in 1936 U.S. athlete Jesse Owens achieved his place in history. Berlin had been selected as the site for the Games in 1916, but the event was canceled because of World War I. In 1931, the International Olympic Committee again selected Berlin to host the 11th Summer Olympics. The German government planned merely to restore the 1916 Olympic Stadium and retained architect Werner March to do this.

However, when Hitler came to power in 1933, he ordered the construction of a giant sports complex covering 330 acres in Grunewald named the "Reichssportfeld" that would include a totally new stadium with 110,000 seats and a special stand for Hitler and his entourage. Werner March was again in charge of the project, with construction taking place from 1934 to 1936. He built the new Olympiastadion on the foundation of the 1916 stadium with the oddity that the field was set nearly forty feet below ground level.

Hitler's desire to wrap his theory of Aryan dominance in grand heroic myth was evident throughout the stadium. Something I found

The cauldron that held the Olympic Flame stood behind the large horses and near the main entrance. Stylized swastikas adorned the fence railings, with the track and field stadium behind. (FCB)

Ed and I stood at the entrance to the stadium at ground level, with the field 40 feet below us. (EF)

Horses of mythic size held by giant men stood outside the stadium. I am not sure where we got the ladder, but Ed and I climbed onto the horse's back and had our pictures taken. Probably not the brightest thing to do. (FCB)

(FCB)

(FCB)

out well after our visit was that the symbols and ceremony built into the games also reflected these myths. The torch relay that starts at Delphi and ends in the lighting of the Olympic flame was introduced by Carl Diem, a German whom Hitler commissioned to organize the 1936 Games. The five interlocking rings that have grown to symbolize the Games were originally used on letterhead for a 1914 World Olympic Congress in Paris, perhaps to symbolize the first five Olympics. The congress disbanded with the outbreak of World War I. Diem had the interlocking rings carved into a three-foot stone altar and placed at Delphi as a prop in the torchbearer's ceremony. Hitler adopted the rings as a symbol and made them part of the Nazi Olympic pageantry.

These tablets affixed to a wall were just inside the stadium and recounted the winners of the field events of the 1936 Olympics. Hitler's name takes center stage in the middle plaque, soon to be replaced, but the first four names on the plaque to the left are the more honored U.S. athletes. Jesse Owens has the honor of the first two spots with his wins in the 100 meter and 200 meter sprints. (FCB)

The Olympic Stadium was in the British sector, and we Americans had no problems touring their area. When we left the stadium, we went around the end that we had only seen from the inside and came across this British tank park in the large open space

Most of the vehicles were covered with tarps, as ours were, but the one out front could easily be identified as a Cromwell cruiser tank. (FCB)

beyond the stadium. They were grouped there probably for the same reason we had our tanks along the autobahn in Grunewald Forest: both were good places to stow a lot of vehicles.

While in Berlin, I had a number of encounters with Russians, both enlisted personnel and officers. The first time was during a visit to the British HQ. I believe it was the main command post for the British. The Russians had moved into a building across the street from the British and set up their own HQ, which we would not have allowed. As one Brit put it, "It was a bit cheeky of them," but the Brits tolerated it, probably to avoid any serious confrontation.

The Brits told us that the Russians were having a continuous party in their HQ, so we decided to walk over and take a look. Almost immediately upon our entering the building, a Russian officer came up to me and yanked my arm up and down in the hardest handshake I have ever experienced. There was an extensive table of food and meats and plenty of vodka. They did not object to our joining the party one bit. Having seen the poor appearance of the average Soviet soldier and the condition of his equipment, I had to wonder how it was that they could set such a lavish table.

In my experience, we had no serious problems with individual Russian soldiers. Some of their officers were a different matter. We got word of a very serious run-in that some of our people had had with a Russian major. The details were sketchy, but I do recall it caused a good deal of concern, and we were on our toes around Russians after that.

The Russians also took security of their sector seriously. Getting clearance to enter their sector was very difficult. They felt free to wander at will throughout our sector. At one point, a company of the 41st Armored Infantry Regiment chased a group of Russians from a warehouse in our sector that they were trying to loot. The fixed bayonets did the job, but we thought officers had to have sanctioned or even planned the well-organized raid on our warehouse.

The Russians on the whole seemed to mix well with Berliners, the Berliners seemingly resigned to their fate.

On our way back to the American zone, we encountered this young Soviet soldier. His uniform and boots were in nearly new condition. Perhaps he and the other young Russians we saw were more occupation forces than there for combat? Measuring in the bayonet, his rifle almost gets to his ear. His cherubic smile made us wonder whether he had any idea what was going on. (FCB)

(FCB)

I particularly liked the two Russian soldiers carrying briefcases. (FCB)

Lieutenant Colonel "Shorty" Powers was not so short in comparison with this young Russian soldier. (FCB)

A Soviet cameraman filming in the Russian sector under the curious eyes of German civilians. (Photo courtesy of the family of Luke Bolin)

The ubiquitous Studebaker US6 with Russian troops, both male and female. One of our jeeps is on the right in the background of the photo. (DAC)

We made our way to the historic Brandenburg Gate (Brandenburger Tor), built in the eighteenth century on the orders of Prussian King Frederick William II (1786–1797), who succeeded Frederick the Great. The entryway was built on the site of a former city gate that marked the start of the road from Berlin to the town of Brandenburg an der Havel, forty miles east of Berlin. In this photo, the gate is visible in the center distance. In the foreground are Russian signs giving directions that were probably not too helpful to Berliners. The top sign indicates a main detour, and the lower sign points in the direction of Spandau, a section nine miles east of Berlin. The detour was probably set up to reroute heavy traffic away from the Brandenburg Gate. (FCB)

The area around the gate and the gate itself were hit hard, but the Berliners had done a good job cleaning up the rubble. (DAC)

Stalin's presence was everywhere in the Russian sector, with large posters of his face plastered where all could see them.

Above: A large poster of Stalin was placed conspicuously beyond the middle arches of the gate. (FCB)

Everyone was going somewhere, except for this gentleman, who seemed to be lost in remembering what had once been. (FCB)

This large display was no doubt prepared before the passing of President Roosevelt, but the Russians decided to honor him here. One has to wonder what they are trying to say about Churchill—always something up his sleeve, perhaps? (FCB)

This display of posters featuring Stalin and his generals was set up outside the Jonass & Co. department store built in the 1920s. In the 1930s, the building became the headquarters of the Reich Youth Leadership organization, and in 1945 it became the headquarters for the politburo of the East German Communist Party. It currently is the Soho House Berlin Hotel, with the building having been declared a cultural heritage monument. A large-caliber gun had to have made that crater located in the left front of the photo. (FCB)

The Stalin tank was one in a series of heavy tanks designed to counter the German Tiger tank. First produced in 1943, it quickly grew in thickness of armor and size of the main gun, finally carrying a large 122mm main gun that was very effective against both infantry and armor. The IS-2 was a match for the Tiger, with the winner in such an encounter depending on the combat situation and the skill of the crew. In total, 3,854 tanks of all IS models were produced from 1943 to 1945.

This memorial is up to date with President Truman, but Stalin now occupies the center position, instead of President Roosevelt. (FCB)

Russian soldiers also received some due with the likes of this monument featuring a Russian IS-2 Stalin tank set on a recently constructed pedestal and painted gold. (FCB)

The more evocative tributes to the Russian troops, however, were the wrecks of vehicles still lying in the streets of Berlin. Here, a T-34 tank sits among wrecks and ruins. (FCB)

The T-34 first saw action against the Germans at the start of Operation Barbarossa, the German invasion of Russia, which began on 22 June 1941. A medium-weight, low-profile tank, its 76.2mm gun was the most powerful gun in the field in 1941. Its sixty-degree-sloped armor was able to deflect shots from anti-tank weapons. The tank also featured the Christie suspension, designed by American Walter Christie for his M1928 tank. As stated in chapter 1, Christie's unique suspension design was not accepted by the U.S. Army, so he sent versions of his tank (without turrets and with documentation that the vehicles were farm tractors) to the Russians, who adopted his design to the T-34. Many German commanders called the T-34 the finest tank in the world and vastly superior to the early German tanks. Others have seen the T-34 as the most influential tank design of the war. A total of 84,070 were built, with a staggering 44,900 lost in battle. As late as 2010, 130 of them were still in service, some appearing in Russian war movies. (FCB)

This mammoth IS-2 Stalin tank did not survive to make it to a pedestal. (FCB)

The Russians must have decided to take target practice with this statue, blowing its tail right off and damaging the pedestal. (DAC)

Photo of me taken while in Berlin by Technical Sergeant Ray Stewart. (RS)

This sign was posted in German by the Russians on a street in Berlin. Translated: "The lessons of history teach us that Hitlers come and go, but the German people and the German state remain. —Stalin." (FCB)

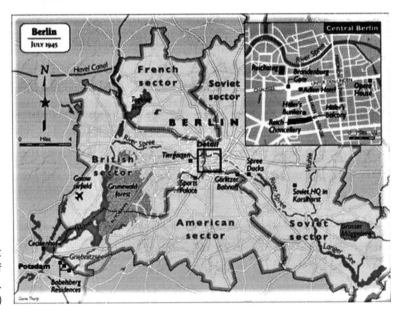

Map of Berlin as it was laid out 1945 indicating the locations of many of the sights I got to see. (Courtesy of Wordpress.com)

17

Leaving Berlin for Frankfurt

We traveled farther east into the Russian sector to see the Berlin Cathedral (Oberpfarr- und Domkirche zu Berlin), located about one and a half miles beyond the Brandenburg Gate.

Friedrich Wilhelm II, in his capacity as king and head of the Protestant Church in Prussia, called for the construction of a cathedral that would measure up to the great churches of the world. Construction of the Berlin Cathedral began in 1894, with the cathedral being inaugurated in 1905. It was built on an island of the Spree River.

Some three hundred yards to the northeast of the Brandenburg Gate were the ruins of the Reichstag. The architect, Paul Wallot from Frankfurt, used Philadelphia's Memorial Hall, the main building of the 1876 Centennial Exhibition, as his model. The German Parliament met in the building from 1884 until it was burned in a mysterious fire in 1933, the fire giving a pretext for the Nazis to arrest Communists and any others seen as threats to the growing Nazi order. The Russians saw the Reichstag as a symbol of Nazi Germany and made it a primary objective of their advance into Berlin.

A postcard of the Berlin Cathedral as it appeared in 1904. (Author's Collection)

We were not sure why there was a World War I tank and an old artillery piece in front of the church, but the island housed many museums, so perhaps this was part of an outdoor display. (FCB)

An 88mm gun in its anti-aircraft position in front of the ruined Reichstag. The fighting had been fierce in this part of the city, as countless bullet marks on the barrel of the 88 and the pillars of the Reichstag prove. (DAC)

The destruction we saw in Berlin was overwhelming, and we were amazed at the way the citizens of the city were bouncing back. Many had to have survived the bombings by living in their basements. We saw their plight, but in the back of our minds, we were aware that they had in many ways been complicit in Hitler's madness and brought this upon themselves.

I took some last photos of Berlin from the upper floors of a building north of the Berlin Cathedral. I took a risk, but the building seemed stable enough. The Berlin Cathedral is the main building in the photo on the left. I faced west for the photo on the right. On the horizon the outline of the Reichstag is just visible. Berlin had been destroyed.

Another 88 farther out from the Reichstag. (FCB)

(FCB)

Though we were more than ready to leave, July saw us still in Berlin. Finally, in early August, we received orders to prepare to move southeast 330 miles to our next post, Gelnhausen, just east of Frankfurt am Main, and take over as the occupying force there. On the day of our departure, we formed all of our vehicles in column and left Berlin. As we moved out, the 82nd Airborne Division moved in, relieving us of our occupation duties in the city.

Soon after we left the Soviet Zone of Occupation and entered the American sector, we were directed to move all of our tanks onto a huge field and park them there. We just left them.

Pup tents had been set up by our advance team in a muddy field nearby, allowing us to shelter for the night and convoy in jeeps, half-tracks and trucks the next day to Gelnhausen. Pup tents were a far cry from the quarters we had become used to in Lebenstedt, Preusslitz and Berlin, but we were tired, and we had done this a lot during basic training. We could handle this for one night.

(FCB)

The field was badly chewed up, with rain puddling in the ruts left by the trucks that had delivered the tents. (FCB)

This energetic soldier is putting his shovel to good use digging a trench around his tent to keep the water from flowing into it. We maintained our Polar Bear titles that we had started using in Lebenstedt. (FCB)

The men of the battalion were tired and ready to go home. (FCB)

Critch enjoying the view from his pup tent. (FCB)

Despite the move and the conditions, we still had an adequate mess set-up; mess tents are seen here to the lower left of the photo. The ability to organize on any scale was still a hallmark of the U.S. Army. (FCB)

The next morning, we revved up our vehicles and formed into column. I was assigned to lead the column to Gelnhausen in the HQ half-track. Somewhere close to the town, I made a wrong turn. I quickly corrected the column, but Colonel Zeien had seen that I made the mistake.

I noticed with approval and perhaps envy that Captain Fawks was dressed for the weather. (FCB)

When we pulled up next to him, he was very disgruntled and snapped at me, "Can't you read a map?"

My immediate response was polite: "I don't have a map, Sir."

The look on his face was of surprise and wonder; perhaps he was amazed that we had made it this far at all. He said no more.

14AUG1945 LETTER HOME

We have taken leave of the city of Berlin and are now in Gelnhausen, just over 300 miles southwest of Berlin and 25 miles east of Frankfurt. I have surely put in the miles here of late. I have your letter in front of me where you apologize for not having written in a week, but please don't apologize because it makes me feel very bad since my writing home has been neglected for about two weeks. Just couldn't be helped with all the moving around we have been doing. We have settled here and will be staying here for some time, I think. The Division is still scheduled to be back home in December . . . maybe we will be together for Christmas? At any rate, we have not heard any changes to that scheduling.

Doc O'Neill. (FCB)

It is a cool evening, and I am sitting in my room. Across the table from me sits Doc O'Neill, who is slamming and banging away on his German Remington portable typewriter. He's very good company, so I told him I'd tolerate the hammering of that machine of his. If the writing in this letter jumps around a bit, you will know why. Doc is our Battalion Medical Officer and strictly an all-right fellow. He accompanied us into Dochamps. Naturally, he is from the Midwest, hailing from Wisconsin. Good. Doc just finished typing his letter, so the table has ceased vibrating.

We are in a valley that seems to catch any passing rain clouds. Had two heavy showers. I signed up for a course in elementary German, which will be conducted right in our regimental area, taught by a German professor who speaks excellent English. Don't know when it will start, but I am hoping that the hours are such that I'll be able to attend. I was finally able to send those glass ballet dancers I was given when we were in Schulenburg, and they should arrive in one piece. I packed them in a stiff cardboard box and surrounded them by sawdust. I also enclosed some medals that I picked up from the Reich Chancellery. A lot of guys stuffed their pockets with them.

I went into Frankfurt to see the movie Hangover Square *with murder and stuff. Not bad.*

Let me know how badly Bob was wounded. Hope it wasn't too serious, but there are so many degrees of seriousness. Bob Ranieri is home again; he was with the 1st AD, no?

It looks as though the situation in the Pacific is winding down, and we are waiting for the radio announcement saying V-J Day has arrived. The fighting there is surely ending much faster than any of us ever dreamed. This atomic bomb surely must pack a wallop.

I improvised a photograph album from a notebook that was produced in Oslo. When it is filled, I am going to take a chance and send the entire book home.

My promotion nomination has gone in again. With things winding down in Japan, it might not make it. However, the end of the war is the best promotion as it means home. All's well. God bless you.

Frankfurt is surely torn up. It hurts to see that destruction. (FCB)

We spotted the approaching oxcart, just visible at the turn in the road, and waited for it, stopping for a photo. (FCB)

(FCB)

(FCB)

While in Gelnhausen, we were able to make day trips and were taken by the scenery, making us even more thankful to be out of Berlin. We passed through the village of Breitenborn, eight miles north of Gelnhausen. We were taken by the fact that it was virtually untouched by the war. We still had our wire cutter attached to the jeep, just in case.

What a relief to be back in the country with its clean air and simpler life!

(FCB)

19AUG1945 LETTER HOME

As you can see, I still have stationery to use up from the Reich Chancellery! The news is that I am now the company commander of the Regimental Headquarters Company. The previous commander is going home. Coming full circle. Back in JUN1941, I was a private in a regimental headquarters company.

Do you remember when I had to select men from my company in the 14th AD to send overseas? Among them, I sent a mechanic, then Private Hoppe. He is now my maintenance sergeant, with a Tech/4 rating.

I've been checking company property all day. What a job. Tomorrow I must sign for it, assuming full responsibility. We had six hours to do a 66-hour job. We were given two new-style historic maps today. They are better than the old ones.

The weather has been bad, with rain every day. I have a good fire roaring under the water heater in the house. I am going to take a big hot bath before going to bed.

Went to mass and communion at 0900 at a fine church in town. Father McPartland said the mass. Usually the local organist and choir are present at our masses, which we have every Monday, Wednesday and Friday at 2030. It is strange to hear Holy God We Praise Thy Name *sung in German. I made all the masses last week—helps so much.*

I met up with Frank Longley in Frankfurt the other night. He told me that Eddie Heist had been killed, which I already knew, and you already know about Hank Woodward. We have so much to be thankful for.

"Rosie," my first sergeant when I was commanding officer of HQ and HQ Company, 66th AR. He had been in command of our lead tank on the road to Dochamps. (FCB)

20AUG1945 LETTER HOME

I've run out of my special Reich Chancellery stationery. So many of the officers are leaving now—some men have 100 points and some officers as many as 122. My 88 points seem so few, but who knows. Just turned on the radio. AFN, the Armed Forces Network, is broadcasting Carmen Cavallero and his orchestra.

My misgiving about this position was that it is much too close to "city hall." Of course it is much too early to say anything definite, but at least it shouldn't be too rough. I know I can handle the job; it's just the idea of being right under the "nose" that gives rise to my misgivings. I'm too used to being in a line company.

There are so many different sections in the officially designated Headquarters and Headquarters Company. I have present for duty 198 men with the S-1, S-2, S-3, S-4, the command section, the band, the communications section and both the reconnaissance platoon and a tank platoon. It's quite an organization to juggle.

I should know sometime soon about the promotion.

I had to go into Frankfurt today. One of my men was picked up by the MPs. I wanted to get a copy of the report as soon as possible. He was arrested because of a curfew violation, but it went beyond that. When the MPs stopped him, he said some highly uncomplimentary and mostly unprintable things. Brutal talk. He surely messed himself up. He was on a shipping list for home . . . that is certainly "was" now. I cannot understand his behavior. Surely he must have realized the risk he was taking. Most men are watching their step. Doesn't pay to goof up now.

Snacks—that's what I want. A package request of not-too-difficult-to-find items: cans of sardines, shrimp, crackers, things, stuff, food . . . anything for snacks. I have quite a reputation as a big eater and am constantly being kidded about it. Can I help it if all the other guys eat like birds? But I surely do have a healthy appetite. A whale of one.

Gelnhausen is a nice little village. On the side of a hill and very picturesque. I am taking photos all the time now since I've gotten that Rolleiflex. It surely has helped me pass the time. I've had all kinds of good offers made for the camera. Journalist Wes Gallagher offered me $400 for it, but no soap. I get too much pleasure fooling around with it.

Speaking of passing the time, I now have an ocarina and can play Good Night Ladies, The Marine Hymn, Whispering, Loch Lomond, *and others. I'll play for you when I get home.*

It is now nearly midnight. Getting sleepy. I have a nice little room again and have my bedroll and air mattress spread out on the bed. The beds in Germany are all a bit short, but they work well enough.

27AUG1945 LETTER HOME

Among the rumors that are flying thick, fast and free is one that has us on board a ship for home on 13OCT. Let's just hope that it will be soon. I am enclosing a copy of our regimental paper, Hot Poop. *The article "Your Address—Kaserne 9" mentions the building in which the HQ Company is quartered. The bomb mentioned in the article surely did tear the middle out of the building. Someone said that it would be better to convert it into two buildings. The hit was practically direct center.*

We have our mess in a building called The Casino, and lieutenants are also quartered there. I share a room with Captain Fawks in the captains' quarters in a fine house near the regimental area. Twin beds, radio, sink, wardrobe—not at all bad.

Stamped on the back of this hand-drawn card: "A souvenir of the Officers' Club, Gelnhausen, Germany." "Kaserne" translates as "barracks." (Author's Collection)

01SEP1945 Letter Home

All is well! The weather has been excellent. No more rain. Had a very enjoyable evening last night. I saw the musical production OK-USA with Mickey Rooney. He really is good and takes quite a beating on that stage. Comedian Red Buttons was in it as well. Scene IV was named "Chicago"—o me o my, the scene was set at the Dearborn Street Station. One of the lines in the song from that scene was "It's a good ol' town." The Special Show Company of the 6817th Special Service battalion was terrific.

Mickey Rooney entertaining the troops. (U.S. Army Photo)

News is, well, it just isn't . . . we're still around sweating it out. Rumors fly fast and thick.

About our leaving for home, the news is, well, it just isn't . . . we're still around sweating it out.

Rumors fly fast and thick.

There is a possibility that some of us could get home before December. It would mean being attached to some other outfit. I would much rather stick with the 2nd and go home with them. Treatment would be much better. At least we are known here. I went through the replacement deal once, and that's enough in any man's life.

We're losing Father McPartland. Another priest came in, and now Fr. Mac feels as though he can go home. He should, too. He's been with the division since it left the States, and that is a long time in any man's army. Surely hate to see him go, but he deserves it.

Doggone, some radio in the building is playing Chicago, Chicago. *It's haunting me. Ah, but soon . . .*

We had the playoff for the battalion softball championship this afternoon. A good close game, although my company lost 5–4.

Sorry for the interruption. It is now Sunday night. This morning we had a parade review for a special visitor, General Harmon. He ate dinner at our mess. My convictions that led me to turn down that aide job were greatly substantiated today. I saw how he had his aides hopping around. Have to sign off. Many of us couldn't get to mass this morning, so padre is having a special mass at 2015.

06SEP1945 Letter Home

I am duty officer tonight, and this just came in: Paragraph #1, Special Orders #244; Hdqs. 7th Army, SEP1945. I am now a captain. It's hard to believe, been a long time. Word got around fast, and Captain Fawks has just come up to Hdqs and pinned a set of his own bars on me. He's a grand fellow.

He was CO of F company when I was with it. He was wounded during the Bulge . . . on his birthday. Hit by a fragment from a mortar shell. I was only with him a little bit before the medics took him to the rear, but I remember saying to him, "Many happy returns of the day, Ol' Man!" We've had many a chuckle since out of that "happy returns" business. At the time it was not meant to be humorous; the situation was too ironic to be humorous. What a way to celebrate a birthday.

We've become good buddies, and we now share a room. The other officers of the company whom we knew are all gone. Fawks and I have similar interests—he's a complete camera fiend—capital letters FIEND. Has a movie camera, a projector, two still cameras and beaucoup accessories. He wants to teach me to play Bridge. So far I've been able to beat him out of that idea. We do play a lot of chess. I'm always kidding him, telling him, "You're a good ol' man—but old." Now that I am a captain, he started calling me Fred . . . for just one day. Then I became "Fritz."

This duty officer shift is quite a deal. There is an NCO on duty all night to answer the phone. I could go to sleep, but the light burns brightly, and the radio blares out, probably on purpose to keep us awake. The time is now 0150. I get to hit the sack soon.

Much of Frankfurt was flattened. No doubt the Imperial Cathedral of Saint Bartholomew (Kaiserdom Sankt Bartholomäus) was a prominent aiming point for Allied bombers. The former coronation church of the Holy Roman Empire took quite a beating, as did everything around it.

Aerial photo of a bombed-out Frankfurt with the Imperial Cathedral of Saint Bartholomew in the center. (U.S. Army Signal Corps Photo in the Author's Collection)

I climbed inside a building, although the stairway was a bit dicey, to get a better view and took these two photos of Frankfurt. (FCB)

09SEP1945 LETTER HOME

Yesterday noon I went into Frankfurt with Capt. Fawks and Major Fuller, who just transferred from the 5th AD to be the new CO of 1st Battalion. With my promotion orders, I was able to buy five sets of captain's bars. We had lunch at the United States Forces, European Theater (USFET) officers' club. What a set-up those yokels have! What a way to fight a war! We had ice cream, sandwiches, cokes; it all reminded me of what it will be like after "the show."

10SEP1945 LETTER HOME

Went around today contacting a few of the civil authorities with an interpreter. What I wanted was a barber chair and some equipment. We had a line on some that was in the hands of a Nazi party member. We got the necessary papers, but the chair had already been picked up by some other outfit, We were able to get a very good electric clipper and a few other items, though. We have a full-time barber in operation now.

Companies are playing a good deal of softball, volleyball, etc. Regiment has also organized a football team. Three days ago the equipment arrived; looks good to see a team practicing in uniforms and all. Another touch of home.

Division CO received a cable from Washington stating that we are tentatively scheduled to arrive at Camp Polk by December. Can you imagine that? This isn't just a rumor. Our new Padre saw the cable.

Capt. Fawks moved over to his battalion commander's house. I will keep his radio. It won't work in his new place. Such a small town and yet the electricity is different where he will be staying.

16SEP1945

The 66th AR versus the 508th Parachute Infantry Regiment! They even printed programs.

17SEP1945 LETTER HOME

By a new ruling, officers can't be declared essential. I can be held long enough to work someone into my job, though. On the 25th there is a quota of officers and men leaving the 2nd AD for the 12th AD, which is a Category IV unit, which means it is going home and will be disbanded when it hits the States.

I went to see the Colonel and stated my case. He was really swell about it, giving me the choice to stay an extra year on active duty with the 2nd AD or to go home and become a civilian as soon as possible. That sure boiled it right down. I know I can go back to Marquette to work, so I told the Colonel that I would like to go home. I'll get on this quota if they take enough officers, and the Colonel had already talked to another officer, Lt. Thursby, about taking over my company. I'll get home before the 2nd AD gets home. I hope the 12th gets a very early

SOUVENIR PROGRAM

66th AR vs 508th PIR

Sunday, Sept. 16, 1945   Kickoff — 2 p.m.

FIELD NO. 2, FRANKFURT AM MAIN

(Author's Collection)

shipping date. Capt. Fawks is doing the same thing, so we might be going home together. He and I came over to Europe together back in 1944, maybe on the same ship, although I do not remember him from that trip.

Ed and I were transferred to the 12th Armored Division, each of us commanding a provisional company of 250 men gathered from various units who were scheduled to go stateside.

We had agreed a good while back that when one of us wanted to go home, the other would as well. I don't know who decided first, Ed or me, but when we learned that the division probably would be there a few more months, that was it. We would miss the "march down Broadway," but we decided to go home anyway.

Don Critchfield had more points than any of us since he had been there from the Fort Benning days. I am not sure when he went home, but I am pretty sure he went home before the division did. I was sorry that Critch and I lost contact with each other and never got together again. He was a good friend.

18SEP1945 LETTER HOME

Confirmed. On or about the 25th, I shall leave the 2nd AD for the 12th AD. All men of the 12th AD will be high-point personnel, and we will be leaving sometime in October. Already an order was published giving command of my Headquarters Company to Lt. Thursby.

Sorry for the interruption. Ed (Capt. Fawks) just came in, along with Capt. O'Neill and Capt. Sheets. Big bull-session about our next mission: getting home. Doc, unfortunately, does not have enough points yet, so he will have to stay longer. Ed and I continue to keep our fingers crossed, as things happen in the army.

23SEP1945

Went to the Officers' Country Club, set up by the Special Service Section of Headquarters Command SHAEF (Supreme Headquarters Allied Expeditionary Force—Ike's HQ). The sumptuous menu, printed with flourishes and designs, featured Crème a la Reine (The Queen's Soup), salami salad, southern fried chicken, mashed potatoes, buttered peas, tossed salad, fresh fruit and a banana tart. We had our choice of coffee, tea, Rhine wine, red wine or champagne! I had the maître d' autograph my menu: "With compliments of John of SHAEF." As you can imagine, the food was the best we had had in quite a while.

02OCT1945 LETTER HOME

We've moved to Grosskuchen now, 170 miles southeast of Gelnhausen, and are with the "Hellcats" of the 12th Armored Division. We hope to be on the high seas sometime this month. Ed and I are still together, and we are in the same company. Two captains in one company is highly irregular; however, the outfit is designed for only one thing—a vehicle to transport all of us home. We have 260 men and eight officers in our company.

Grosskuchen is strictly a rural town—electricity is about the only modern convenience. Ed and I are living in a swell room in the local priest's house. Ed has a bad cold, so Padre gave him a small pitcher of hot wine—it's altar wine—told him to drink it, go to bed and sweat it out.

My address is Company B, 714th Tank Battalion, APO 262 c/o PM NY, NY. You can still write, but don't send any packages. Our APO will close temporarily since we are scheduled to move to France soon.

It will be great to really get going. I'm an eager beaver these days and can't sit still. It's funny, but understandable, that our morale is at low ebb. All of us have a lost-like sensation all the time. Guess it's because things are still rather in a fog.

Ed and I playing chess at our billet in Grosskuchen. We were staying in the rectory of the Catholic Church. Ed beat the pastor, Father Mueller, in every game of chess they played. (FCB)

Father Mueller was priest of the parish of Grosskuchen. He was probably the only male in the entire town. Father Mueller's brother was a Jesuit and had been taken by the Nazis, but somehow Father Mueller managed to visit his brother, who told him about the horrible things the Nazis were doing.

One night, a dance was arranged by our men for the locals. Father Mueller came to Fawks and me and told us that we should not do this—that his brother had told him that the Germans had done very bad things and that they should not be treated well. Despite Father Mueller's misgivings, we held the dance anyway, with only one special order to obey—do not blow up the condoms and give them to the kids.

I visited Grosskuchen on a tour in 1986 to see whether I could get any information on Father Mueller. I was able to find his grave, and I paid my respects.

During that visit I saw three older women talking on a street corner. I decided to go over and start up a conversation. The first thing I told them was that I had been in Grosskuchen after the war. They said they loved Americans, and as we talked, they mentioned the dance—all three had attended the dance that night. One woman disappeared and quickly came back with a large beer stein that she presented to me as a souvenir to remember my two visits to Grosskuchen.

07OCT1945 LETTER HOME

Our APO is now open again. The move to southern France and our ship home has been postponed. We might leave next Saturday. We hope we'll go directly to the port instead of the area assembly command that is in Rheims, France, where they supposedly ready you for shipment.

Father Mueller. (FCB)

The pastor's sister brought a small bouquet of blue and yellow flowers into my room and put them behind your photo to celebrate our wedding anniversary. Wish you could see your photo now.

I hope to be back in the U.S.A. around the first or the middle of November. Time is sure dragging along. Ed and I play cribbage and chess, then we read, get plenty of sleep and eat well. Actually, we are taking it too easy and feeling rusty.

We have been listening to the World Series games on AFN Radio. Come on, you Cubs. The broadcast starts at 1900 each night.

09OCT1945 LETTER HOME

Ed and I are still roommates, and he is an excellent companion. We did a bit of calisthenics this morning, and we're feeling better for it. This noon we are going on a cross-county walk and picture-taking tour. Too much lying around and getting sluggish.

Wow, what a ballgame last night. Detroit 8—our Cubs 7 in the last of the 12th. We lost, but a real game. It's surprising how well we hear it. We'll take in a couple of Bear games when I get home. I have a bit over two months accrued leave that I can take as terminal leave just prior to final checkout of the army.

11OCT1945 LETTER HOME

Ed is sitting across the table from me writing a letter to his wife. He started it by saying, "Just finished beating Fritz in a game of cribbage." I played two games of chess with the Padre, winning one and losing the second. He speaks little or no English, but we get along with my meager German. He came into our room while AFN Radio was playing popular music. He shook his head and said, "Nichts gut"—not good. He makes it clear that he thinks there is too much bouncing in our dancing, and he demonstrates. I get a kick out of him.

The 12th AD paper came out today saying, "The Division will stay here." The good news is that we are to by-pass the assembly area and move directly to the staging area in preparation to load personnel and equipment aboard ship by 28OCT.

12OCT1945 LETTER HOME

We have a good number of men from the 2nd AD here, and they have been getting passes to go back to the Division to visit their buddies. Ed and I have asked a few of them to pick up our mail. Company A of the other battalion of our unit has taken in the remaining Company F men who are going home. Too bad we do not command Company A. All the men in both battalions have enough points for discharge—I now have 96, which is more than enough.

Before the war ended, units were put in one of four categories: Category One was made up of those units who would stay in Europe as occupation troops; Category Two were to be redeployed to the States or to the Pacific (the 2nd AD was in this category, but now there is no need of our presence there); Category Three units were here waiting to be placed in one of the other categories; and Category Four were units made up of all high-point men who would be sent directly to the States and discharged and their units disbanded. The 12th AD is a Category Four unit. Most of our buddies have already left the 2nd AD, so it is the 2nd AD in name only now. I could have stayed with the 2nd, which will reach home only a couple of weeks after we do, but my chances of discharge with the 12th are a sure thing.

The war is over and all that, and we know that we are going home, but, surprisingly, the morale is not as high as you would expect. I guess it's the let-down. The job is finished. We want HOME, and we want it now. Time drags. Combat is a lousy dirty business, but during that time we had a purpose and many things to keep us occupied. Now it is just the waiting.

14OCT1945 Letter Home

Our shipping date has been cancelled for an indefinite time, but we, supposedly, have priority, and, as soon as things straighten out, we are on the way. This has been the best day I've had with the 12th. We have very little actual work now, as there are ten officers in the company of 296 men. We end up taking jeep trips around the area.

We went to Neresheim today, the abbey of the Benedictine Fathers. A bearded monk took us to Fr. Emmeram, who is the head of the abbey and speaks excellent English. He took us on a tour, showing us paintings from 1770 that looked like they had been completed yesterday and a book that had been printed in 1500. I will show you all the photos when I get home.

Neresheim Abbey. (FCB)

19OCT1945 Letter Home

Yup, doggone it . . . we are still here. Grosskuchen, a town of 500 people, and here we are 300 strong. What a dead town this is. We get movies and there is an officers' club, but what an existence the locals lead.

The word now is that we'll start loading 06NOV. Yesterday, Ed and I covered 316 miles by jeep. We went to the Swiss border and actually stood on Swiss soil and talked to a guard. We went through over a dozen picturesque towns. The weather was foggy, so we did not take many photos, but we did enjoy the day. Good just to get out.

We imposed on the French (we are in the French Zone of Occupation) for lunch, and we ate at the officers' mess. The steak was good, but we have a sneaking suspicion that it was a slice of horse.

I have been thinking that in about ten years or so, when maybe these countries have settled down a bit—maybe in five years—we should come over here. Switzerland first and then a train into Germany.

27OCT1945

Ed, Lieutenant "Pete" O'Neill and I took off for a five-day trip in a jeep, leaving Grosskuchen at 1130, picking up the autobahn north of Ulm and cutting east to the site of the Dachau concentration camp, twelve miles northeast of Munich.

Visiting Dachau was horrible. It was difficult to believe what we'd heard about the atrocities, but to actually see Dachau and realize that human beings could plan and systematize such horror and inflict it on other human beings shook us to the core. A former inmate guided us through.

The trains that carried thousands upon thousands of prisoners stopped where I stood to take the photo above. The boxcars would be opened, the prisoners who had survived the trip would step out onto the platform, and all would be marched into the camp.

The main entrance to Dachau. The British had set up a tour, putting up signs in English throughout the camp. (FCB)

Part of the British tour was an exhibit with mannequins illustrating what would happen to prisoners who escaped and were recaptured.

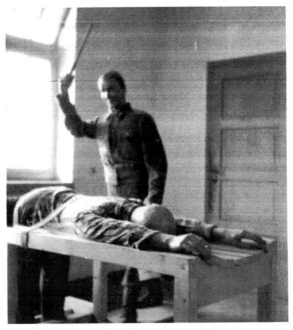

"Ich bin wieder da!" (meaning "I'm back"). A mannequin wearing chains around his ankles represented a prisoner who was caught after he had escaped. The next exhibits showed punishments for this offense. (FCB)

(FCB)

The ovens were intact. Barrels of charred bones were still at the outside entrance to the ovens. A sand pit was nearby; the sand was to soak up spilled blood. (FCB)

Ed took this photo of me next to one of the ovens. I had been horrified and angered at what we'd seen at the work camp at Leau outside Preusslitz, but the concentration camp at Dachau was beyond the pale. If you do not fight to end tyrannical genocide, there is nothing you will ever fight for. (EF)

After the officers' tours, the camp opened for the enlisted men. (FCB)

We checked in at the Excelsior Hotel in Munich, and then, to lighten the mood as best we could, we went to Seehaus, a beer garden located in the heart of Munich, for the opening of the Officers' Club. By the end of the day, we'd put on about 120 miles, and we were emotionally drained.

28OCT1945

The next morning we drove to Prien am Chiemsee and took the ferry to Herreninsel Island, site of Herrenchiemsee, one of three extravagant castles of King Ludwig II of Bavaria (1864–1886).

(FCB)

The New Herrenchiemsee Palace (Neues Schloss Herrenchiemsee) was designed to look like Versailles and begun in 1878, but construction ended when Ludwig died in 1886. It was the last and largest of his building projects and remained incomplete. The partial building covers 90,050 square feet, with only fourteen rooms completed.

The cost of the unfinished castle was outrageous at $30 million. Ludwig's bedroom alone cost $5 million. Two vases we saw were valued at $70,000 each. Gold, gold plate, gold thread, silver and ivory were everywhere. His love for grandiose construction works most likely led to his mysterious drowning in 1886. He was stuck with the label "Mad King" and another nickname, perhaps more apt, the "Fairy Tale King." The tour of the castle was well worth the visit.

(EF)

Lieutenant O'Neill, me and Ed at the Italian border at Brenner Pass. (EF)

We took the autobahn back to Rosenheim and went south seventy-five miles up winding mountain roads to the Brenner Pass. We talked a British "leftenant" into letting us drive into Italy but only went in a few miles and turned around.

We settled in for the night at a hotel on the Austrian side of the pass.

29OCT1945

The next morning, we doubled back to Innsbruck and ended up in Garmisch-Partenkirchen. The distance was only sixty miles, but it was slow going down the winding mountain roads. Garmisch was the setting of the 1936 Winter Olympics. We made arrangements for supper and breakfast and rooms at the Post Hotel, but then we had to make some "arrangements" with battalion.

We were supposed to be back to battalion the next day, 30 October, for a dry run of a parade to be held on Wednesday, 31 October, but a "very strange thing" happened to our jeep. It developed "mechanical trouble." We walked into a military government office and tried to telephone battalion to tell them of our "trouble" and that we would be delayed one day. An operator had to relay our conversation (telephone service was still rather makeshift), but battalion got the idea.

After the call, our jeep got miraculously better, so we drove to Oberammergau, where the world-famous "Passion Play" is presented every ten years. We got to tour the stage and see the costumes.

Linderhof, another one of Ludwig's castles, was our next stop. We called it a day and headed back to the Post Hotel for the night.

30OCT1945

At 0900, we took the cable car up the Zugspitze, which at 9,731 feet is the highest point in Germany. The altitude and the views of Germany, Austria, Switzerland and Italy took our breath away. We took the opportunity to ski, although I know we spent more time taking in the view.

I had no choice but to wear this atypical ski outfit, tie and all, but it worked. In the photo on the right (from left to right) are Lieutenant Peter O'Neill, me, Ed Fawks and a new friend. In the back of both photos is the Hotel Schneefernerhaus sitting at 8,694 feet. (FCB)

TOURS FROM 4TH ARMORED DIVISION REST CAMP
PRIEN AM CHIEMSEE, BAVARIA, GERMANY

Although we did not take advantage of the site, the 4th AD had a rest camp in the area and printed this brochure describing the local sights and with a detailed map on the back. (Author's Collection)

The show we saw at Oberammergau was definitely not the "Passion Play." (FCB)

We had supper at the Post Hotel, where the waiter gave me a huge beer mug. My "looting" days were over, but I accepted graciously and packed it for home. It is still displayed prominently on our living room shelf, next to the one given to me by the women in Grosskuchen.

Knowing that we had to head back to Grosskuchen in time to make the Wednesday parade, we hit the road at 2000, made a stop in Oberammergau to catch the evening show and then flew up the autobahn, arriving at our billets at 0020 on 31 October. We were there in plenty of time to get some rest before the parade. A very successful trip; it was a great relief from the slow pace of Grosskuchen.

01NOV1945 LETTER HOME

We were hoping that by the time we got back from our trip the redeployment news would have changed, but it stands the same. We are supposed to sail from Marseille, with the Division closing into the port area on 16NOV. The trip to the States will be, in all probability, completed before the end of the month. I have 17 rolls of film (12 pictures on each) to be developed. That's a lot of pictures, but they include all the photos from our trip into the Alps.

Over the next days, we prepared and packed our things for the trip to Marseille. And we waited.

Father Mueller's sister Maria Odette on the right with her mother in Grosskuchen, 1945. Maria stayed in contact with Helen and me via letters for a number of years after the war. (FCB)

18

Marseille and Going Home

The process of separating from the army began while I was still on active duty in Germany. After learning that I was to be allowed to go home early, I found out that I had ninety days of leave coming, days that I had been accumulating over the years. These days were a very nice cushion when I got home. I had one last item to take care of, which I accomplished while getting ready to board ship for the trip home. Given the choice of changing my captain's commission from AUS (Army of the United States) to RA (Regular Army, which would have meant a career for me in the military), I decided to stay with the AUS, thus making it clear that I wanted to join the Active Reserves, as this would preserve my rank.

I was certain that, exact words said silently to myself as I filled out the forms, "We'll be fighting those Russian bastards and quite possibly very soon." If I were to be called back, I wanted to come back as a captain. If I had retired completely from the army and then was called back, I feared it might be as a private. Staying in the reserves allowed me to go back to Marquette Paper Corporation full time and still keep my commission, a decision I have never regretted.

Grosskuchen, Germany, was 150 road miles from a rail line at Strasbourg, France, that headed south to Marseille, where our ship home would be waiting. We were trucked over to Strasbourg and boarded boxcars for the 480-mile trip to Marseille.

Operation Dragoon, the Allied landings along France's Mediterranean coast on 15 August 1944, had just one major objective: to move north and link up with the D-Day forces driving east to Germany. A by-product of Dragoon's main objective was the capture of the port of Marseille and its railroad lines leading north. Once cleared of the damage caused by Allied bombing and German demolition, the port was put back in service, eventually handling a third of all the Allies' supplies. It was also going to handle our departure.

The officers' boxcar meant we all had good seats to watch the passing countryside. (FCB)

A rest stop along the way to Marseille. Time to take some pictures! (FCB)

The boxcars we boarded were designed in 1870. Called forty and eights (40&8), they were made to hold forty men or eight horses. The French army used them in both wars, and now we were using them to go home.

At a stop on our way to Marseille, a local woman sold us breads and biscuits. Our graffiti is everywhere on the boxcars, perhaps "WHERE IS THE BOAT?" being the best one. (EF)

We burned our waste in the can provided, along with some gas to help with the job. That's me on the right. (FCB)

When we got off the train, we entered an area where we had to turn in any weapons we had been thinking of taking home as souvenirs. Word was out that if you were caught carrying weapons of any sort, you risked your spot on the ship. I did not want to take any chance of that, so, like most guys, I dumped the contents of my duffel bag onto the cot. We had to wonder who got all these items.

Our arrival in Marseille. We would have to travel across the city in trucks to get to our ship. (FCB)

We piled onto the trucks, though the officers got to sit in the cabs. It wasn't a long trip, and after the train ride it was good to be out in the air. (FCB)

After our duffels were searched, we turned them over to be loaded onto the ship. We sat back and "enjoyed" a lunch of K-rations while we waited for the ride to the ship. Ed Fawks is on the left. (FCB)

We passed a movie theater/amphitheater built into a quarry. Perhaps this was a place for troops newly arrived in France to be oriented and/or for those waiting for their ships home to relax and be debriefed. (FCB)

Marseille had not been hit too hard by bombers, so most of the buildings still had roofs on them. (FCB)

The port, however, had not been completely cleared of all the damage done by both the Allies and the Germans. (FCB)

There it is. Our very own Victory ship and our passage home. A total of 531 Victory ships were built between 1944 and 1946. Built to replace losses caused by German U-boats, these cargo ships had a more modern design, being larger and faster than the earlier Liberty ships. The extra speed allowed them to keep up with high-speed convoys and made them more difficult targets for the German submarines. (FCB)

23NOV1945

We departed Marseille on the *Westminster Victory*. The important part of its cargo was our company of 250 men, Ed and me.

(EF)

(FCB)

The *Westminster* about to depart from Marseille and, about time for us, the European land mass. (FCB)

A tug pulls us away from the dock. (FCB)

At least one man along the rail is waving goodbye to France . . . at least it looks like it could be a wave. (FCB)

I had a ringside seat to watch the port of Marseille slip off into the distance. (EF)

Finally out into the Mediterranean, heading west. (FCB)

Ed and I enjoying the fresh air. (FCB; EF)

We sailed past the Rock of Gibraltar at night, and the captain of the ship invited two of us to join him on the ship's bridge for the event. Four GIs on special duty on the bridge were assigned to operate the radar, and we got a radar view of the Rock as we sailed through the Strait of Gibraltar.

The chaplain said Mass for us on deck. We had great weather all the way across the Atlantic. (FCB)

(FCB)

While passing through the strait, one of the GI's, a corporal, jumped up, ran out of the bridge and went straight to the rail. We wondered what was wrong with him. One of the other GIs on the bridge said, "Poor guy, he's been on this duty for months and he still gets seasick!"

(FCB)

(FCB)

03DEC1945

We arrived at Camp Kilmer in New Brunswick, New Jersey. Camp Kilmer was activated in June 1942 to be the embarkation point for transport of troops to Europe. After VE Day, the post processed troops returning from Europe. I was sent from Kilmer to my local separation center, which in my case was Camp Grant in Illinois, where all this started out. During the course of the war, more than 2.5 million soldiers passed through Camp Kilmer.

04DEC1945

I received my movement order to travel by train from Camp Kilmer to Camp Grant, Illinois.

Ed and I at Camp Kilmer. This is the only photo we have from there. By this time we were thinking more about home than taking any more photos. (FCB)

I was home for Christmas. Thanks, Bing! (FCB)

(FCB)

EPILOGUE

Everything After This Will Be Gravy

08DEC1945

I received my appointment to the Army Reserve Corps as a captain. I also received a letter thanking me for accepting a position as an officer in the reserves.

10MAR1946

My ninety days of leave ran out, and I was relieved from active duty, the separation taking place at Camp Grant, Illinois.

We never did get called up to fight the Russians, nor did I go to Korea. My first reserve assignment was to the 21st Armored Division, which had units in Wisconsin, Illinois and Indiana.

I was given command of a company in the 749th Tank Battalion with the slogan "Fear Our Rage." In the group photo, that is me standing farthest to the left. (FCB)

(FCB)

(FCB)

I served in the reserves until 1977, attending monthly weekend meetings of the companies and summer camp for two weeks every year at Camp McCoy, Fort Knox or Fort Leonard Wood. I ended my career as a battalion commander in the 85th Training Division, retiring as a lieutenant colonel.

I had a soft landing back at Marquette Paper Corporation, which had its offices in downtown Chicago. After thirty years there, I was asked to take on the position of general manager when Marquette was taken over by Jim Walter Papers. I held that position until my retirement in 1984.

Our son Fred (Ricky) was born in 1948. We lived in Wood Dale, Illinois, at the time. When he was nine years old, I took out the Nazi wall banner I had gotten at Kaldenhausen, laid it out on the floor and told Rick to stomp on the swastika. I explained why that was the right thing to do. (FCB)

I am on the left with one of our salesmen, Dick Schwartz, a representative from Jim Walter Papers up from Florida, and salesman Jerry Mason. We are at our office in Schaumburg, Illinois. (FCB)

I served in six armored divisions, one tank battalion and an infantry division.

3rd AD—Basic training and promotion to sergeant and technical sergeant
8th AD—Assigned here after Officer Candidate School
14th AD—Transferred to become part of the cadre to build up this new division
2nd AD—Joined the 2nd AD in September 1944, always considering the 2nd my "home" division
12th AD—Co-commanded with Captain Fawks a provisional company of 250 men, all of us on our way home
21st AD—U.S. Army Reserve division, with units in Wisconsin, Illinois and Michigan

I retired from the Army Reserve Corps in 1967 after serving for twenty-six and a half years.

When I retired from the paper business, Helen and I moved to our dream lakefront home outside Fredericksburg, Virginia. Sadly, Helen was not able to enjoy our time there for very long; she passed away in late 1985. We enjoyed forty-two happy years of marriage. I remarried in 1987 to Margaret Walker and added twenty-seven more years of happy marriage to my life.

Some frosting on the cake was the invitation to be flown out to California along with several other veterans of the 2nd AD to meet with the writers, producers and cast of the movie *Fury*. I was sent a copy of the script to review, and Rick sent two pertinent chapters from this book to the writers in case there was anything in those chapters that they could use.

749th Tank Battalion—served as commanding officer of Company C and as executive officer. (Author's Collection)

The movie focuses on the actions of a platoon with markings on the featured tank indicating that it is part of the 66th AR of the 2nd AD. Although this story is supposedly about a platoon in a Company L, there was no L Company in any of the army's tank battalions. Additionally, the tank is named *Fury*, a name beginning with "F," indicating it was part of Company F. This movie was us.

I was unable to take them up on the invitation due to health reasons, but Ray Stewart of our platoon was able to go along with Don Evans of our reconnaissance company. Turns out our units had worked together many times, but the two of us only met at several reunions. We became good friends. Two other 2nd AD vets also made the trip.

Ray and the others got to interact at length with the cast playing the crew of *Fury*, including Brad Pitt. Ray and his wife Dottie both are in the credits at the end of the movie (Ray by his given name, Rodney Stewart). I am sure that these vets were able to say everything I would have said, but I wish I had been well enough to go.

Ray with Brad Pitt and Logan Lerman. (Courtesy of Sony Pictures)

The group photo: the stars of *Fury* with the four visiting veterans of the 2nd Armored Division. Brad Pitt signed the photo "WITH RESPECT." (Courtesy of Sony Pictures)

I have to admit that I read only twelve pages of the script and stopped because I objected to the language in the dialogue that had been written for the cast members. When I told Rick, he asked me whether the men actually talked this way during the war, and I said, well, yes, they did, but I didn't want to give anyone the wrong impression. He just laughed. I guess I was thinking too much about the movies I grew up with and the war movies from the 1940s and 1950s in which such language was prohibited.

I've often said, "Everything after the war has been gravy"—not that it has been easy, but rather that I very easily could not be here at all. I considered myself extremely lucky to have survived active duty, and, indeed, luck it was: luck that I survived the dangerous combat I experienced and luck that I survived when others didn't. I carried the loss of my fellow soldiers with me for the rest of my life, often feeling that perhaps I shouldn't be alive either. My fallen comrades were very special people. I have tried to honor them and all my fellow companions in my daily actions and words.

The war was a singular, moving and tough time in my life. Life itself has been gravy ever since.

Lieutenant Colonel Frederick C. Brems, USAR (Retired) 02JAN1919–17AUG2014 (FGB)

APPENDIX

My Visual Short Snorter

General John "Pee Wee" Collier, commanding officer of the 2nd AD (June–September 1945), awarding medals to tankers from the 2nd AD. Five stripes on this man's left sleeve indicate two and a half years overseas. (EF)

Colonel Stokes, 66th AR commanding officer, at the 2nd AD dismounted review in Wolfenbüttel. (FCB)

Lieutenant Colonel Carl Parker, 1st Battalion commanding officer. (FCB)

I'm on the left, Captain Fawks is on the right, probably at a rest stop on one of our trips out of Gelnhausen. (EF)

Lieutenant Trinen, commander of the 1st Platoon, winner of three Silver Stars and a battlefield commission. A feisty guy in every positive sense of the word! Sadly, he was killed in Korea. (FCB)

Lieutenant Don "Critch" Critchfield, commander of the 3rd Platoon. (FCB)

First Sergeant Harris and Captain Fawks; Harris was my platoon sergeant, a good 'un, cool as can be. Here at Lebenstedt. (FCB)

Schnapps! At Lebenstedt. When we left, he went AWOL. (FCB)

Critch in front of his M4 Sherman with the 75mm howitzer. (FCB)

Steve Jutras, my gunner while I was with F Company, and Ralph Melchior sitting on *Fay*, the tank. (FCB)

I'm on the left with Lieutenant Di Simone. (DAC)

Chaplain Luke Bolin at the 2nd AD review in Wolfenbüttel. (FCB)

Mike Marino and Ray Stewart of F Company. (RS)

Steve Jutras hanging out in Berlin. (RS)

Ray Stewart at one of the reunions. (FGB)

Standing (left to right): Ramos and Stewart; sitting (left to right): Conner, Shafer and Marino. All of Company F. (RS)

Kurt Eisenmann, me, Steve Kelly (our best man) and Ed Furman at Camp Polk in 1941. (FCB)

Steve Kelly. (FCB)

Steve Kelly and me. (FCB)

Ed Furman standing second in from left with me standing on the far right. (FCB)

Kurt Eisenmann at ease in the barracks. (FCB)

Left to right: English, McBride, Payne, Mieczynski, Eisenmann, Strefling, Whittington, me, Sandy, Olson, Furman, Kelly, Heape, Prass, Maroni. The upper window was my corner, with the mailroom, where Kelly worked, just below me. (FCB)

Steve Kelly and Ed Furman. (FCB)

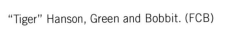

"Tiger" Hanson, Green and Bobbit. (FCB)

On the right, Sergeant Hunt, sergeant major of the 32nd AR. (FCB)

Lieutenant McClung, formerly of F Company, outside our HQ in Lebenstedt. (FCB)

William R. "WR" Harris had been my platoon sergeant and became our first sergeant. (FCB)

Sergeant White, our mess sergeant, with a motorcycle and two enlisted men standing behind our barracks in Lebenstedt. I am not sure whether we got any vegetables out of what was left behind by the previous occupants, but White would have found what was there to be had. (FCB)

Tec 5 Ray Stewart, from my platoon,
in a German winter camouflage jacket.
Great thing about it, besides being
warm, is that it was reversible: white
and camouflage. He is standing in front
of Critch's tank *Fancy Pants*; not sure
where this photo was taken. (RS)

Captain Raines. (FCB)

Company F commanding officer wounded at Amonines and returned
to Company F before we entered Berlin. (FCB)

Ed on the left and Chaplain Luke Bolin on the
right in Frankfurt. Beth Cooper, Chaplain Bolin's
daughter, had never seen this photo. (FCB)

Ed on the lake near King Ludwig's castle. (FCB)

At a town on the Elbe River. Notice the white flag hanging out the window. Ed is in the middle. (EF)

Ed on one of the ubiquitous piles of bricks in Berlin. Multiple bullet strikes are on the wall behind him. (EF)

Ed with his command tank *Fawks Family* at the beginning of the Bulge. Soon after, he was wounded. (EF)

Ed in front of our 66th AR sign noting our campaigns. (FCB)

Ed (center) with his crew and the identification flag taken from one of the two tanks they knocked out with one shot. Anytime a German tank was under its own air cover, it would drape the flag over the rear deck of the tank to make sure its own planes would not shoot or bomb it. (EF)

A wrecked German column somewhere in France. (EF)